A Nation Conceived and Dedicated

VOLUME ONE • Prehistory to 1824

By Ira Peck with Steven Deyle

HISTORICAL CONSULTANTS

Elaine Tyler May
*Professor of American
Studies and History
University of Minnesota
Minneapolis, Minnesota*

Susan Levine
*Historian
University of North Carolina
Chapel Hill, North Carolina*

IRA PECK is a professional writer. Born in New York City, he attended public schools there and Harvard College, where he majored in history. As a journalist, he worked as a newspaper reporter and a magazine editor. He has written numerous biographies and historical books for young people.

STEVEN DEYLE is a professional historian and teacher. He has received degrees in American history from the University of California—Santa Cruz and Columbia University. He was a historical consultant and contributing writer for Scholastic's *African American History: Four Centuries of Black Life.*

ON THE COVER
The painting called *The Right to Know* appeared as an illustration in *Look* Magazine on August 20, 1968. Printed by permission of the Estate of Norman Rockwell. Copyright © 1968 Estate of Norman Rockwell. The following caption appeared with the painting: "We are the governed, but we govern too. Assume our love of country, for it is only the simplest of self-love. Worry little about our strength, for we have our history to show for it. And because we are strong, there are others who have hope. But watch us more closely from now on, for those of us who stand here mean to watch those we put in the seats of power. And listen to us, you who lead, for we are listening harder for the truth that you have not always offered us. Your voice must be ours, and ours speaks of cities that are not safe, and of wars we do not want, of poor in a land of plenty, and of a world that will not take the shape our arms would give it. We are not fierce, and the truth will not frighten us. Trust us, for we have given you our trust. We are the governed, remember, but we govern too."

For reprint permission, grateful acknowledgement is made to:
Joan Daves, agent to the estate of Martin Luther King, Jr., for the excerpt from I HAVE A DREAM by Martin Luther King, Jr., copyright © 1963 by Martin Luther King, Jr.

Scholastic Inc. ISBN 0-590-35699-2

Copyright © 1991 by Scholastic Inc.
All rights reserved. Printed in the U.S.A.

American Adventures is a trademark of Scholastic Inc.

12 11 10 9

PUBLISHER
ELEANOR ANGELES

EDITORIAL DIRECTOR
CAROLYN JACKSON

PROJECT EDITOR
DEBORAH GORE

SKILLS EDITOR
MOLLIE COHEN

MANAGING EDITOR
KEVIN GILLESPIE

.ASSISTANT EDITOR
LISA KEATING

EDITORIAL ASSISTANT
LISA CRAWLEY

PRODUCTION
CLAUDIA BRUCE
VIRGINIA DUSTIN
MIDGE MARONI

◆

DESIGN DIRECTOR
CAMPION PRIMM

ART DIRECTOR
JUDITH ORLICK

PHOTO & ILLUSTRATION
RESEARCHERS
PHOTOSEARCH, INC.

CARTOGRAPHER
DAVID LINDROTH

ILLUSTRATOR
CHIP WASS

COVER DESIGN
ROSEMARY INTRIERI

CONTENTS

AMERICAN ADVENTURES

A Nation Conceived and Dedicated

A small group of men, women, and children move swiftly but steadily across a grassy field. They wear animal skins around their waists. Some of them carry long, heavy sticks with pointed stones at one end. Others use the branch of a tree as a weapon. These people are looking for food. If they are lucky, they will find a herd of wild horses. They will then chase the horses and kill them with their spears. If the hunters fail, however, they will eat seeds, berries, and roots.

Experts believe this scene might have happened about 20,000 years ago on the North American continent. The first native peoples of North America, **Native Americans**, lived in

These ancient cliff dwellings were once home to the Anasazi, a native culture of the American Southwest.

CULTURES

1500 B.C.		1400 A.D.		1450	1500	1550
1500-1000 B.C.		**1400**	**1434**		**1492**	**1519**	**1540**

1500-1000 B.C.
Anasazi Pueblos begin growing corn.

1400
Iroquois form Five Nations.

1434
Gil Eanes navigates African coast.

1492
Columbus lands in San Salvador.

1519
Aztecs encounter Spanish.

1540
Coronado seeks legendary cities of gold.

MEET

1600   1650   1700

1680
Pueblos
revolt against
Spanish.

1682
La Salle reaches
mouth of the
Mississippi River.

UNIT 1

Thousands of years before guns and gunpowder were made, Native Americans hunted with handmade tools—and clever disguises. These hunters have cloaked themselves in deerskins to keep their jumpy prey from sensing danger.

caves and brush lean-tos. They used fire to cook, keep warm, and hunt. By lighting fires in the grass, hunters coaxed animals over cliffs or into valleys where they could be killed.

The first humans arrived in North America between 20,000 and 30,000 years ago. They came from Asia and crossed an ancient land bridge onto what is now Alaska. Over the centuries, the water level of the ocean rose and the land was buried under water. These people were left in isolation from the rest of the world.

Their descendants fanned out over North and South America. Many different **cultures** (ways of living) evolved because these Native Americans lived in such a large area. Hundreds of separate languages emerged. People developed different physical characteristics, customs, and ways of making things. Most groups crafted tools out of stone—axes, spears, arrowheads, and knives. Aztec (AZ-tec) people, for example, invented calendars and created their own forms of writing. As time went on, the Aztecs in present-day Mexico developed a very advanced culture.

In these years, people in North and South America knew little or nothing about the rest of the world. And the rest of the world knew little or nothing about the people in the Americas. One of the earliest contacts occurred centuries before. Around the year 1000, Leif Ericson and other Vikings from Scandinavia (present-day Sweden, Norway, and Denmark) reached the coast of North America. However, they were unable to establish a permanent settlement. Few Native Americans had met them and the influence of the Vikings was soon forgotten.

Age of European Exploration

By 1492, improvements in technology made long sea voyages possible. Growth of trade with Asia gave European governments an incentive to sponsor voyages of exploration. The increase in population made overseas settlement possible.

Early on the morning of October 12, 1492, the Italian sailor Christopher Columbus and his three small ships of sailors saw land. The sailors had traveled more than 3000 miles from Spain. Columbus thought they had reached the East Indies (present-day Japan and China). Instead they landed on an island off the coast of North America. Columbus never realized his mistake. But his voyage was one of the single most important events in history.

Columbus was helped by the experience of earlier explorers. For years other Europeans were braving unexplored

Europeans introduced many changes—good and bad—to the New World. Horses were one of their most useful contributions.

waters in search of a new passage to the riches of the East. Columbus was the first to try finding it by going west.

Almost 75 years before Columbus arrived in North America, Prince Henry of Portugal sent out his first expedition. Henry thought the best way of sailing to the Indies was by heading south, then east. He sent many ships down the African coast. In the 15th century, Portugal became the leader in seafaring discovery. The Portuguese built new sailing ships called caravels to help them travel long distances in unknown waters. Columbus relied on this technology in his trip across the Atlantic.

One result of Prince Henry's exploration of Africa was the capture of Africans for slavery. Some Africans were brought back to Europe. But many more were shipped to the New World to work as slaves in European settlements.

Without the Native American's help, the European settlements might not have survived. The Native Americans, or Indians as Columbus called them, taught the Europeans their ways of farming. They introduced new crops to them. Some of the crops that were unknown in Europe before 1492 were corn, potatoes, tomatoes, and peanuts.

However, for Native Americans much of the contact with Europeans was

Migration of Early Peoples to the Americas

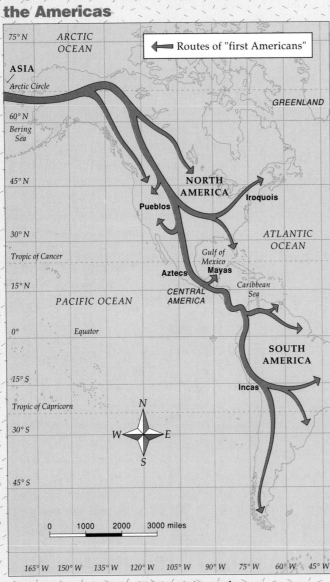

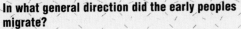

In what general direction did the early peoples migrate?

harmful. Many Native Americans were killed in wars with the newcomers. The Europeans had guns and other weapons which the Indians lacked. Even more disastrous were European diseases, such as smallpox. Millions of Native Americans died because they had never before been exposed to these diseases.

Exploring North and South America

In the early 16th century, the Aztecs' vast empire covered much of Mexico. Their main city was larger than any European city of that time. It boasted impressive roads, waterways, and buildings.

Spanish explorers met the Aztecs in 1519. They were impressed with the Aztec culture. For a short time, the Aztecs and Spanish got along, but soon conflicts arose between the two groups. War broke out. Because the Spanish had better weapons and Indian allies, they conquered the Aztec empire.

Riches such as gold and silver filled the land conquered by the Spanish. Using both Native Americans and Africans as slaves, the Spanish created large estates and amassed a great fortune from their New World settlements.

Spanish explorers kept moving north and south in search of more wealth. One such adventurer was Francisco Coronado. He tried to find the legendary seven lost cities of gold. Coronado never found these mythical cities. But he did explore far into the present-day states of Arizona, New Mexico, and Kansas.

AMERICAN ADVENTURES

Spanish explorers helped their nation gain control over Florida and much of the American Southwest. Spain established a settlement at St. Augustine, Florida, in 1565. This is the oldest European city in the present-day United States. In 1609, the Spanish founded Santa Fe in what is now New Mexico. And Spain sent explorers along the California coast as early as the 1540s. However, it was not until the 18th century that they set up permanent settlements there.

This 20th-century painting illustrates the daily life of the Algonkins. The Algonkins were among the first Native American peoples to befriend French explorers in what is today Canada and the northeastern United States.

The largest group of Native Americans living in the Southwest were Pueblos (poo-EB-lohs). The Pueblo were peaceful people who lived in many-storied houses made of straw and mud bricks. They grew corn and other crops. When the Spanish arrived in the Southwest, fighting broke out. The scars of the conflict remained between the Europeans and Pueblo peoples long afterward.

Other European nations raced to establish colonies in the New World. The French sent explorers and settlers to Canada. French missionaries came to spread Christianity to the Native Americans. The French found great wealth in the fur trade. Thanks to explorers like Robert La Salle, they also established settlements along the Mississippi River.

One group of Native Americans encountered by the French were the Iroquois of present-day New York State. The Iroquois nation was a league of five (later six) tribes. Together, they were one of the strongest Indian nations in North America. They were warriors and excellent farmers. They remained a powerful factor in Indian-European relations until the American Revolution.

Within 150 years of Columbus's voyage to America, European colonies were set up throughout much of the Americas. This greatly affected the lives of Native Americans, Africans, and Europeans.

1 THE EAGLE AND THE SNAKE

In the 1500s, the Aztec capital of Tenochtitlán was home to hundreds of thousands of people. Grand temples towered over busy streets and canals, while a network of dikes controlled the flow of water.

Imagine a city built in the middle of a lake. Farmers work on lovely floating gardens of tropical flowers. People travel in canoes down canals, which are the main streets of this watery wonderland. Luxurious homes made of volcanic rock and gardens with ponds for swans and for ducks line the waterways. In the island's main square, two tall pyramids rise above the royal palaces built of stone. The square, which covers a full 125 acres, is also a huge marketplace where 60,000 people come each day to trade goods and talk. The artists who flock here skillfully carve large, dramatic statues in stone. They make fine jewelry of gold, silver, and precious gems and weave the feathers of many different birds into colorful designs.

Here was the heart of a mighty empire that extended over most of central and southern Mexico. By about 1500, the Native American peoples called Aztecs ruled more than 11 million people. Their capital city, Tenochtitlán (tay-noch-TEET-lan), had a population of 250,000. This was far more than even the largest cities of Europe at this time.

Search for a Capital City

Who were the people who created this advanced civilization long before Europeans arrived in the New World? They were the Aztecs, who rose from the poorest beginnings to fashion a rich and powerful society. A **nomadic** (wandering from place to place) tribe, they first lived in the arid north of Mexico. Over many decades, they traveled southward in search of a better climate, water, and forests filled with game. The early part of their long journey is described in Aztec legends. These are stories that were handed down from one generation to the next. In them, the storytellers freely mixed truth and fiction.

The legends say that the first Aztecs emerged into the world from a cave in northwest Mexico. This cave was on an island in a lake where cranes dove for fish. The name of the island was Aztlan (ahs-TLAHN), which means "the place of the cranes." From it came the name Aztec.

A stern Aztec god, named after a hummingbird, ordered them to leave their island cave and search for a new home. The Aztecs neared the Valley of Mexico early in the 13th century and were eager to settle down. But they were extremely disliked by the people who had already settled in the valley. The older settlers regarded the Aztecs as crude, dangerous barbarians, and forced them to move from place to place. The king of the city of Culhuacan (cool-wah-CAHN) banished them to a piece of land that was infested

with rattlesnakes. He hoped that the snakes would destroy them. But he hadn't counted on the toughness of the Aztecs. In their wanderings, they had become used to eating almost anything. They killed the snakes, cooked them, and thoroughly enjoyed eating them.

The Aztecs were not content to live under the domination of the Culhuacan. After an unsuccessful rebellion, the Aztecs were driven into the marshes of Lake Texcoco where they hid among the reeds. Their hummingbird god spoke to them again. He told them to look for an island where they would find a huge eagle perched on a cactus. The eagle would be devouring a helpless snake in its beak. They did not have to search for long. On a small island that was little more than some rocks poking above the marshes, they found the cactus, the eagle, and the snake. The eagle devouring the snake later became the symbol of Mexico and appears on the nation's flag.

Building the City

In 1325, the Aztecs began building a city on this island, the site of present-day Mexico City. They named it Tenochtitlán, which means "the place of the cactus." In time, it grew to become the magnificent capital city of the Aztec empire. The water protected the Aztecs' stronghold from enemies and made it safe. The Aztecs soon learned to enlarge

The Aztecs honored a powerful god called Quetzalcoatl portrayed in this turquoise mask. Someday, they believed, Quetzalcoatl would return to rule them.

The Aztec Empire

Where was the Aztec empire located in North America? How far was Tenochtitlán from the edge of the Aztec empire?

their island by filling in marshes with soil from the lake bottom.

The Aztecs were first-rate warriors who often fought for pay in the armies of other kingdoms. In time, they began to conquer these kingdoms. Their success as warriors was closely related to their religion. Their hummingbird god became the god of sun and war. He demanded many human sacrifices so the sun would rise every day. Without the sun, crops would die and people would starve. So warfare was necessary to conquer people who could be sacrificed.

The wealth of Tenochtitlán was made possible by tributes paid to the Aztec rulers by the conquered peoples. Gold, silver, pre-cious stones, jaguar skins, feathers, corn, and other food poured into the capital.

This wealth was reflected in the great buildings of the central square. Here was the 100-foot high pyramid crowned with the temple where human sacrifices were made. From this central square, the city spread outward to the homes of the nobility. These were usually two-stories high and had as many as 50 rooms. The common people lived in bamboo huts on the rim of the island. These were raised on stilts because heavy rains sometimes flooded the city.

Daily Life

The Aztecs placed great importance on the education of their children. Every Aztec boy and girl went to school. At the age of 15 or younger, boys of the nobility attended schools run by priests. Discipline was very strict, and the hours of study long. They learned holy songs, how to read the picture writing in their books, astrology, poetry, and the calendar. Girls were taught by older priestesses, and learned to become experts in embroidery and weaving.

Children of the lower classes went to other schools where the teachers were ordinary citizens. Boys were taught military skills. Those who did well became soldiers. Others learned a trade. Girls were taught how to run a home and care for children.

Aztec society had strict rules for all its citizens. Criminals were dealt with firmly. For minor offenses, people might have their hair cut off. But offenses such as drunkenness, stealing, or lying could be punished by death.

Coming Disaster

In 1502, a young man named Moctezuma (mok-te-SOO-ma) took control of the Aztec empire. He was 22, and his courage as a warrior was proven. He had led Aztec armies to victories in more than 40 battles.

Moctezuma was skilled in reading the books and calendars of his people, and was a priest in their religion. The Aztecs considered him a god. Few were allowed to look him in the face, or even sit in his presence.

Moctezuma lived like a king. Three thousand servants and workers waited on Moctezuma in his royal palace with 300 rooms. His lush gardens contained every kind of plant and flower in the empire. He kept snakes, eagles, and jaguars in cages. These creatures ate about 500 turkeys a day. Each day, Moctezuma had the choice of 100 kinds of food, brought to him by 20 of his wives. After dining, he was entertained by jesters, musicians, magicians, and dancers.

Despite his great power and wealth, Moctezuma was not a happy man. He was filled with a sense of doom. His prophets told him that the Aztec empire would come to an end during his reign. Moctezuma saw many signs of coming disaster. In 1517, for example, a comet streaked across the sky and seemed to drip fire on the earth.

An Aztec legend told about Quetzalcoatl (keh-tsah-KWATL), a pale, bearded ruler who was a god to his people. One day, Quetzalcoatl sailed off to the east. The legend said he would return again where the sun rose. For two years, the legend of Quetzalcoatl haunted the Aztec leader. Would the pale, bearded ruler come back to claim his throne?

CHAPTER CHECK

WORD MATCH
1. nomadic   **a.** a story or myth from the past
2. legend   **b.** wandering from place to place
3. conquer   **c.** a high level of culture
4. civilization **d.** to gain control by force
5. empire   **e.** a group of cities, states, or territories under the rule of one person

QUICK QUIZ
1. How did the Aztecs obtain their wealth?
2. Why were the Aztecs considered an advanced civilization?
3. How did the education of Aztec boys and girls differ?

THINK ABOUT IT
1. In what ways was the city of Tenochtitlán like your hometown? How was it different?
2. Think about the importance of human life and the part people's religious beliefs played. Were the Aztecs justified in sacrificing human beings?

2 CLIFF DWELLERS OF THE SOUTHWEST

When the Spanish first came to the American Southwest in the 1500s, they found the people there living in huge adobe buildings like this one. One multilevel pueblo could house many families.

After getting out of prison, Popé (poh-PAY), a Pueblo medicine man from San Juan Pueblo, went into hiding with only one thing on his mind: revenge. Popé and 47 other Pueblo Indians had been imprisoned for clinging to their religious beliefs. The Spanish, who were Catholic, forbade any practice of Native American religion.

Popé planned a rebellion that would rid the area (what is now New Mexico) of the Spanish conquerers forever. Runners secretly carried news of his plan to all the Pueblo people, who were spread out over an area of 300 miles. One by one, the villages enthusiastically joined the plot.

For hundreds of years, Native Americans had lived peacefully in what is now Arizona and northern New Mexico. They were successful farmers, made handsome pottery, and wove fine cotton cloth. Above all, they were very religious.

But when Spaniards came to the area about 1540, they forced the Pueblo people to pay taxes in the form of goods or slave labor. The Spanish renamed villages after Catholic saints. Old religious practices were forbidden.

On August 10, 1680, the Pueblos revolted. Many Spanish were killed and the remaining Spaniards fled. Popé became the honored leader of the Pueblos.

Living in Giant Cliffs

The Pueblos had always been a peaceful people. Unlike the Aztecs, they fought only when they were attacked. They cared much more about harvesting corn than they did about war.

The Spaniards called these people *Pueblos* after their houses that looked like villages. Pueblo means "village" in Spanish. Each village had its own government. The people were linked by their customs, beliefs, and way of living.

Their desert land of steep **mesas** (flat-topped hills) and deep canyons was a beautiful but harsh place to live. The Pueblos and their ancestors had been building villages and growing crops successfully there for hundreds of years. Their **hunter-gatherer** (people who moved often to hunt and gather food) ancestors were living in the Southwest thousands of years before that.

Sometime between 1500 and 1000

The Hopi and Zuñi used kachina dolls to teach their children about honored spirits.

B.C. these ancestors, called the *Anasazi* (a-nah-SAH-zee), or Ancient Ones, learned to grow corn. This discovery changed their way of life. It was no longer necessary to wander in search of food. They built stone and clay houses. They were able to stay in one place for many seasons until disease, drought, or some other natural disaster forced them to move to a more promising location.

The Anasazi constructed their most magnificent villages around an area known today as the Four Corners—where Arizona, New Mexico, Utah, and Colorado meet. They made their homes in giant cliffs of reddish-brown rock.

After about 200 years, the Anasazi deserted their cliff dwellings. The main reason for the move was a 23-year period without rain. They then moved to the fertile valley of the Rio Grande River in present-day north central New Mexico.

This time they stayed. Most of the villages built after 1300 were inhabited by the same peoples. Pueblos have lived in the same place longer than any other people from Canada or the United States.

The Pueblos built houses out of stone and **adobe** (a sandy clay that molds easi-

Native American Tribes of North America

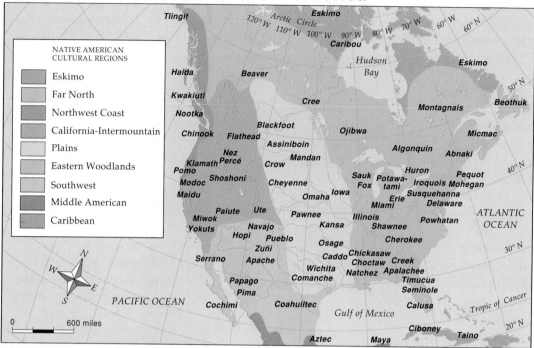

What other tribes are in the same geographical area as the Pueblos? What Native American culture was in the region where you live?

ly when wet and dries hard). Villages were made up of clusters of these box-shaped dwellings, often several stories high like apartment buildings. In fact, one Pueblo village—Pueblo Bonita in New Mexico—was once the biggest apartment house in the world. A thousand people probably lived in it.

Daily Pueblo Life

Religion was the center of all Pueblo life. Pueblos tried to live in harmony with nature. Mountains were holy places, homes for supernatural spirits. Lakes were sacred and often seen as doorways to other worlds.

Pueblos held many ceremonies to promote peace and order in the universe.

Kachinas were good spirits that would bring rain, health, and plentiful crops. Pueblo men performed kachina dances in which they wore masks that symbolized the spirits.

Religious ceremonies were performed in *kivas*. Kivas were circular ceremonial rooms built underground. They were an imitation of the original home beneath the earth in which Pueblos believed life began. Women, though rarely allowed to enter, helped to build and maintain the kivas. Kivas were also used for council meetings and as workshops for weaving.

By the time the Spanish explorer Coronado came to the Pueblo homeland in 1540, the villages spread out along the Rio Grande River. The Hopi (HOH-pee)

AMERICAN ADVENTURES

and Zuñi (ZOO-nee) broke off from the Pueblo and remained in the isolated desert country. They kept their customs and ways of life of their ancestors.

In most Pueblo villages, the house was the property of the woman. A man went to live with his wife's family when he married, and children belonged to the **clan** (family) of their mothers. Homes were used for sleeping and shelter. Most daily activities such as cooking and eating took place outside.

Each family also had a small garden near the village. They ate meat when they could get it, usually rabbits or squirrels. Men hunted regularly for larger game, such as deer and antelope. These animals provided meat, but they also were sources for thread, drums, clothing, and tools.

Blending Cultures

The Pueblos were free for a period of 12 years. After brief fighting, Spanish rule was reinstated in 1692. More Spaniards moved to the area. Both cultures began sharing ideas and ways of doing things. The Pueblos began growing new crops—wheat, chilies, and peppers. They learned to mold adobe into bricks and to build fireplaces and chimneys. The Spanish learned the Pueblo method of making pottery and weaving cloth.

The new Spanish government relaxed the rules forbidding old Pueblo religious ceremonies. Religion became a blend of Christian and ancient Pueblo beliefs. Unlike the days in which Popé lived, it was a time when the Spaniards and the Pueblos learned to live together in peace.

CHAPTER CHECK

WORD MATCH
1. clan
2. hunter-gatherer
3. adobe
4. fertile
5. mesas

a. person who moves often to hunt and gather food
b. flat-topped hills
c. very rich and productive
d. family
e. a sandy clay that molds easily when wet and dries hard

QUICK QUIZ
1. How did Pueblo life change under Spanish rule?
2. What role did religious beliefs and practices play in the lives of the Pueblos?
3. How did learning to grow corn change the lives of the Anasazi?

THINK ABOUT IT
1. Compare the role of Pueblo women to that of women in today's society.
2. Pueblo villages were made up of box-shaped, apartment-like dwellings.
(a) Why do you think this particular design was chosen by the Pueblo?
(b) What are the advantages and disadvantages of this design?

3 PRINCE HENRY'S DREAM

Portugal's Prince Henry (1394-1460) was a hero in war. He is remembered, however, for his bold efforts in opening up new sea routes to the riches of the East Indies—even though he remained at home in the port city of Lagos.

On a rocky cliff high above the ocean, a man stood motionless, looking out to sea. The night was dark but clear. Below him, waves slapped against the cliff.

The man was Prince Henry of Portugal. The year, 1434. Henry was watching—and praying — for the safe return of a Portuguese ship. He had sent the ship out on a dangerous voyage to explore the coast of Africa.

For more than 15 years, Henry had been sending explorers on these sea voyages. Each time, the new wooden sailing ships, called caravels, got a little farther down Africa's western coast.

There was one place that no one had yet dared to pass. For centuries, many people in Europe had believed that this place was the end of the world. It was a desolate and empty stretch of land called Cape Bojador in what is now Western Sahara.

Beyond Cape Bojador, legend said, the sea boiled. Monsters lurked underwater. The sun was so hot that it would burn away one's skin.

It was a bold explorer indeed who would venture into these regions. Now, standing alone on the cliff, Henry waited, hoping. He had sent a trusted squire, Gil Eanes, on this last journey. The prince had begged Eanes to "strain every nerve to pass that cape." He had told the sailor, "You cannot find a peril so great that the hope of reward will not be greater."

The next day, Henry's hopes and prayers were fulfilled. Eanes returned with a welcome tale. He had sailed past Bojador and found no monsters, no boiling sea. Instead, he brought Prince Henry some flowers pulled from the ground at the place he had landed.

Henry loved planning these journeys. He made his home at the very southwestern tip of Portugal, practically in the Atlantic Ocean. There, sailors and mapmakers from Portugal and other parts of Europe gathered to plan their voyages. Although Henry never led a voyage himself, he became known as Henry the Navigator.

Exploring the Unknown

Why was Henry so eager to explore Africa? There were many reasons. For one thing, he hoped to find new wealth for Portugal. Perhaps his sailors would find gold in West Africa. Or maybe they would reach new markets for Portuguese goods.

Henry may have even dreamed of sailing around Africa to find a water route to Asia, or the East Indies in present-day Indonesia. In the 1400s, Europe traded with countries in the East Indies for highly prized items like fine jewels, silks, ceramics, and spices.

Spices were extremely important. In those days, there was no way to keep meat fresh for long periods of time. In the winter, meat might be stored for months. Spices like pepper, cinnamon, and cloves helped to preserve food a little bit. And if the meat was served rotten, as it often was, the spices could disguise the bad taste.

These precious spices did not grow in Europe. The only place they grew was in the islands of Indonesia.

The spices were imported to Europe. But the overland trade route to the East Indies was long and dangerous. Some of it lay in Muslim countries that were often at war with European nations. There were many stops along the way where the goods changed hands. Each time they did, someone would make a profit. By the time the silks, jewels, and spices got to Europe, they were extremely expensive. European rulers grew intent on finding a safe, direct sea route to the East. Portugal and Spain were leaders in this search. They had many experienced sailors and boat builders. By the end of the century, they were fiercely compet-

Early explorers used astrolabes like this one to measure the altitudes of the stars. They'd determine longitude, latitude, and other information by which to navigate their ships with this tool.

European-Asian Trade Routes, 1450

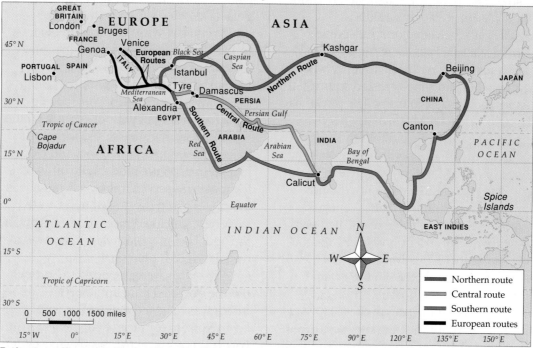

Estimate and compare the lengths of each trade route. Which trade route requires more water travel? More land travel? Which route do you think would have taken the most time in 1450? Why?

ing. Each wanted to be the first to reach the Indies by ship.

Religious Wars

Portugal and Spain had religious reasons for exploration as well as economic ones. For centuries, Christians and Muslims had fought in Europe, Africa, and Asia. Like most Christians of the time, Henry thought of Muslim peoples as enemy **infidels** (non-believers). In his lifetime, Henry took part in three battles against Muslim armies in North Africa.

Henry hoped that Portugese explorers would contact Christians living in Africa or Asia. These Christians, he thought, could then help him in his wars against the Muslims. Even if there were no Christians living there, he reasoned,

the voyages would still be useful. They would help him find out as much as possible about the Muslim enemy.

After Gil Eanes passed Cape Bojador, Portuguese explorers had many more successes. Moving south along Africa's coast, they discovered the gold Henry sought. They found exotic animals: elephants and sea lions, which they called sea wolves. Soon Portugal was making a profit selling sea lion oil and skins.

Slave Trade Roots

The Portuguese were the first Europeans to meet the African peoples of the Kongo (in present-day Angola). Like other African states of the period, the Kingdom of the Kongo had an army, court system, and an internal revenue department. It

AMERICAN ADVENTURES

also traded with other African kingdoms.

One European explorer later described his meeting with a South African people known as the Hottentots: "Here people [are] … dressed in skins and furs. The women wear turbans of sheepskin on their heads. The people's speech is clipped. Instead of gold, they exchange their goods for iron. They carry white staffs. Their weapons are long spears and slings. They wear white leather sandals upon their feet."

In 1444, Henry's explorers found another source of profit: the African people themselves. In that year, two ships returned to Portugal with ten captive Africans. It was the beginning of the European slave trade that would last almost 400 years.

During that time, millions of Africans would be kidnapped and taken from their homes and countries. They would be sent to Europe, and to colonies the Europeans were building in the New World. The slave trade would yield great wealth to merchants. Only after the slave trade began, did Europeans begin to describe Africans as savage-like. Some Europeans tried to justify the slave trade by saying they were bringing Christianity to Africans. But slavery would just bring degradation, despair, and suffering to generations of African victims.

Prince Henry died in 1460. In 1488, a fellow Portuguese, Bartolomeu Dias, sailed around the southern tip of Africa. Ten years later, another Portuguese, Vasco da Gama, sailed farther—around Africa and all the way to India. Portugal had found a long-sought sea route to Asia. Lisbon, Portugal's capital, soon flourished as Europe's center for the spice trade.

Prince Henry's dream had come true. Portugal grew rich and powerful from its explorations. Henry's adventurous spirit had opened the way for a new age.

CHAPTER CHECK

WORD MATCH
1. desolate
2. cloves
3. infidels
4. exotic
5. Muslims

a. a fragrant spice
b. non-believers of a dominant religion
c. believe in the God, Allah
d. lonely and abandoned
e. rare and colorful

QUICK QUIZ
1. Why were spices extremely important to the Europeans in the 1400s?
2. What caused silks, jewels, and spices to be so expensive in Europe?
3. Why did Lisbon, Portugal's capital, become Europe's center for the spice trade?

THINK ABOUT IT
Prince Henry had several reasons for wanting to explore the coast of Africa. (a) State those reasons. (b) Which of the reasons do you think was most important? (c) Why?

CHAPTER 4 COLUMBUS IN THE NEW WORLD

Columbus made four voyages to the Americas, but none was as important as the first. This painting by Edward Hicks (1780-1849) portrays that landing, when he was greeted by native Arawaks.

Christopher Columbus was worried. His ships, the *Niña*, the *Pinta*, and the *Santa María*, had left Spain on August 3, 1492. His goal was to reach the Indies by sailing west into unknown waters of the Atlantic ocean. At that time, most Europeans knew of only three continents—their own, Africa, and Asia. These continents, they believed, formed a big island that was surrounded by the sea. Columbus and others were sure that the world was round, like a large ball. So it seemed only natural to the great sea captain that by sailing west he would reach the Indies.

Yet it was now October 10, 1492, and the ships had seen no land for weeks. Columbus' men were becoming rebellious. They feared that they would never see home again. They demanded that Columbus turn back to Spain.

"The men could stand it no longer. They grumbled and complained of the long voyage," Columbus wrote in his diary. "I [lectured] them for their lack of spirit. I told the men that I had started out to find the Indies and would continue until I had accomplished the mission."

20

AMERICAN ADVENTURES

These were brave words, but Columbus had to **compromise.** He promised the men that if they did not find land within three days he would turn back. Then, two days later, they saw land. It was an island in the Bahamas off the coast of present-day Florida that Columbus named San Salvador. Columbus did not know that he had "discovered" a new continent—America. He believed that this island was close to China and Japan. Columbus took possession of the island in the name of King Ferdinand and Queen Isabella of Spain, who with others had paid for the voyage.

Christopher Columbus (1451-1506), once named Admiral of the Ocean Sea for his discovery, died almost forgotten.

Meeting the Arawaks

The people of the island fled inland when they first saw the "monstrous" Spanish ships coming near. But curiosity got the best of them. They approached the tall, strange-looking men on the beach and offered them gifts.

Because Columbus thought he was in the Indies, he called these people Indians. They were, in fact, Arawaks (AR-ah-waks). Arawaks lived on the chain of islands which stretch from the tip of Florida to South America.

"They are friendly people who bear no arms except for small spears, and they have no iron [guns]," wrote Columbus in his diary. "I want the natives to develop a friendly attitude toward us. I therefore gave red caps to some and glass beads to others. They took great pleasure in this and became so friendly that it was a marvel.

"In the afternoon they brought us parrots, balls of cotton thread and a kind of dry leaf [tobacco] that they hold in great esteem. They ought to make good and skilled servants, for they repeat very quickly whatever we say to them," wrote Columbus. Several Arawaks learned to speak Spanish and served as guides for the group.

Hoping to Find Riches

Columbus sailed for the Indies hoping to find great riches—gold, jewels, silks, and spices. Because he found only a few gold trinkets, he was disappointed. But in sailing to other islands, he had many enriching encounters with the people he called Indians.

The Indians did have a religion, Columbus realized. "They are not idolaters [people who worship idols]," he wrote in his diary, "but rather they are very meek and know no evil. They are very trusting. They believe there is a God in Heaven, and they firmly believe we come from Heaven."

The Arawaks shared their way of life with the Europeans. The Arawaks introduced Columbus to tobacco (the

The Four Voyages of Columbus

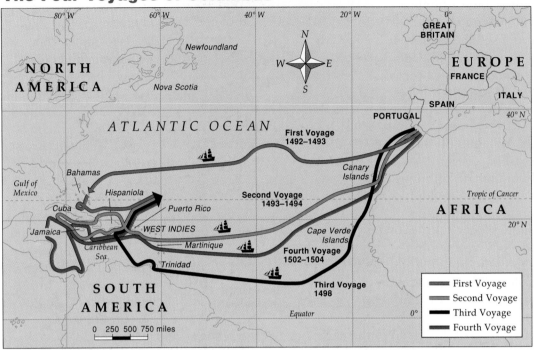

Study the key. Which islands did Columbus go to on his first voyage? Which did he visit on his second voyage? On which voyage did he go to South America?

name comes from the Arawak word for cigar), as well as hammocks (comfortable swinging beds), and foods such as corn and potatoes.

On the coast of another island, Columbus met a young chief and invited him to visit the *Santa María*. This is how he described the visit in his diary:

"After the meal a servant of his brought a belt. He gave this to me, along with two very thin pieces of gold. I saw that a cover on my bed pleased him, so I presented it to him along with some very good amber beads. I also gave him some red shoes and a flask of orange flower water. This pleased him wonderfully. I sent him ashore with great honors and fired a salute with the cannons."

Admiral of the Ocean Sea

Columbus took notes about the trip for King Ferdinand and Queen Isabella. "Your Highnesses," he wrote, "may rest assured that these lands are so good and fertile that there is no one who can describe it. Your Highnesses may believe that this island and all the others are as much yours as is Castile [Spain]."

Like most Europeans of the time, Columbus viewed the Arawaks as people to be conquered and converted to Christianity. He wanted to make them **subjects** of Spain. It was also a time when explorers wanted to spread Christianity to the New World. To bring Christianity to the Indians was considered very noble. "All that is needed here is to build a town

AMERICAN ADVENTURES

and order the Indians to do your bidding," wrote Columbus. "They are suitable to be governed and made to work and to build villages. They can be taught to wear clothes and observe our customs." The friendly Arawaks, on the other hand, only wanted to live peacefully.

Columbus sailed back to Spain in January 1493. He rode horseback across Spain to meet with the king and queen. He forced a few Arawaks to travel with him. In a great reception, Columbus was named Admiral of the Ocean Sea.

He went on three more voyages to the New World. Until he died, Columbus believed that he had reached the offshore islands of the Indies. It was only later that explorers learned Columbus had landed in islands off the coast of a new continent,

named America. His voyages to the New World led to lasting contact between Europe and the Americas.

Christopher Columbus and his crew braved the vast unknown "Ocean Sea" in tiny ships like this one, known as caravels.

CHAPTER CHECK

WORD MATCH
1. compromise
2. monstrous
3. idolators
4. subjects
5. rebellious

a. characterized by opposition to one in authority
b. owing allegiance to the crown
c. overwhelming
d. people who worship idols
e. mutual agreement

QUICK QUIZ
1. How did the Indians react to the arrival of Columbus?
2. What caused Columbus to believe that the Indians had a religion?
3. How did Columbus's trip to the New World change Europe and the rest of the world?

THINK ABOUT IT
Assume that you were one of the Native Americans who met Columbus and his sailors when they arrived in the New World. How would you have reacted? How would you have described your visitors?

CHAPTER 5

CONQUISTADORES

Found on a high canyon wall in what is today Arizona, this Navajo painting depicts the arrival of the Spanish explorers, missionaries, and conquerors.

The white beach sparkled like diamonds. Eleven Spanish ships with 550 men, 16 horses, and 14 brass cannons approached the coast of Mexico in 1519. The men on the ships were Spanish soldiers who came to the New World seeking fame and fortune. Hernán Cortés, their leader, had gone first to Cuba, where he gained much land. When he heard stories of Mexico—a land rich in gold, ruled by the Aztecs—Cortés wanted to visit the Aztec empire.

After landing and marching inland, Cortés, the Spanish **conquistador** (kahn-KEES-tuh-dawr), or conquerer, and his army reached the outskirts of Tenochtitlán. "There were great towers and temples and buildings rising from the water," wrote Bernal Díaz, a soldier traveling with Cortés. "Some of our soldiers even asked whether the things that we saw were not a dream."

Moctezuma met Cortés and his men in a golden-covered chair carried by four nobles. Moctezuma treated Cortés as if he might be the god Quetzalcoatl. He presented Cortés with flowers and golden necklaces. "You have come to your city," said Moctezuma. "Now you have come out of the clouds and mists to sit on your throne again."

"Tell Moctezuma that we are his friends," replied Cortés through a translator. "There is nothing to fear." Cortés lied. Within one year, Cortés took Moctezuma prisoner and stole his gold. Cortés, and his Indian **allies** destroyed the Aztec empire.

Other Spanish conquistadores soon heard about the riches in North and South America. Francisco Vasquez de Coronado (fran-SEES-koh VAHS-kayz day koh-ro-NAH-doh) was a young Spanish nobleman. He came to the New World in 1535 to seek riches of his own. By 1538, he was governor of a frontier province northwest of Mexico City.

All of Mexico, at the time, was abuzz with rumors of the seven fabulously wealthy cities of Cíbola (SEE-boh-lah). They heard one was the capital of a great Indian empire. They were told that the streets were paved with gold and that the buildings were set with precious stones. The Spanish had a legend of their own about seven bishops who had left Spain hundreds of years before to settle new lands in the Atlantic Ocean. So the stories of Cíbola seemed like they might be true.

Trek to Cíbola

A Spanish explorer, Alvar Cabeza de Vaca (kah-BAY-sa da VAH-kah), had returned in 1536 from a long expedition on which he claimed to have seen these cities. A Franciscan priest, Marcos de Niza, confirmed Cabeza de

Vaca's account after his own expedition in 1539. De Niza said that his black companion Esteban had visited the cities before being killed by Indians.

Coronado persuaded his friend Antonio de Mendoza, **viceroy** (governor) of Mexico, to send him out to conquer them. The viceroy urged Coronado to report on the customs of the people he met along the way and to **convert** them to Christianity.

With de Niza as a guide, Coronado left Mexico City in February 1540. They were accompanied by 300 heavily armored Spanish soldiers, 1000 Indians, and several priests. Coronado himself wore gold-covered armor and a plumed helmet. With this colorful group traveled hundreds of mules, pack horses, and herds of cattle.

In less than a month, the party had traveled across the rough, dry Mexican terrain in northwest Mexico. Then Coro-

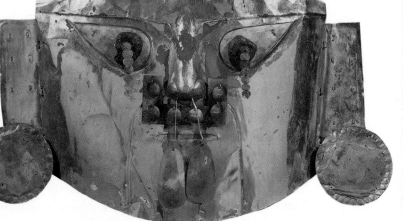

Like the Aztecs, many Indian cultures of South America made ornate masks. Chimu Indians of Peru created this gold funeral mask some time between the 10th and 15th centuries.

nado took a smaller group with him across mountains and desert into what is today Arizona and New Mexico. In the intense heat of July, after traveling more than 1000 miles, they finally reached Cíbola.

There was no gold. There were no jewels. There were only several hostile Zuñi Indians. Coronado's demand that they surrender and convert to Christianity was met with arrows. Only after a difficult battle were the Spanish victorious. Father de Niza was disgraced. Coronado sent him home before the angry men could turn on him.

The Search Continues

Deeply disappointed, Coronado decided there must be gold somewhere nearby. He sent out scouting parties to see what they could find. One party, under Pedro de Tovar, headed northwest were it found some dusty Hopi villages—but no gold. Another party reached the Colorado River running through the Grand Canyon. They were the first Europeans to set sight on this incredible American landmark.

Meanwhile, to the east, other Spanish scouts explored a Pueblo settlement around Tiguex (tee-GWAY) in the Rio Grande River valley. A Plains Indian they called the Turk, probably because

of his turban-like headdress, became their guide. They wandered around the high plains of north Texas. There they saw herds of strange, shaggy beasts—buffalo.

The Turk told them stories about a great city to the north named Quivira. Bells of gold supposedly hung from trees. In the winter of 1540 to 1541, the main group left Cíbola and camped in Tiguex, preparing for yet another conquest.

But by the time they reached Tiguex, the Indians were not so impressed by Coronado and his armed men. They resented having to feed and clothe the Spanish. They decided to be rid of them once and for all. It took 50 days for the Spanish to put down the rebellion. They burned one pueblo and destroyed another. Finally, when order was restored in April, Coronado set off again in search of the fabled cities of gold. The Turk was bound in chains for the trip.

This time Coronado marched through present-day Texas and Oklahoma. The

This painting called "The Great Explorers III—Coronado" by Frederic Remington (1861-1909), shows Coronado with his men in the American Southwest.

AMERICAN ADVENTURES

trip was very difficult. Each man carried about 30 pounds of armor. There was little fresh water. When supplies began to run out, Coronado sent the main group back to Tiguex. But he plunged on until he reached Quivira. He was near what is today Great Bend, Kansas.

More Disappointments

Once again, however, he was disappointed. There was still no gold, jewels, or riches of any kind—only the straw huts of the Wichita Indians. At least they were friendly. They talked with Coronado and his men.

When the Turk confessed to misleading him, Coronado had the Turk executed. Coronado returned to Tiguex for the winter. There he was kicked in the head by a horse. He never quite recovered from the injury.

Coronado's return was a great disappointment to Viceroy Mendoza. He had spent a great deal of money. Many lives had been lost. In 1546, Coronado was accused of mistreating the Indians in his group, unjustly ordering the Turk's execution, and abandoning the trip without government permission. Although Coronado was later acquitted of these charges, his health and spirit were broken. He died in Mexico City in 1554.

Coronado's explorations were considered a great failure at the time. Yet through them, Europeans learned much about North America. His expeditions had extended from the Gulf of California through Arizona, New Mexico, Texas, and into Oklahoma and Kansas.

Chapter Check

WORD MATCH
1. viceroy   **a.** cause to change from one belief to another
2. convert   **b.** office similar to governor
3. conquistador   **c.** type of animal native to the American West
4. allies   **d.** conqueror
5. buffalo   **e.** people united for a specific purpose

QUICK QUIZ
1. Why did Coronado believe that the fabled seven cities of gold did exist in the New World?
2. What effects did Coronado's explorations have on the Indians?
3. What did Europeans learn about North America as a result of Coronado's explorations?

THINK ABOUT IT
1. What obstacles did Coronado encounter during his explorations?
2. Coronado's explorations were considered a failure by his fellow Spaniards. Do you agree? Why or why not?

6 THE FIVE NATIONS

These murals show two sachems—council chiefs of the League of the Iroquois. This league of five great Native American nations is one of the models for our democratic system of government.

Dekanawida, a Huron Indian who lived in present-day Canada, spoke to a large Native American group called the Iroquois (IHR-uh-kwoy) around the year 1400. He told of a dream in which he envisioned a Great Peace. In his dream, a giant fir tree grew on a cliff. At the top of the tree, an eagle hovered, keeping watch. Dekanawida interpreted his dream to mean that the five Iroquois tribes—the Mohawk, Oneida, Onondaga, Cayuga, and Seneca—should live in harmony and stand united against their common enemies.

Iroquois villages extended from the Hudson River Valley in what is now eastern New York State to the Great Lakes. The Iroquois had been fighting one another and with other tribes over boundaries and hunting and fishing rights for generations.

In one village, Dekanawida met an Onondaga chief living among the Mohawks. Named

Hiawatha, he put Dekanawida's ideas into practice to end a war between his tribe and the Onondagas. They had been fighting for so long that the people were in rags.

Hiawatha traveled around other Iroquois villages trying to abolish feuding through peace. Through him, Dekanawida's dream was fulfilled. The five great tribes formed the Ho-De-No Sau-Nee, or League of the Iroquois. By uniting, they became very strong. They became known as the Five Nations, and their wilderness **confederation** (a bond between groups) lasted for 400 years.

Longhouse Builders

The League's symbol became the tree and the eagle in Dekanawida's dream. It included five arrows bound together in unity and five strings of beads, standing for the five tribes. The Iroquois called the League a confederacy of five fires. Later, they would call the United States the 13 fires, because of the 13 original states.

The Onondagas became the firekeepers of the League. Each year, 50 representatives from member tribes met in the Onondaga council house. The council chiefs (including some women), called **sachems**, and lesser chiefs dealt with mat-

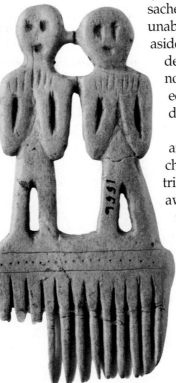

Iroquois women used feathers and porcupine quills to decorate their hair and clothing. This Iroquois woman's hair comb was made out of bone.

ters common to all of the tribes. Before any action could be taken, all the sachems had to agree. If they were unable, the issue had to be set aside. The council passed laws to deal with crimes, but they had no say in how the free and equal tribes ran their day-to-day affairs.

Sachems, who wore deer antlers on their heads, were chosen by the women of their tribes. The women could take away the deer horns if they thought a sachem was unworthy. The lesser chiefs were great speakers for the people, but they did not have the power to vote in the council.

The Iroquois lived in deep forests. Their food, clothing, homes, and transportation all came from their environment. The men hunted deer and bear. In canoes hollowed out of elm trees, they fished in the region's many lakes and rivers.

The women grew corn, beans, and squash in **communal** (shared ownership) fields. Corn was pounded in hollowed logs to get meal or flour. This was often mixed with beans, berries, or nuts. In spring, they tapped maple trees for syrup, which they used to make sugar.

The Iroquois name means "we long house builders." Their **longhouses**, covered with elm bark, were home to as many as 20 families. Each family had its own apartment with a fireplace on either side of a central room. Though men built the longhouses, they were owned by women.

Iroquois Beliefs

The Iroquois believed that animals were spirit helpers, and that every person had his or her own spiritual guide. But some spirits caused sickness. Members of the False Face Society could break these evil spells in their ceremonies. They wore masks with twisted features, strained eyes, and long, stringy hair. Masked men went from house to house, shaking large rattles made from turtle shells, and they spread ashes on those who were ill.

Fierce and ruthless warriors, the Iroquois painted their faces with bright colors to frighten enemies. Often, they adopted captives into the tribe.

Though the Iroquois had no written language, they recorded their history with **wampum** beads. These beads, made from clamshells, were extremely valuable. Making them took great skill and patience. The white, purple, and black beads, woven into belts or strung on strings, each had their own meaning, and their designs could be read like a book.

By custom, all important statements were accompanied by a gift, to indicate that the statement was both serious and true. Treaties between the Iroquois and other Indian nations customarily were accompanied by an exchange of wampum. Europeans, who later became neighbors of the Iroquois, quickly learned that they could buy furs with wampum.

This watercolor-and-ink drawing of Native American warriors appeared in a book written by a French missionary in the mid-1600s.

AMERICAN ADVENTURES

The League traded with the new Dutch settlers for firearms in the early 1600s. These weapons helped them to control a strategic region in the North American continent—from present-day Maine to Michigan and from the St. Lawrence River to Tennessee. The Iroquois also regulated fur trade and boat travel in the Great Lakes.

When the French and English began to establish colonial empires in the 17th century, they took great trouble to win the League's friendship because of its power. The League traded furs with the British. It sided with the British against the French in the war for control of North America from 1754 to 1763. The British won the war.

Europeans had brought firearms, 3 iron cooking pots, horses, wheeled vehicles, and diseases, for which the Native Americans had no immunities. They also brought whisky. This led some Native Americans, who had never had strong drink before, into giving up their lands and furs for almost nothing. The Iroquois became more and more dependent on the European goods. They began to lose the self-reliance that had made them strong. By the time of the American Revolution (1775 to 1783), the Iroquois League of Nations had splintered.

When the Constitution of the United States was written, American leaders looked at the Iroquois League's form of government. Dekanawida's dream of a Great Peace was used as a model for the federal government that would unite the 13 colonies as free and equal states.

CHAPTER CHECK

WORD MATCH
1. confederation   **a.** multiple residence houses
2. communal   **b.** shared ownership
3. wampum   **c.** a bond between two groups   alliance
4. sachems   **d.** beads made from clam shells
5. longhouses   **e.** council chiefs chosen by each tribe

QUICK QUIZ
1. Describe the life and culture of the Iroquois.
2. How did the Iroquois benefit from trading with the Dutch, French, and English?
3. What factors contributed to the decline of the powerful self-reliant Iroquois Indians?

THINK ABOUT IT
1. Both the Iroquois and the Europeans placed a high value on wampum. How did their value systems differ?
2. What aspects of the Constitution of the United States closely resemble the government of the Iroquois Indians?

7 LA SALLE'S QUEST

René Cavalier, Sieur de La Salle (1643-78), was a bold explorer and great pioneer from France. In this painting by American George Catlin, La Salle meets with the Indians.

His enemies called him a madman and a traitor. He was too ambitious and greedy, they said. All he wanted was to become rich and powerful.

In fact, none of these things mattered to the young French explorer, René Cavelier, Sieur de La Salle. He did not deny being ambitious. His dream was to create a great empire for France in the heart of North America in the late 17th century. It would mean exploring the vast, unknown region through which the Mississippi River flowed. At that time, Native Americans lived there. La Salle

wanted to open it up to French settlers and traders.

French Canada was a cold country. But the land south of the Great Lakes was mild, Indians told him. There were countless beavers, otters, and minks whose furs would make fortunes. The soil was fertile and would grow anything.

Everyone would prosper. The flag of France would fly over this great land between the Appalachian Mountains on the east and the Rocky Mountains on the west. At the same time, La Salle would win fame, glory, and wealth for himself.

He endured great hardships for his ambition. In the end, it cost him his life, but his explorations would lead to France's control of the entire Mississippi River valley.

The Spirit of Adventure

La Salle was born in 1643 in Rouen, France. His father, a wealthy merchant, wanted him to become a priest. At 16, René took the vows of the Jesuit order and two years later became a teacher. But La Salle was not happy. He wanted to go to Canada as a missionary. When his wish was refused, he quit the Jesuits. In 1666, he sailed for Canada on his own.

In Montreal, La Salle became a farmer and a fur trader. Seneca Indians told him about rivers flowing through rich valleys. The Senecas' stories fired him with the desire to explore. Selling his land, he organized an **expedition** to sail down the Ohio River. La Salle learned from the Senecas that it flowed into a large river, the Missisippi. From then on, he would not rest until he claimed that river for France.

At times, La Salle and his men withstood great difficulties. They often had to carry canoes and supplies around waterfalls for as much as ten miles. When the rivers froze, the men had to go on foot through forests deep in snow. Sometimes they were so hungry they would eat the remains of an animal killed by wolves.

Some Indian peoples were friendly and helpful. Others were hostile and threatening. One day, an Illinois chief warned the explorers not to go on with their search for the Mississippi. Fierce tribes would attack them, he said. The river was full of "monsters, alligators, and serpents." It had many falls that ended in bottomless pits. La Salle and his men would be swallowed up and disappear underground.

La Salle began to fear that it was the Illinois Indians who would attack him if he went on. Some of his men thought so too and deserted him. But La Salle would not surrender to threats. The next morning he and the rest of his men continued and eventually found the Mississippi.

After years of exploring the upper Mississippi River and its branches, La Salle finally reached the mouth of the river at the Gulf of Mexico. He was the first French explorer to do so.

On April 9, 1682, he placed a French flag and a cross there. La Salle claimed all the land from the Great Lakes south to the Gulf of Mexico for the French king, Louis XIV. In honor of the king, he named this territory Louisiana. France now had the largest colonial empire in North America.

Winnebago Indians on the Upper Mississippi River used their blankets as sails. La Salle spent years exploring the Mississippi.

Enemy Plots

La Salle had reached the highest point of his career. From then on, he was beset by ene-

This detail, from the ornate border of a 1718 map, shows the city of Quebec as La Salle knew it.

mies who did everything possible to ruin him. Who were these enemies? Mostly they were powerful fur traders in Montreal and Quebec. They were jealous of La Salle's success. The French king had rewarded the explorer with many gifts. He had given La Salle Fort Frontenac on Lake Ontario. Indians brought their furs to the **fort** (permanent army post) rather than make the long trip down the St. Lawrence River to Montreal and Quebec. La Salle could now become the richest fur trader in all of French Canada.

But La Salle was not just interested in gaining wealth. He wanted to make the French empire in North America safe against all enemies. Most of all he feared the powerful Iroquois, who were allied with the British. The Iroquois were attack-

ing and crushing other Indian tribes in French territory. If the Iroquois attacks were not stopped, the French would lose the fur trade.

La Salle wanted to unite the Indian tribes in the Louisiana Territory against the Iroquois. He would build a chain of forts to protect them. Many tribes favored his ideas and joined his alliance. More than 14,000 Native Americans joined the Illinois Indians and settled in the Fort St. Louis area.

But in Montreal and Quebec, La Salle's enemies plotted against him. The new governor of French Canada was joined with La Salle's enemies. He accused La Salle of dealing with the British. The governor took over Fort Frontenac and refused to send supplies to

Fort St. Louis. He also encouraged the Iroquois to attack La Salle.

More Trouble Develops

To defend Louisiana, La Salle needed the help of the French king. He sailed for France and met with Louis XIV, the most powerful ruler in Europe. La Salle told the king that he wanted to build a fort and a colony at the mouth of the Mississippi. The king gave La Salle everything he wanted. In the summer of 1684, four ships sailed from France with 230 settlers and supplies for the new **colony** (settlement).

Trouble soon developed. The ships completely missed the mouth of the Mississippi. Instead they landed on the coast near present-day Galveston, Texas. La Salle was furious with the sea captain. In a huff, the captain sailed back to France, taking some of the colonists with him.

La Salle built a fort on the Texas coast. In this dreary **wilderness** (undeveloped area), the colonists were attacked constantly by Indians. Many of them died of disease. La Salle himself became ill and almost died. The settlers were overcome with fear and misery.

When La Salle recovered, he set out on foot with 16 men to find the Mississippi River. They wanted to sail to Canada for help. But the trail was rough and the men suffered greatly. Finally they could stand it no longer. A mutiny broke out somewhere in eastern Texas. La Salle was murdered. His body was left for the wolves.

So ended the great explorer's life. But because of his efforts, France took possession of the huge Louisiana Territory in the heart of North America.

CHAPTER CHECK

WORD MATCH

1. fort
2. wilderness
3. colony
4. traitor
5. expedition

a. undeveloped land area
b. trip taken for a specific purpose
c. permanent army post
d. settlement or community
e. one who betrays another's trust

QUICK QUIZ

1. Compare how the French king treated La Salle to how his enemies treated him.
2. What were La Salle's reasons for exploring the Mississippi Valley? List them in terms of their relative importance.
3. (a) Why did La Salle fear the Iroquois Indians? (b) Was his fear justified? Why or why not?

THINK ABOUT IT

1. How did La Salle help to make France the greatest colonial power in North America?
2. What facts presented in this chapter cause one to believe that La Salle was a determined, courageous person?

CULTURES MEET

History Detective

1. I dreamed a pale, bearded ruler sailing from the east would take my throne. Who am I?
2. I was a great, floating island capital—center of the Aztec people. What am I?
3. Named Pueblo Bonita by the Spaniards, my walls once rang with the voices of a thousand people. Where am I?
4. My dreams of exploring Africa helped launch a new age in Europe. Who am I?
5. I trekked across much of the present-day American Southwest in search of Cíbola. Who am I?
6. Dekanawida called me the Great Peace; the Iroquois called me the "five fires." What am I?
7. Claimed by La Salle, I formed the heart of the French empire in North America. What am I?

Voices From the Past

In May 1502, Christopher Columbus set out on his fourth and final voyage across the Atlantic. On board was his 13-year-old son, Ferdinand, who later wrote a biography of his famous father. Read the selection below and answer the questions that follow.

Now the gate was open, anyone could follow the coast [of America]… after the Admiral [Columbus] had shown them the way… For he was convinced that new treasures would be found daily, as he had earlier written… in reference to his discovery: "It must be followed up, because it is certain if not now, then later some new thing of great value will be found." New Spain and Peru have since shown the truth of this observation, but at the time nobody believed what he said.

1. Does Ferdinand believe his father's accomplishments were properly recognized? What evidence supports your answer?
2. Why is Ferdinand's account a valuable source of information on Columbus? What inaccuracies might it have? Why?

Hands–On History

1. *Reading a Map*—Use a historical atlas to find a map of the various Indian cultures at the time of European arrival in the 1500s. Locate the different groups named in this unit.
2. *Thinking Historically*—Pretend you are on one of the first Spanish or French expeditions to the Americas. In diary form, record what it was like to walk the American land.

The *Niña* Limps Into Portugal

Lisbon, March 4, 1493—An armed guard under the command of Bartholmeu Dias sailed into Lisbon harbor this morning to meet the battered ship of Admiral Christopher Columbus. Admiral Columbus is claiming to have just returned from a voyage to the Indies. Columbus presented Dias with a letter of identification from the King of Spain. He then requested permission to fix the *Niña's* torn sails. Dias agreed, but not before inquiring about the strangely clad people on board that Columbus called Indians. By midday, ships filled Lisbon's harbor, as throngs of people tried to catch a glimpse of the *Niña's* "passengers."

Instead of just gold and spices, Columbus found a new world.

1.

Valparaiso, March 9, 1493 — Before setting off for Spain, Columbus paid King John II a visit at the Portuguese royal palace outside Lisbon. Columbus's story, said the king, sounded like a tall tale. Having refused twice to back Columbus's trip across the Atlantic, the king asked to see the Indians for himself. Surely they must be Africans, said John.

The Indians, however, were like no Africans the Portuguese had ever seen. Two of them drew maps of unknown islands to the west and presented the king with an odd food called beans. Convinced that Columbus had stumbled across new lands, the king beat his chest and cried out "Why did I let slip such a wonderful chance?"

Columbus Marches Triumphant Into Spain

Barcelona, April 20, 1493—People all over the city of Barcelona turned out to cheer the return of their hero. Columbus looked every inch the title bestowed upon him by the king and queen of Spain—"Our Admiral of the Ocean Sea and Viceroy and Governor of the islands discovered in the Indies."

Tanned by the many months at sea, the Admiral rode at the head of a grand procession. His gray hair gleamed in the sun. Behind him walked six Indians and dozens of servants carrying brilliantly plumed parrots, golden masks, and rare spices. These were things, said one observer, "never before seen in Spain nor heard of."

Imaginations Run Rampant in Spain

Cadiz, September 25, 1493—This morning, Columbus weighed anchor and set off on a second journey across the Atlantic.

2.

You Be the Reporter

Match each question with its news item above.

1. What headline would you write for this article?

2. How would you complete this article to explain what Spaniards may have expected of Columbus's second voyage?

READING A HISTORICAL MAP

Imagine that you are a reporter for the *New France News* and the year is 1688. You have been assigned to write a factual account of La Salle's explorations. Your only source of information is a map, like the one on the opposite page, drawn by La Salle's guide. It is a **historical map,** because it shows where events took place at different times. Where did La Salle's explorations take him, and when was he there? The map holds some answers.

Study the map's key. Then note the answers to these questions on a separate sheet of paper.

1. La Salle first set out in 1669 from the settlement of Ville-Marie. Find it on the map. **(a)** On what river was Ville-Marie located? **(b)** What other settlement was about 150 miles northeast of it?

2. To find "the land of rich valleys and flowing waters," La Salle made several expeditions. They are shown on the map by colored arrows with dates. In what years did La Salle **(a)** explore the land along the Belle Riviere? **(b)** first travel on the Mississippi River? **(c)** explore the Great Lakes?

3. Find the route of La Salle's first expedition. **(a)** In which direction did he travel? **(b)** How far from Ville-Marie did he get? (Use the map's scale to estimate the distance.) **(c)** Which Native American tribes did he encounter? **(d)** How long did this expedition take?

4. Follow the route of La Salle's second expedition on the map. **(a)** Where did it begin? **(b)** In what year did it begin? **(c)** Describe the route. **(d)** On his second expedition, La Salle passed through a mission and established two forts. What were their names?

5. Use the map's scale to estimate the distance in miles along the route of La Salle's second expedition. **(a)** Was the distance longer or shorter than La Salle's first expedition? **(b)** Which route took less time? Why?

6. Early in 1682, La Salle and his party reached the Mississippi River. **(a)** They entered it from what other river? **(b)** How far was it from this point to the mouth of the Mississippi? **(c)** How long did it take La Salle to travel this distance?

7. In 1684, La Salle made a costly mistake. Sailing from France, he hoped to enter the mouth of the Mississippi from the Gulf of Mexico. **(a)** The mouth of the river was located at what position of latitude and longitude? **(b)** At what latitude/longitude position did La Salle go ashore? **(c)** How far off course was he?

8. After setting up a fort in 1685, La Salle traveled inland. **(a)** How far from the fort was he killed? **(b)** How long had he been in the region? **(c)** Why do you think he had been there that long?

9. Write an article for the *New France News*. Describe La Salle's explorations, and explain why they were important.

10. La Salle claimed the area of the Mississippi valley for France, and named it "Louisiana" for King Louis XIV. Compare this map with the political map of the United States, on page 812. What states now exist in La Salle's Louisiana?

    For Extra Credit: Make a timeline of La Salle's journeys, using information from this map.

La Salle's Expeditions, 1669-1687

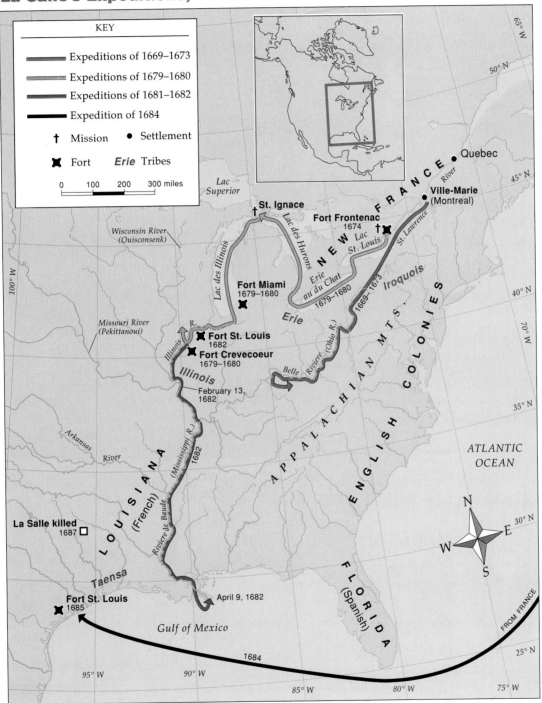

KEY

Expeditions of 1669–1673
Expeditions of 1679–1680
Expeditions of 1681–1682
Expedition of 1684

† Mission   • Settlement
✠ Fort   *Erie* Tribes

0   100   200   300 miles

Lac Superior

† **St. Ignace**

Wisconsin River (Ouisconsenk)

Lac des Illinois

Lac des Hurons

Fort Frontenac
1674

Lac St. Louis

N E W   F R A N C E

• Quebec

St. Lawrence River

Ville-Marie
(Montreal)

Erie au du Chat

Fort Miami
1679–1680

Erie

1679–1680

1669–1673

Iroquois

Missouri River (Pekittanoui)

R.

✠ **Fort St. Louis**
1682

Illinois

✠ **Fort Crevecoeur**
1679–1680

Illinois

February 13,
1682

Belle Riviere (Ohio R.)

A P P A L A C H I A N   M T S.

E N G L I S H   C O L O N I E S

Arkansas River

(Mississippi R.)
1682

La Salle killed
1687 ☐

L O U I S I A N A
(French)

Riviere de Baude

Taensa

✠ **Fort St. Louis**
1685

April 9, 1682

Gulf of Mexico

F L O R I D A
(Spanish)

ATLANTIC OCEAN

N
W   E
S

FROM FRANCE

1684

65° W
50° N
45° N
40° N
35° N
30° N
25° N
70° W
75° W
100° W
95° W   90° W   85° W   80° W

SETTLING THE
WILDER

1580	1600	1610	1620	1630

1585
Raleigh sends expedition to explore American coast.

1607
British settle Jamestown colony.

1613
First tobacco shipment from Jamestown to England

1620
Separatists sail to America on *Mayflower.*

1621
First Thanksgiving in Plymouth colony

The first British settlement in North America was planned by a bold fortune-seeker, Sir Walter Raleigh (RAWL-ee). In 1585, Raleigh sent 100 adventurous men and boys to explore the North American coast. They landed on Roanoke Island, off the coast of present-day North Carolina. The explorers returned to England and told of America's sunny weather. They reported that ripe fruits hung from trees, forests were thick with deer, and the Croatan Indians were friendly.

In 1587, another group of men, women, and children set sail for Roanoke Island intending to establish a settlement there. When the colony

Plymouth Colony, in present-day Massachusetts, was settled by Europeans seeking freedom for their religious beliefs.

NESS

1650	1700	1750

1681

William Penn and Quakers sail from England to America.

1744

South Carolina ships indigo to England.

UNIT 2

The Dutch were among the many peoples to colonize parts of the New World in the 17th and 18th centuries. This painting from the early 1700s shows the homestead of the Marten Van Bergen family in New York State.

began to run out of supplies, John White, the expedition's leader, sailed to England. He had hoped to return quickly, but a war in Europe delayed his return. When White came back two years later, his family and the other settlers had disappeared!

White searched the island for any clues to explain the disappearance of his family and friends. He found the word "CROATOAN" carved on a post and the letters "CRO" on a tree. White searched the nearby Croatoan Island, but found nothing. What happened to these early British settlers remains a mystery.

The story of the lost colony of Roanoke spread. But the dangers of settling in the wilderness did not stop the British from exploring and settling in North America. Their colonies lay south of the French in Canada and north of the Spanish in Mexico. The British also established colonies in the West Indies (present-day islands like Barbados and Jamaica).

The British established more than settlements on vast areas of land. The mainland British colonies evolved into what is now the United States. From the British, later generations of Americans took some customs, the language, and a system of laws.

A New Colony

After the disastrous start on Roanoke Island, the British succeeded in starting a colony at Jamestown, Virginia, in 1607. At first, times were hard. Most colonists refused to work at planting crops. Only with the help of the

Powhatan (pow-HAT-uhn) and Algonkin (al-GONG-kee-n) Indians, and the leadership of Captain John Smith, did the colony survive. Still, it was not until the settlers began growing tobacco that the colony became a success.

Not long afterward, a different group known as the Puritans started a colony in Massachusetts. Unlike the colonists in Virginia, these settlers did not come to the New World to find wealth. The Puritans were discriminated against by the Church of England. So they came to worship in their own way in America.

Soon other colonies were founded. Some were similar to Virginia. They were established to obtain wealth. In these colonies, settlers usually produced one crop. In the West Indies, it was sugar. In North Carolina, it was tobacco. Rice flourished in South Carolina and Georgia. South Carolina also grew **indigo** (a plant that gave a deep-blue dye) in the 18th century.

Colonies such as Maryland were founded by a group of men, usually the king's friends. They were called proprietary colonies. In 1634, Lord Baltimore, a Roman Catholic, established Maryland for himself and other Roman Catholics. In the 17th century, most English people who did not follow the Church of England were punished. So Lord Baltimore, who believed in religious freedom, allowed both Protestants and Catholics to settle in Maryland.

Even in Massachusetts, not all the settlers agreed on religious matters. The colony of Rhode Island became a **haven** (safe home) for those who held religious views different from those of the Puritans. And William Penn established Pennsylvania as a shelter for Quakers. In Pennsylvania, men and women were free to worship in any way they wanted.

Many New England settlers sought religious freedom. This New England church was stitched into a quilt in the late 1700s.

Why People Came

All of the colonies faced the problem of attracting laborers. This was especially true in the early years of settlement. Unlike in England, in America there was plenty of land. But there were never enough people to work it.

Colonial Regions

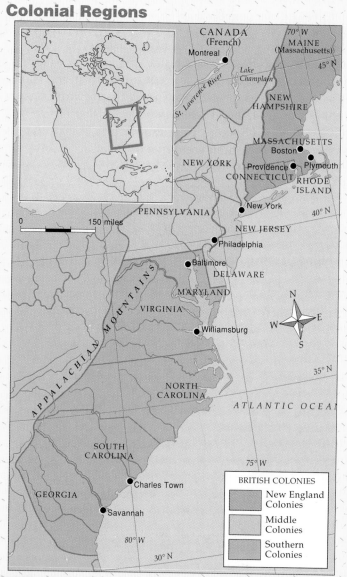

Which region has the most colonies? Is Pennsylvania a New England colony?

The most common method of attracting colonists was called **indentured servitude**. This meant that a woman or man would work for a set number of years in exchange for boat passage to America. After the indenture, or term of service, was completed the person was freed. This was a popular option for poor people in the 17th and 18th centuries. Roughly half of all colonists from Britain came as indentured servants. Many came from other European countries as well.

Most worked as indentured servants because they thought their lives would be better in the New World. Land was plentiful and wages were higher than in Europe. All they needed to do was survive their indenture and they had a hope of prospering.

The most brutal form of labor was slavery. At first, colonists tried to enslave the Native Americans, but this failed. The colonists turned to enslaving Africans because it was cheaper than using indentured servants.

Many methods were used to obtain workers. British criminals were often sent to America to work as punishment—at least 50,000 were brought over during the 18th century alone. Other people were kidnapped and sent against their will.

Blacks had been present in America from the early years of settlement. They first came as indentured servants. By the mid-17th century, they were forced into slavery. During the 18th century, the number of Africans brought to America soared.

Slavery on Plantations

African slaves were present in every British American colony. But most were found in the colonies which depended upon growing a single crop, such as cotton, for export. This was because the work on the large plantations was difficult. Few Europeans voluntarily came to such colonies, and indentured servants eventually became free. So the planters started holding laborers for life.

Forced from their homelands into slavery, African people held on to valued traditions.

The British colonies in the West Indies were the most dependent on slave labor. Living conditions on the islands were harsh. Few British men and women settled there. Most land owners remained in England. They sent representatives to supervise their plantations and imported many Africans to work their land. On some islands as many as 80 to 90 percent of the people were black slaves.

On the mainland, the Southern colonies had the most African slaves. There, one-third of the population were black slaves. In South Carolina, almost two out of every three people were black slaves.

Blending of Cultures

Despite early hardships, the population of the colonies grew. British North America was a patchwork of peoples and cultures. Many settlers came from Germany, Scotland, and Ireland. There were also many non-European people. Approximately one out of every five people in the colonies was of African heritage. Native Americans were always present, mainly living in colonial towns, and frontier settlements.

By the mid-18th century, three distinct economic regions had developed in mainland British North America. In the New England colonies, people lived on small farms or worked on the sea. In the Middle Atlantic colonies like Pennsylvania or New Jersey, people lived on large farms and grew crops like wheat. And in the Southern colonies, large plantations used black slaves to raise crops for export.

This is the story of thousands of people who sailed across the Atlantic Ocean and made new homes in a strange land.

8 WILL JAMESTOWN SURVIVE?

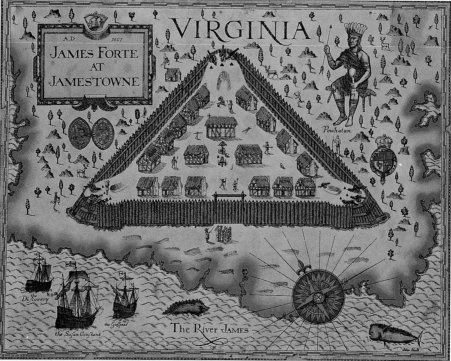

Jamestown was the first permanent English settlement in the New World. The settlers lived inside this small fort, while outside reigned Chief Powhatan [top right].

It was an odd mix of about 105 English men and boys who landed in Virginia on May 13, 1607. Half were gentlemen who had never done a day's farm work with their hands. Others were adventurers and wanderers. Only a few were farmers and craftsmen. Some expected to find gold and make fortunes. Others were looking for more liberty than they had in England. Some wanted to bring Christianity to the Native Americans. But all of them shared the hope of finding a better life for themselves in Virginia.

The new settlers built a fort near a river that flowed into Chesapeake Bay. They named this site Jamestown in honor of their king, James I, who had granted them the land called Virginia. They chose this site because it was on a river and accessible to ships. It could also be defended easily against Indian or Spanish attackers. But in other ways, it was an unfortunate choice. The land was low and swampy. It bred mosquitos that carried a deadly disease, malaria. The water was salty, the soil was sandy and poor. The men lived in flimsy huts surrounded by the walls of the fort.

Saved from Starvation

Most of their food was used up on the long trip across the ocean. Soon men began to die of hunger and disease. By December, less than half were left alive. Amid all this misery, the leaders of the colony quarreled and plotted against each other.

At this point, Captain John Smith took command of the colony. Smith was a soldier who had fought for money in some of Europe's wars. When wealthy English merchants formed the London Company to colonize Virginia, Smith was made a leader.

Smith cracked the whip hard when he took control of the colony. He had a simple rule for making the men work. "If any would not work," he wrote, "neither should he eat." He threatened to drive into the forest those who loafed. Smith himself went among the neighboring Powhatan and Algonkin Indians to trade for corn. On one of these trips he was captured and brought to the great chief they called Powhatan.

Years later he wrote that Powhatan sentenced him to death for killing two Algonkins. It was reported that Powhatan's 12-year-old daughter, Pocahontas (poh-kuh-HAHN-tuhs), saved Smith's life.

Is the story true or did Smith make it up? No one knows for sure. But it is known that Powhatan agreed to give the colony corn, saving the people from starvation. A period of peace between the settlers and the Indians began. The Christmas of 1608 was celebrated with the Indians. "We were never more merry," Smith wrote. "Nor were we fed on more good oysters, fish, meat, wild fowl, and good bread."

Pocahontas, whose name means "playful one," was known as Rebecca in England.

More Disasters

The period of ample food did not last long. Instead of farming, many of the settlers looked for gold in the forests. In August 1609, seven ships arrived from England with hundreds of settlers. Among them were many women and children. Even with the extra help, there was no way the little colony could feed all the new arrivals. Before long, all the food in Jamestown was gone.

The winter of 1609 was a terrible one for the settlers. Those who were not too sick or weak searched the woods for acorns, roots, and even the bark from trees. Some hunted for snakes, rats, and toads. Of the almost 500 settlers in Jamestown, only 65 were still alive when spring came. That winter became known as the "starving time" in Virginia's history.

Virginia Grows

Lord De La Warr, the new governor, arrived with three large ships loaded with supplies for Jamestown in June 1610. He acted quickly to restore discipline and order in the colony. Strict laws were passed. For stealing food, a colonist could be punished by having his or her ears cut off. But it would take more than strict laws to put the colony on its feet.

What it really needed was a crop that could be sold at a profit in England, that would bring **prosperity** to Virginia.

The person who developed the needed **export** crop was a young man by the name of John Rolfe who arrived in Jamestown in 1610. Soon the Powhatans and Algonkians began showing him how to raise tobacco. Tobacco had already been brought to England from the West Indies (the islands where Columbus landed).

Smoking tobacco was becoming more and more popular. (People of the time were unaware it caused cancer and other diseases.) So Rolfe developed a tobacco leaf that would appeal to the tastes of English smokers. The first shipment arrived in England in 1613 and was quickly bought up. Soon other settlers were planting tobacco and selling it at a profit in England.

While he was experimenting with tobacco, Rolfe met Pocahontas, the young Powhatan woman who John Smith said had saved his life. Rolfe and Pocahontas fell in love and were married in 1614. Two years later, Rolfe took her and their infant son to England. Pocahontas met the English king and queen and made a fine impression. Rolfe and Pocahontas were about to return to their home in Virginia when, sadly, she became ill with smallpox and died.

John White, a mapmaker and early English settler of Virginia, painted this scene of a Native American village.

Labor Problems

In 1617, 20,000 pounds of tobacco were shipped to England and Virginia's economy was booming. There was, however, a troubling problem in growing tobacco. There were not enough settlers to tend to the crop. At first the colonists tried to solve the problem by bringing over indentured servants from England. After they fulfilled their indenture, many became planters themselves.

Another solution to the labor problem was slavery. The first blacks came to Jamestown from the West Indies in 1619. They were treated as indentured servants. But as time went on, more and more blacks were **imported** as slaves.

Virginia grew and prospered. But Jamestown itself

Retum Optimum Subter Solem
Le meilleur Tabac de sous le Soleil
The Best Tobacco under the Sun

went into a steady decline after 1699, the year that Williamsburg became the new capital of colonial Virginia.

Today only a few ruins and a graveyard remain of the original Jamestown. Yet it was here that the first permanent English colony was established in America.

Tobacco was the first cash crop grown by Virginia's English settlers. On this 1600s tobacco label, slaves toil under a hot sun.

CHAPTER CHECK

WORD MATCH
1. malaria   **a.** a state of plenty
2. accessible   **b.** goods sent to another country
3. prosperity   **c.** a deadly disease carried by mosquitoes
4. export   **d.** brought in from another country
5. imported   **e.** capable of being reached

QUICK QUIZ
1. Describe the English people who first settled at Jamestown.
2. What events and conditions in the New World almost caused the new colony to fail?
3. Explain the significance of corn and tobacco to the Jamestown colony.

THINK ABOUT IT
1. On the part of the Jamestown planters there was a growing need for more people to tend the tobacco crop. Describe the two solutions the planters developed. How were they similar; how were they different? Which system do you think was more effective?
2. What facts in this chapter support the generalization that societies need law, order, and strong leadership in order to survive?

9 THEY WERE FREE AT LAST

This modern-day painting shows the first Thanksgiving celebration, held in 1621. Grateful English settlers share their bountiful harvest with the Native Americans who had helped them survive.

The harvest was in and it was a good one. Twenty acres of Indian corn had yielded a bumper crop. The woods were full of wild turkeys and other game, and there was an abundance of fish in the streams. There would be plenty to eat in the coming winter. So why not celebrate?

That was what Governor William Bradford of the Plymouth Colony in Massachusetts thought in the fall of 1621. He was one of a small group of hopeful Pilgrims who had landed there from England less than a year before. But the bitter, cold winter and a poor diet of salted meat, dried peas, and hard biscuits took a heavy toll of lives. Of the more than 100 settlers who had arrived on the *Mayflower*, one of them wrote, "scarcely 50 remained, and sometimes two or three persons died in a day."

The First Thanksgiving

Help came in the spring. One day a tall Indian named Samoset walked into the settlement. He greeted the astonished Pilgrims in broken English, which he had learned from English sailors who fished off the coast of Maine. A few days later he returned with another Indian, Squanto, who spoke much better English. Squanto had been kidnapped by English sailors and had lived nine years in London with a merchant. Later Chief Massasoit (MAS-uh-soyt), leader of many New England tribes, arrived. He signed a treaty of peace with the settlers that lasted 54 years.

Squanto taught the colonists how to grow corn, using fish as fertilizer. He also taught them the Indian ways of hunting and fishing. Without Squanto, many more Pilgrims would have died.

When Governor Bradford decided to celebrate and give thanks for the good harvest, he invited his Indian friends to join the Pilgrims. Bradford sent four men into the woods to hunt for turkeys. Then Massasoit arrived with 90 tall, husky braves, all of them hungry. Massasoit sent hunters into the woods and they returned with five large deer, which they presented

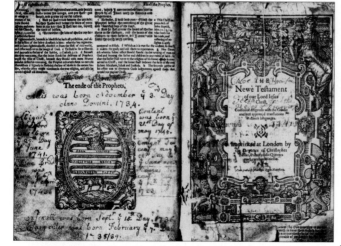

The Pilgrims came to the New World seeking religious freedom. This Bible belonged to Plymouth Colony governor William Bradford (1590-1657).

to the Pilgrims.

For three days the Pilgrims and Indians feasted. They ate turkey, geese, deer meat, fish, corn, and wild berries. Almost all the cooking was done outdoors by 10 women and girls. Between meals, the Pilgrims and Indians engaged in sports. The Indians showed their skills with bows and arrows, the settlers with their muskets (rifles). Massasoit and his braves were delighted when some young settlers joined them in their races and wrestling matches.

By the time the first Thanksgiving was over, the peace treaty between the Plymouth Colony and Massasoit's Indians was bound by strong ties of friendship. Before parting, Indians and settlers vowed to repeat the feast for many years to come.

Settling in Plymouth

Why had the Pilgrims made a dangerous trip across the ocean to settle in the wilderness of the New World? Some people came for jobs or to start a new life. Most came for religious freedom. In England, only one religion was allowed, the Anglican, or Church of England. Its head was the king. People of other religions were persecuted. Sometimes they were publicly whipped and sent to jail.

Within the Church of England was a group that thought the church's services were much too fancy. They wanted to do away with elaborate altars and ornate priests' robes. These people called themselves **Puritans.** They wanted to "purify" the church, or make it plainer. Puritans

Elizabeth Freake and her daughter, Mary, were painted by an unknown artist around 1674.

decided that it would be better to leave England and go to Holland. In that country, people could worship as they pleased.

A large group of Separatists moved to Holland in 1608. The Dutch people made them feel welcome, but still they were not happy. Their children began to speak Dutch, and the older Separatists wanted to remain English-speaking. Many began to think about starting all over again somewhere else—in America. They didn't know much about America, but they thought they could be free there.

In July 1620, the first group of Separatists left Holland for Plymouth, England. There they were joined by others who wished to journey to the New World. Finally, they crowded onto a little ship called the *Mayflower* and set sail on September 16, 1620. For two months they were tossed by storms and many became sick. When they reached Cape Cod, Massachusetts, they could hardly wait to go ashore. For now, they were free at last.

believed that only they could understand the true meaning of the Bible.

Some Puritans thought it was hopeless to try to change the Anglican church. They wanted to separate from it and form their own church. They were called **Separatists.** At first they held services secretly in their homes. But finally some

While still on board the ship, they signed a **compact** (agreement). They agreed to obey all the "just and equal" laws that were made for their colony. The Mayflower Compact was a big step toward self-government in the New World.

Banished from the Colony Read

Before long, many more Puritans and others settled in Massachusetts. The Plymouth Colony became part of the larger Massachusetts Bay Colony. The Puritans who came to the New World for religious freeeedom did not believe in religious freedom for others. Quakers and other groups that disagreed with their ideas were banished from Massachusetts.

Roger Williams, the pastor of a church in Salem, thought the Puritans had no right to impose their beliefs on everyone. Williams was banished from Massachusetts and, in 1636, started a settlement that he named Providence. In time, it became the colony of Rhode Island.

Another person to find religious freedom in Rhode Island was Anne Hutchinson. At the time, Puritan women were expected to obey husbands and male clergy. But Anne held religious meetings in her Massachusetts home. She was told to leave the colony after criticizing ministers of the established church. After her arrival in Rhode Island, Hutchinson taught and preached in public.

Today we still admire the Pilgrims who withstood hunger, disease, and a cold climate to establish their colony in New England. They also took one of the first steps toward self-government in the New World: they wrote the Mayflower Compact, an agreement to obey all fair laws.

CHAPTER CHECK

WORD MATCH
1. compact
2. Puritans
3. Pilgrims
4. muskets
5. Separatists

a. people who wander
b. rifles
c. people who wanted to make the church plainer
d. people who wanted to separate from the church
e. agreement

QUICK QUIZ
1. Describe the relationship that existed between the Pilgrims and Indians in the Plymouth Colony.
2. How did Governor Bradford show appreciation to the Indians for their help?
3. Why was survival so difficult for the original settlers of the Plymouth Colony?

THINK ABOUT IT
1. What historic document was signed on board the *Mayflower*? What was the importance of this document? Why is it important to us today?
2. In what ways do you think the Mayflower Compact was one of the stepping stones in the development of the U.S. Constitution?

10 SO WISE A RULER

William Penn (1644-1718) making his historic treaty with Pennsylvania's Native Americans. Penn was honored far and wide for his honesty and sense of fairness.

"My prison shall be my grave before I will budge one bit. I owe my conscience to no man."

These words were written in 1668 by a "born fighter" named William Penn. He wrote them while he was in jail in the Tower of London. His cell was a tiny, bare room under the roof. It was icy cold in the winter. It was steaming hot in the summer. Bad prison food made him thin and weak.

Penn didn't have to be in prison. He could have had an easy life. His father Admiral Sir William Penn was a British navy hero and a rich man. His home was a castle with servants and many acres of land. His father had sent him to a famous English college, Oxford University. Many of the students there were the sons of noblemen. Penn was friendly and good at sports.

But after a while, Penn began to question one English law. The law said that all English people had to belong to the Anglican church. Puritans and people who belonged to other churches were often beaten. Sometimes they were put in prison, and even hanged. Penn saw many college students attack Puritans and

Quakers in the streets. He tried to defend the people who were beaten, and was called a "troublemaker." Penn and some of the other students stopped going to the Church of England as a protest. Then Penn was forced to leave college.

Penn's father was very angry with him. At first he threw his son out of the house. Later he felt sorry and took him back. Then he sent the young man on a trip to France and Italy to make him a "gentleman."

Penn did become a gentleman. He wore fine silk clothes and carried a sword. In London he met the king and many great **noblemen**. Then in 1665, a terrible disease hit London—a **plague,** or "black death." Many thousands of people became sick and died. Others ran away from London to save themselves. But the Quakers stayed to take care of the sick and the dying. Penn liked these brave people. Before long, he became a Quaker himself.

Quaker Beliefs

What were the **Quakers** like? They lived simply and wore plain clothes. They did not have churches or regular ministers.

They met in plain buildings called "meeting houses." Members could speak at meetings whenever they felt moved by the spirit of God. In the Church of England, this free speaking behavior was frowned upon. The Quakers believed in strict honesty in business, and were against violence and war. They would not serve in the king's army. They were against any kind of unfair treatment of one person by another. They also believed in helping the sick and imprisoned. Quakers would not take off their hats in the presence of royalty— lords and ladies. It was the Quakers' way of saying that all women and men were equal. They called themselves the Society of Friends.

After William Penn became a leading Quaker, he was jailed in the Tower of London for nine months. He was told to give up his Quaker beliefs. His refused to deny his faith. Later Penn was sent to prison two more times.

Penn began to feel that freedom of religion was impossible in England. More and more, he thought of starting a colony in America. In this colony, men and women would be free to worship in whatever way they wished. Men would also be free to vote as they pleased.

Penn's father was now dead, but the king had owed him $80,000. Penn asked the king to give him, instead of money, a grant of land in America. The king was glad to give Penn some land—anything to get rid of this Quaker troublemaker. He gave Penn the land that is now Pennsylvania. The name means Penn's Woods.

Colonial Agricultural Regions

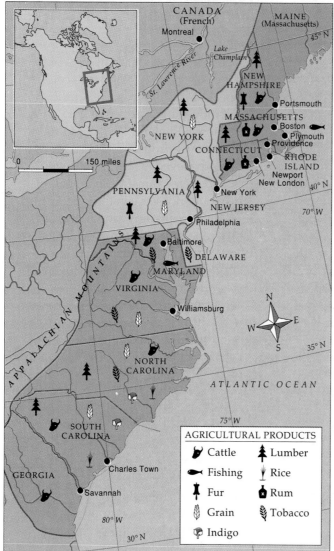

AGRICULTURAL PRODUCTS

Cattle		Lumber	
Fishing		Rice	
Fur		Rum	
Grain		Tobacco	
Indigo			

What agricultural products are produced in South Carolina? What other states produce the same products? Do these states fall into one of the regions in the map on page 44?

Charter of Liberties

In 1681, Quakers from England and other countries such as Scotland, Ireland, and Wales set sail for America. Some African Americans from southern colonies had settled in Philadelphia. Penn had rul-

ing power in the new colony, so he wrote a Charter of Liberties. Many years later it may have served as a model for the U.S. Constitution. The Charter stated that the lawmakers of the colony would be elected by the citizens of the colony. Every male citizen of the colony could vote. There would be freedom of religion for all. There would be freedom of speech for all. There would be trial by **jury** (a group chosen to make a judgement) for anyone accused of a crime.

Thomas Jefferson, who wrote the Declaration of Independence in 1776, called Penn "the greatest lawgiver the world has produced."

Penn was also a good friend to the Delaware Indians of Pennsylvania. He was honest and fair, and the Delaware respected him for it. Penn once told a group of Indians: "All will be brotherhood and love. I consider us all the same flesh and blood, joined by one heart."

Penn agreed to several treaties with the Delaware. The Indians replied that they and the colonists "must live in love as long as the sun and moon give light." The treaties were not broken in Penn's lifetime.

What was it like to live in Pennsylvania in the early 1700s? "The neighbors for many miles around were all well known to each other," wrote Rhoda Barber about Lancaster County. "There was harmony and friendship among

This is the Pennsylvania seaport of Philadelphia as it appeared in 1720.

them that was beautiful to behold. I well remember the gatherings at my father's house on Sunday afternoons. The people enjoyed apples and cider, bread and butter, and smoked beef. "

Many of Barber's neighbors worked as tradesmen, weavers, shoemakers, or farmers. "The people wore clothes that were chiefly homemade, for there were no stores nearer than Lancaster," she wrote. "I remember the difficulty of getting shoes, especially for children."

Penn made Pennsylvania "a free colony for all mankind." It was free not just for English people or Quakers, but for people of all nations and religious beliefs. One colonist said this about Penn: "He is loved and praised by all. The people have never seen so wise a ruler."

CHAPTER CHECK

WORD MATCH
1. Quakers
2. jury
3. noblemen
4. plague
5. meeting house

a. a serious epidemic
b. plain building used by Quakers for church
c. a group chosen to make a judgement
d. a Christian religious group
e. of high birth or high rank

QUICK QUIZ
1. What goals did William Penn have for his colony?
2. List the major points of the Charter of Liberties. Why were these important?
3. Why was the name "Friends" appropriate for people who were Quakers?

THINK ABOUT IT
1. William Penn was born with wealth and high social status. By defending the individual rights of the poor, he lost both and was imprisoned. If you had been Penn, would you have made the same choices?
2. Freedom of religion is one of the fundamental rights guaranteed by the U.S. Constitution. Have all Americans always enjoyed this freedom?

11 ELIZA'S CROP OF BLUE

Rice Hope was a large and prosperous plantation in South Carolina. In the early 1700s, rice was the colony's main cash crop. But all that was changed by a young girl's experiments with a plant called indigo.

She was only 16 when her father asked her to take charge of his three plantations in South Carolina. It was a big responsibility for one so young. But Eliza Lucas not only made her father's plantations prosper, she made all of South Carolina prosper. She did this by developing a new crop, indigo, which produced a valuable (worth a great price) blue dye used in the manufacture of cloth. "Indigo proved more beneficial to Carolina than the mines of Mexico and Peru were to Spain," wrote one historian. "The source of this vast wealth was the result of an experiment by a girl."

How did this experiment come about? The Lucas family came from the island of Antigua (an-TEE-gwuh). It was a British colony in the West Indies with close ties to the mainland colonies. The family moved to South Carolina in 1738 when Eliza's father, George Lucas, inherited **plantations** (large farms or estates) there. But the next year, a war broke out between Britain and Spain. George Lucas, an officer in the British army, had to return to Antigua for military duty. He left his wife, who was ill, his younger daughter, and his plantations in Eliza's care. This was quite unusual for the time!

Seeds of Wealth

From Antigua, Lucas sent his daugher some indigo seeds and urged her to try to grow this crop on the family plantation near Charleston. Why was this so important? At that time, South Carolina's economy depended on only one crop, rice. Dependence on a single crop was the rule in southern colonies. In Virginia, Maryland, and North Carolina the planters grew tobacco. In South Carolina and Georgia, they grew rice. Later, when the plantation system spread to Georgia, Alabama, Mississippi, and Louisiana, cotton became the big crop there.

But dependence on one crop was risky. Britain's war with Spain, for example, cut off the market for South Carolina's rice in Europe. Now indigo would provide the colony with another crop to support its economy. Experiments with indigo had been tried 70 years earlier, but had been dropped because of crop failures.

Could young Lucas make the seeds that her father sent her grow? Later she recalled, "I was ignorant both of the proper season for growing indigo and the soil best adapted to it." But Lucas kept trying, and by 1741, she was growing indigo suc-

cessfully. Producing the dye from the plants was a difficult process, so Eliza's father sent her an experienced dyemaker (one who colors fabrics) from the West Indies. The dyemaker was anything but a help. He was afraid that if Eliza Lucas developed an indigo trade, his island would be ruined financially by the competition. So he threw lime water into the dye, spoiling its color.

Lucas kept experimenting every year. In 1744, she shipped six pounds of the dye to England where it was found to be better than any other. Lucas also gave seeds from her crop to any planter in South Carolina who promised to grow indigo and export it. Two years later, she and other South Carolina planters shipped 135,000 pounds of the blue dye to England. To encourage the planters, the British Parliament voted to pay them six cents for every pound of indigo they grew. By the 1760s, more than a million pounds of indigo annually were sent to England, and South Carolina's economy was booming.

By persevering through many trial-and-error experiments, young Eliza Lucas finally found a way to make a rich blue dye from a colorless substance found in the indigo plant.

Family Life

As a teenager, Lucas did more than manage her father's plantations. She taught reading and writing to her younger sister, Polly, and to two slave girls. In some areas, teaching slaves to read was illegal. She spoke French, played the flute, and read so many books

Reasons for Founding the Colonies

COLONY	YEAR FOUNDED	REASON FOR FOUNDING
VIRGINIA	1607	Trade
MASSACHUSETTS	1620	To escape religious persecution
NEW HAMPSHIRE	1623	Agriculture, trade
NEW YORK	1624	Trade
CONNECTICUT	1636	Trade, to escape religious/ political persecution
MARYLAND	1634	Land sales, to escape religious/political persecution
RHODE ISLAND	1636	To escape religious persecution
DELAWARE	1638	Trade
NEW JERSEY	1664	Land Sales, to escape religious/political persecution
PENNSYLVANIA	1682	To escape religious persecution
NORTH CAROLINA	1653	Trade, farming, protection against Spanish Florida
SOUTH CAROLINA	1670	Trade, farming, protection against Spanish Florida
GEORGIA	1733	Refuge for debtors, protection against Spanish Florida

Imagine that you were living in Europe in 1650. Why might you decide to move to the New World? What sort of people do you think were satisfied with conditions in Europe? What sort of people were not?

that one neighbor said she would surely damage her brain. She studied law and used her knowledge to help others who could not afford a lawyer.

The plantation on which Eliza Lucas lived, Wappoo, was near the city of Charleston. Charleston was located on the Cooper River, near the South Carolina coast. At that time, the city had many rich people and a busy social life. But Lucas was more interested in her experiments than in going to parties and dances with young men. "As to the other sex," she wrote, "I don't trouble my head about them. I take all they say to be words."

Yet Lucas was impressed with a lawyer more than 20 years older than she, Charles Pinckney. Lucas married Pinckney in 1744. At their plantation,

Belmont, she raised silkworms and made silk. But she was close enough to Wappoo to keep up her experiments there with indigo.

Eliza and Charles Pinckney had four children, one of whom died soon after birth. Eliza now devoted herself to the upbringing of her daughter, Harriott, and two sons, Charles Cotesworth and Thomas. Eliza Pinckney taught Harriott herself, but her two sons were educated in England. Later they would become leaders of the young United States.

After her husband died in 1758, Eliza Pinckney successfully managed the family's plantations for more than 30 years. In 1792, she became ill with cancer, and died the next year in Philadelphia where she had gone for treatment. She was buried

AMERICAN ADVENTURES

there in St. Peter's churchyard. President George Washington, a good friend of the Pinckney family, served as one of the pall-bearers at his own request.

In Eliza Lucas's day, as now, indigo was mainly used to color and decorate fabrics. This cotton print was made with two shades of indigo blue.

CHAPTER CHECK

WORD MATCH
1. Antigua
2. plantations
3. valuable
4. dyemaker
5. economy

a. large farms or estates
b. one who puts color in fabrics
c. British colony in West Indies
d. financial affairs of a community
e. worth a great price

QUICK QUIZ
1. Why did it become necessary for plantations to move away from growing just one cash crop?
2. "Indigo proved more beneficial to the Carolinas than the mines of Mexico and Peru." Explain the meaning of this statement.
3. What personal characteristics of Eliza Lucas helped her succeed in accomplishing very difficult goals?

THINK ABOUT IT
1. Have the reasons for women wanting to get an education in America today changed since Eliza Lucas lived? Explain.
2. Compare Eliza Lucas' life as a teenager to the life of a teenager today.

ELIZA'S CROP OF BLUE

SETTLING THE WILDERNESS

History Detective

1. "Work or do not eat!" I delivered this tough order to help save Jamestown. Who am I?

2. In 1619, we set foot in Jamestown, but unlike other arrivals we came against our will. Who are we?

3. Here, 90 of Massasoit's braves joined with the Pilgrims in the first Thanksgiving. Where am I?

4. My words, with the agreement to obey all "just and equal" laws, are evidence of the Pilgrims' belief in self-government. What am I?

5. The Puritans banished me for criticizing the established church—a rebellious act for a woman. Who am I?

6. "Brotherhood and love"—these were principles upon which I founded my colony. Who am I?

7. Experiments by Eliza Lucas made my dye one of South Carolina's most valuable crops. What am I?

Voices From the Past

By 1749, Philadelphia amazed British visitors with its sophistication. Read the description written by Lord Adam Gordon. Then answer the questions that follow.

The city is perhaps one of the wonders of the World, if you consider its Size, the Number of Inhabitants, the regularity of its Streets, . . . the Magnificence and diversity of places of Worship (for here all Religions are tolerated equally), the plenty of provisions brought to Market, and the Industry of all its Inhabitants, one will not hesitate to Call it the first Town in America, but one that rivals almost any in Europe.

1. Based on this account, would you expect Philadelphians to support an established church? Explain.

2. Because of Philadelphia's carefully laid-out plan, some Europeans called the city boring in design. What adjectives might Lord Adam use to describe the city? Why?

Hands–On History

1. *Creative Writing*—Using pictures and words, design an advertisement convincing people to settle in either Jamestown or Plymouth.

2. *Researching a Topic*—Using the library to find articles or books on colonial dress, make sketches to show some of the fashions popular in the colonies. Show styles from the farm and the city, frontier and plantation, working class and upper class.

YESTERDAY'S NEWS

The American Adventures Newspaper

Puritans Pass "Good and Wholesome Laws"

Boston, Mass., 1681—The arrival in recent years of non-church members has caused Puritan leaders in Boston to worry about the moral decay of their "City Upon a Hill." Evidence of idle behavior—dancing round a Maypole, bowling on the green, and playing cards—has been cited at numerous town meetings. Such corruption, said one official, leads to "great mispense of time."

Explained the official: "An hour of idleness is as bad as an hour of drunkenness."

The Massachusetts General Court has enacted laws punishing "unprofitable pastimes." In compliance with the laws, Governor John Winthrop has given up hunting, his favorite sport. Why? "My conscience twinges, "moaned Winthrop, "each time I miss a bird and waste powder."

Virginia Governor Hosts Party

Alexandria, Virginia. 1685—At least 100 people attended a three-day wedding party given by the governor of Virginia. Elegant tables displayed platters of meat, sugary punches, wines, chocolate, and teas. The governor held horse races by day and as evening descended, couples danced minuets equal to those seen in the royal courts of Europe. But as the night wore on, dancers broke into lively country jigs as fiddlers played tunes learned from African slaves.

One French visitor remarked that the "frolic lasted till morning." At daybreak, marveled the visitor, the "gentlemen and ladies took to the saddle. I was astonished that they held themselves on."

A guest from Boston, however, took a different view of the merrymaking. Said the Bostonian:

1.

Family life in the New World is shown in this portrait of the Van Bergen family.

2.

Philadelphia, Penn., 1709—The English government stepped in to overrule the Pennsylvania Blue Laws providing fines for **masquerades** (costume balls), stage plays, and dice games. Royal officials in London objected to the laws on the grounds that they restrained "loyal English subjects from Innocent Sports and Diversions."

You Be the Reporter

Match each question with its news item above.

1. Write a concluding paragraph telling what the Bostonian thought of the wedding party.

2. What headline might a Puritan write for this item? As a Puritan, respond to the article in the form of a letter to the editor.

THINKING ABOUT PLACES ON A MAP

Between the 15th and 19th centuries, millions of people were kidnapped from their homes in Africa and transported across the sea to the New World. Those who did not die of mistreatment on the slave ships faced hard lives in strange lands. What was it like to be a captured African arriving in the American colonies? The map on the opposite page shows where many such captives came from in Africa and where the traders of Europe took them in the Americas.

Refer to the map to answer these questions.

1. Study the map's title and key. **(a)** What year in history is represented by this map? **(b)** What do the color symbols stand for?

2. Which African peoples in 1775 lived **(a)** just south of the Senegal River? **(b)** south of the Congo River?

3. You can use the map's scale to estimate approximate distances. About how far apart in miles were **(a)** Ashanti and Oyo? **(b)** Angola and Mozambique? **(c)** the Gold Coast and British North America?

4. Find Europe on the map. **(a)** Which European nation is closest to Africa? **(b)** What body of water separates Europe from northern Africa?

5. **(a)** Which five European nations had colonial empires in 1775? **(b)** Which one of these was not involved in slave trade?

6. The Portuguese were the first Europeans to trade for slaves on the West African Coast. **(a)** Which areas of Africa did the Portuguese control in 1775? **(b)** Which African peoples lived there? **(c)** Where were the enslaved Africans from these areas taken in the New World?

7. Africans from the Ashanti region were considered "strong and obedient" by the slave traders. **(a)** Which European nation dominated the slave trade from this area? **(b)** Where did slaves from the region end up in the New World?

8. Most of the enslaved Africans had originally lived in the warm area called the **tropics,** between the Tropics of Cancer and Capricorn. These people found themselves living in very different climates in the New World. In which area of the New World would they have experienced the greatest change in climate? Explain.

9. Slaves from different parts of Africa spoke different languages. **(a)** Why do you think this fact made slave revolts in the New World difficult? **(b)** If you were a captive Mandingo African in British North America, what other African peoples might you encounter?

10. Imagine that you were a captive Mandingo African who was brought to Charleston, South Carolina, in 1775. **(a)** What features of this new place would seem most strange to you? **(b)** What would you notice about the people here? **(c)** What would you miss most about the places and people in Africa?

For Extra Credit: Write a letter or a diary entry as if you were an African who was brought to the New World as a slave. Describe your first few days in the New World.

Colonial Slave Trade, 1775

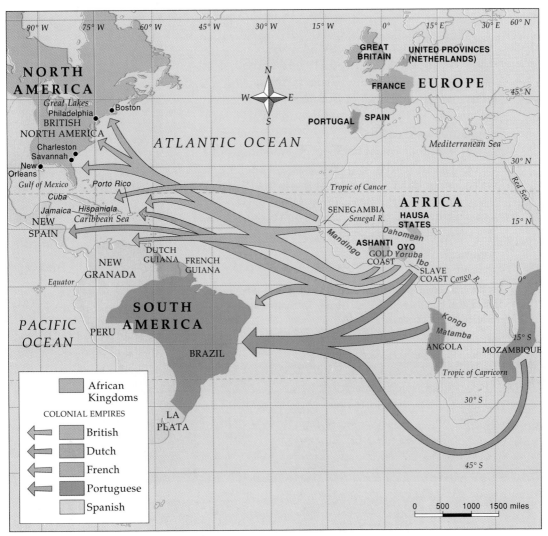

In 1750, a teenager named George Washington was proud to be a subject of the king of England. True, he lived 3000 miles away from London. But like most colonists in 1750, he expected to be a loyal Englishman all his life.

At least that was what George Washington thought as an 18-year-old. Yet 25 years later, he was a leader of a revolt against the British king, British laws, and the British flag. What happened? What changed the minds of Washington and thousands of other loyal British subjects in America?

By the time eight Minutemen died at Lexington in this exhange of gunfire with British troops, the American Revolution had begun.

SEARCH FOR FREE

1760		1765				1770
	1764	**1765**	**1765**	**1766**	**1768**	**1770**
	British Parliament passes Sugar Act.	British Parliament passes Stamp Act.	Patrick Henry denounces Stamp Act.	British repeal Stamp Act.	George III sends soldiers to Boston, Massachusetts.	Boston Massacre

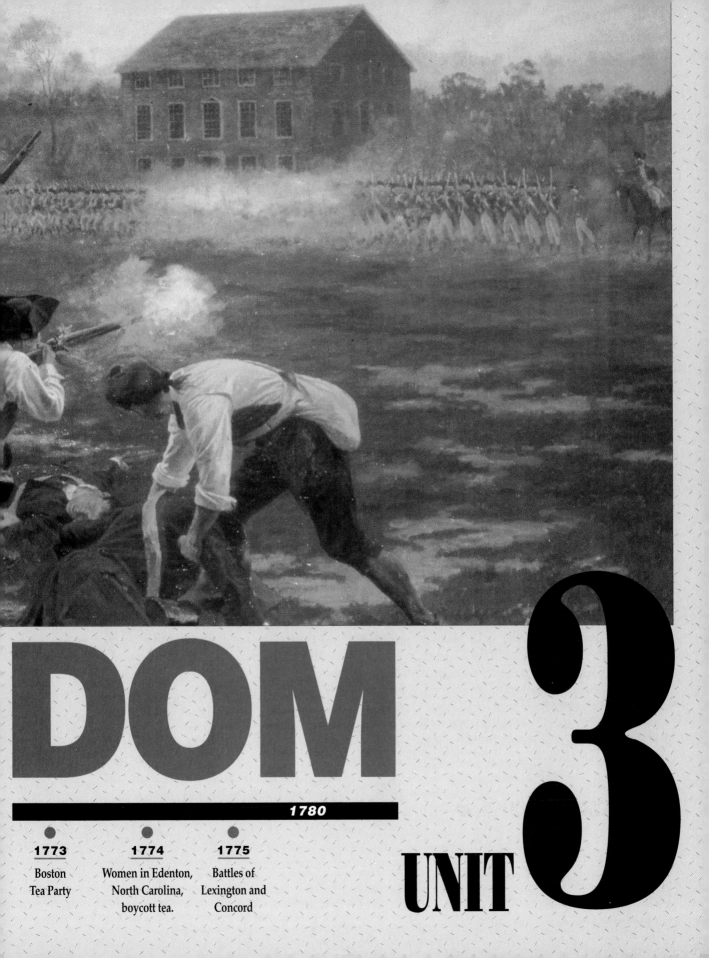

DOM

1780

UNIT 3

After the British defeat of the French in 1763, peace returned to the American colonies for only a short time. This painting shows the Great Seneca Falls at Lake Ontario in 1766.

There is no single explanation of how the American Revolution came about. There were many causes which led to this event.

The American colonists had long been an independent people. For most of the 18th century, Britain had ruled its American colonies with a light hand. In fact, the colonies had enjoyed more self-rule than any colonial people, anywhere. Most of the colonists had a similar government. There was a governor chosen by the British king. White male voters in the colonies elected an assembly that had most of the power for making new laws.

Then the relationship between the American colonies and Britain was disrupted. In the 1750s, Britain went to war with France. Fighting occurred in many places, including North America. In America, this conflict was known as the French and Indian War.

The American colonists played an important role in helping the British win the war. In 1755, George Washington and a group of colonists joined the British army in a march through the western woods. The colonists warned the British that fighting in American forests was different from fighting on a battlefield in Europe.

But the British would not listen. They marched into an Indian attack. Many of the British soldiers panicked. They did not know what to do. But most of the colonists stood and fought.

AMERICAN ADVENTURES

After seven years of bloodshed, the British finally won the war against France. The French and British signed a peace **treaty** (a formal agreement between nations) in 1763. This treaty made the British Empire much bigger. Britain gained control of French Canada. Now most of North America east of the Mississippi River belonged to the British.

British Crackdown

The British government decided to get more involved in governing its huge American empire. It decided to stop ruling with such a light hand. A new king, George III, was on the throne. He was young and wanted to establish his power. He and **Parliament** (the British legislature) worked together to change colonial rule.

First, they tried to stop the fighting between the colonists and the Indians. They decided that the two groups must be kept apart. In 1763, they drew a line on a map down the middle of the Appalachian Mountains. The colonists were banned from settling west of this line. The British government hoped this would keep peace between between Native Americans and colonists. But the colonists wanted more land. They became very angry when they heard

This British cartoon suggests some colonists expressing their anger at Britain by attacking tax collectors.

about this rule.

Second, the British government decided to station troops in the colonies. It did so to guard its empire. While the troops helped protect the colonists, most Americans were angered by their presence. The colonists were forced to lodge the soldiers in their inns and taverns.

Third, the British government needed help in paying the expenses of the empire. The French and Indian War had been costly. The British thought that the colonies should help to shoulder some of the debt.

Britain had passed navigation laws for its American colonies. But during most of the 18th century, it did little to enforce them. However, after the French and Indian War, it decided to crack down on these laws.

Parliament passed the Sugar Act in 1764. This law put a tax on molasses and other goods bought outside the British Empire. The extra money raised from the taxes went to pay off Britain's war debts. The next year, Parliament passed the Stamp Act. This law created another tax in the form of a stamp. Now every business and legal paper had to have a special stamp on it.

The British government meant business. They wanted see to it that people obeyed the new laws. But they were not prepared for the colonists' reaction.

American Protests

To the shock of the British, the American colonists protested against the new taxes. Most of the money being raised was to be used in defense of the colonists themselves, British leaders said. The colonists had been paying taxes for years—mostly to support their colonial governments. But the Americans were paying much less of their income in taxes than citizens in Britain.

Why then did the colonists refuse to pay the new taxes? Many of them were upset by the way the taxes were created. The colonial **assemblies** (meetings of lawmakers) had not voted on them. Therefore, the colonists were being taxed without their consent. "No taxation without representation," they cried. Many of the them thought that a king who tried to make them pay such a tax was a **tyrant** (a cruel and unjust ruler).

Men like Patrick Henry led the attack against the new taxes in the colonial assemblies. The American officials appointed to collect the new taxes soon received notes threatening them with death. Their houses were torn apart by angry mobs. Some tax collectors were punished by being covered with tar and feathers.

Finally, the British **repealed** (did away with) the Stamp Act in 1766. But

Triangular Trade Routes

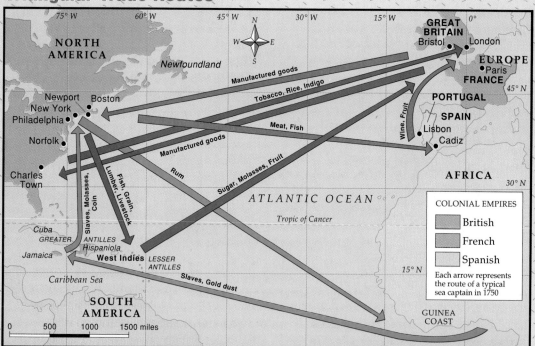

What goods were exchanged between London and Charleston? What other places and goods were part of that triangle?

Britain's King George III, shown here with his wife, Queen Charlotte, and some of their children, was hated by many of his subjects in the colonies. His harsh rule sparked a revolution that tore America from its motherland.

American opposition continued as the British government passed new taxes on goods such as tea and glass.

The American colonists saw their actions differently. They believed they were trying to protect themselves. The government in London was taking away their liberty. They were only fighting for their rights as British citizens.

The result was a struggle between the colonists and the British. A series of events, such as the Boston Massacre and the Boston Tea Party, increased the distrust between the two groups. In 1775, the tension finally erupted in armed conflict at Lexington and Concord in Massachusetts.

Rarely had the American colonies been united in the past. Now Britain's hated laws and taxes brought the colonies together.

Skillful leaders such as Paul Revere and Samuel Adams organized support for the rebellion. Committees wrote letters to people in other colonies. They spread news and suggested ways to oppose British tyranny. Abigail Adams wrote to her friends about the political situation in Boston. Other women united in **boycotting** (refusing to buy) British goods.

By 1775, only 10 years had passed since the first trouble over taxes. But enough had happened at this time to make some Americans think that British soldiers were their enemies. Not all of the British colonies revolted. Canada (recently acquired from France) and the islands in the West Indies did not join in the rebellion. But the 13 mainland colonies took up arms against the British government. They now had more in common with each other than they had with the people in Britain.

12 IF THIS BE TREASON

In 1763, a young Virginia lawyer named Patrick Henry went to court to oppose The Parsons' Cause. At the time, few Americans were bold enough to speak against the wishes of the English king.

He was lazy and a good-for-nothing. That was what some people said about young Patrick Henry. It was a waste of time sending him to school. He didn't seem to learn anything. All he wanted to do was fish, or hunt in the woods. Patrick's father, a Virginia farmer, didn't know what to do with the boy. Sometimes he whipped him, and other times he prayed for him. But nothing seemed to help.

Finally Patrick's father took him out of school. It was a happy day for both Patrick and his teachers. At home, Patrick's father taught him the Bible, math, and Latin. Patrick really wasn't stupid. He could learn—when he wanted to. The trouble was he did not like school. He liked being out in the woods.

Patrick's father worried about the boy. How would he ever earn a living? The elder Henry decided to start his son in business. When Patrick was 16, his father bought him a country store to manage. But Patrick was no businessman. And there were many wild animals in the forests of Virginia in 1751. On nice days, he would just close the store and go hunting. After a while, Patrick's father had to close the store for good.

At 18, Patrick fell in love with the daughter of a poor farmer and married her. Now he tried to make a living by raising tobacco. But he had no luck at farming and soon had to give it up. Then he started another store, but he had to close this one, too.

By this time, Patrick Henry had three children as well as a wife to support. He knew he had to make a living somehow. There was one thing he did well: He was a very good speaker. So he decided to become a lawyer. He studied law books night and day for six weeks. Then he took a test and passed. At 24, Patrick Henry began to practice law.

Questioning the King

Henry's gift for speaking helped him win many cases. His first important case came when he was 27. It had started out as an argument between the Virginia House of Burgesses, (a group responsible for making laws), and some church ministers. Virginia at that time had a church supported by public **taxes.** Many people thought that the ministers of this church

American colonists hated the tax they had to pay for stamps like this one, which King George required "on every piece of paper."

were overpaid. So the Virginia legislature passed a law that cut the ministers' salaries.

The ministers were quite angry about this. When King George III heard about it, he was angry too. He threw out the Virginia legislature's new law. Then the ministers went to court. They wanted all the money they had lost through the pay cut.

This was where lawyer Henry stepped into the case. He argued that Virginia didn't owe any back pay to the ministers. Nobody thought he would win. What jury would dare go against the king? But when Henry got up to speak to the jury, there was magic in his voice.

Henry asked, what right did the king of England have to throw out a law passed by the people of Virginia? The voice of the people, he said, is the voice of God. When a king rejects a law passed by the people, the people do not have to obey him.

This was pretty strong talk in the days when kings were very powerful. Some people in the courtroom were shocked. But Patrick Henry won this important case.

Questioning a Tax

The young lawyer was now a hero in Virginia. He was especially admired by the small farmers and woodsmen. They elected him to serve in the Virginia legislature in Williamsburg. Soon after, Henry really gave the people of Virginia something to talk about.

This time his subject was King George's Stamp Act. The act had put a tax on "every piece of paper" used in the American colonies. The primary purpose of the Stamp Act was to raise money to pay off British war debts. This meant that every legal piece of paper had to have a stamp on it. Not even a marriage license would be valid without a stamp. Many Americans were angry about this. They didn't want to pay for a stamp every time they signed a paper. Besides, they believed that only their own legislatures had the right to tax them. But few people were brave enough to protest aloud.

Then, on May 29, 1765, Patrick Henry got up to speak in the House of Burgesses. The stamp tax was against the law, he said. Under the law, the people could be taxed only by their own **representatives** (those chosen to speak or act for others). The colonists had no representatives in the British government. So how could the British

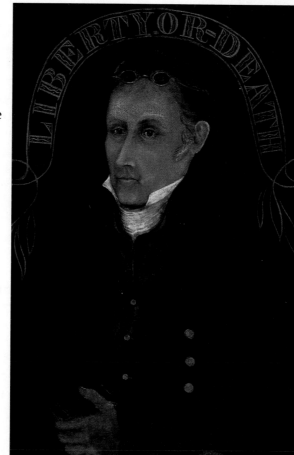

American patriot and orator Patrick Henry (1736—1799) is crowned by a portion of his most famous speech: "For me, give me liberty or give me death !" He became one of the most outspoken leaders of the American Revolution.

government place a stamp tax on the colonists? It couldn't, Henry argued—unless it broke the law.

Henry said that nobody in Virginia should obey the Stamp Act. What he said next really shocked many of his listeners. He compared King George to a tyrant. And he warned the king that tyrants were sometimes killed.

Suddenly, there were shouts of "Treason! Treason!" from those who were loyal to the king. Henry waited until the shouting died down. Then he said, "If this be treason, make the most of it!"

News of Henry's speech traveled fast. Before long, Americans in all the colonies refused to pay the stamp tax. Sometimes they burned stamps and beat up the tax collectors. In Boston, there were riots.

Did the British learn anything from the uproar over the stamp tax? Some Americans thought so. The British repealed the Stamp Act in 1766. But at the same time, they passed another law—the Declaratory Act. This act said that Britain had full power to make laws for the colonies and the people of America—"in all cases, whatsoever."

Henry continued to speak out against the unjust British laws. In a passionate speech, Henry cried out to the House of Burgesses: "We must fight! Is life so dear, or peace so sweet, as to be purchased at the price of chains and slavery? Forbid it, Almighty God! I know not what course others may take, but as for me, give me liberty or give me death!"

These were fighting words.

This teapot, marked with a call to repeal the hated Stamp Act, was probably made in England by supporters of the American cause.

CHAPTER CHECK

WORD MATCH

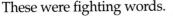

1. treason
2. House of Burgesses
3. representatives
4. Stamp Act
5. taxes

a. elected officials
b. disloyalty
c. tax on legal papers
d. money paid by citizens for government and public services
e. group responsible for making laws in colonial Virginia

QUICK QUIZ

1. How did the Stamp Act and the Declaratory Act contribute to the separation of England and the colonies?
2. Why were colonists afraid to protest the actions of Parliament out loud?
3. Patrick Henry's ability to speak and his knowledge of the law helped him to win many cases. Describe two of these cases.

THINK ABOUT IT

1. As a boy, Patrick Henry didn't like school and didn't seem to understand the importance of an education. Explain how and why his attitude changed later.
2. Explain the meaning of the phrase "taxation without representation." Does this issue continue to be important today? Discuss.

The American colonists' long-held bitterness against England erupted into the famous Boston Massacre of 1770. Five Bostonians died in the brief and sudden burst of violence.

It was a cold winter night in Boston. The moon was shining brightly over the snowy streets. A British soldier stood guard near the Customhouse, where British records were kept. The soldier had already been in an argument with several young people. Tension was in the air.

Suddenly, an icy snowball flew past the soldier's ear. Another nearly knocked his hat off. A third caught him right in the chest. The snowballs were thrown by a group of boys across the street. Soon the boys began to yell at the soldier. "Lobster back! Lobster back!" they shouted. British soldiers wore red uniforms in those days and Americans often called them **redcoats** or "lobster backs."

There had been many fights between British soldiers and Boston citizens in recent years. What were the fights about? The British had enforced their unfair Declaratory Act. They had placed several new taxes on the colonies. The people hated these taxes. In Boston there were **riots** (violent disturbances of the peace by a group) against them. The people hated many other laws made for them in far-off England. "Why should we obey these laws?" many colonists asked. "We had no part in making them."

King George III became angry. In 1768, he sent 4000 soldiers to Boston to stop the riots. The people of Boston hated these soldiers even more than the taxes. They had to give housing to the soldiers in inns, taverns, and other privately owned buildings. Some soldiers were put up in people's homes. And that wasn't all. Many soldiers took off-duty jobs that the colonists themselves needed. Dock workers often attacked soldiers who were off duty.

Screams from a Crowd

On this night, March 5, 1770, the

Paul Revere's drawing of the "5 Coffins for Massacre" appeared in broadsides (printed newsletters) protesting the killing of American patriots in the Boston Massacre. Such broadsides helped to fuel the anti-English passions spreading through the colonies.

BLOOD ON THE SNOW

This is Boston as it appeared on September 30, 1768, during the arrival of redcoat troops from England. Paul Revere made this engraving, which shows the redcoats marching off their ships and into the city. Colonists' resentment of this "insolent parade" sowed the seeds for the Revolution to come.

British guard was nervous. A bell had rung from somewhere. A number of men and women had joined the shouting boys. Soon there was a large crowd. The soldier then fixed his **bayonet** (knife attached to the end of a rifle) on his rifle. The crowd nearly went wild. "Kill him! Kill him!" they screamed. A group of dock workers and sailors joined the crowd. One of them was a free black man named Crispus Attucks.

The British guard called for help. Seven redcoats led by a captain came to his aid. The captain told his men to load their rifles, but ordered them not to fire. He tried to break up the crowd, but it was no use. Soon the crowd began getting out of control. A British guard was knocked down. Suddenly, someone shouted, "Fire!" No one ever knew who shouted it, but the British soldiers began shooting.

When the smoke cleared, Attucks and two other men were dead. Two more lay dying in the snow. Though it was really a street fight, the event became known as the Boston Massacre.

The angry crowd charged forward again. Soon other soldiers arrived to halt the rioters. Governor Thomas Hutchinson of Massachusetts rushed to the scene and made a speech to quiet the crowd. He promised the people that the soldiers would be put on trial.

Speeches from a Patriot

The next day Samuel Adams spoke

out. He said "redcoat butchers" had to be punished. But others felt that the crowd was partly to blame for the massacre. Little doubt existed that the first argument had been started by young people, not by the British troops.

John Adams, who was a cousin of Samuel Adams, agreed to defend the soldiers in a court **trial** (a formal examination of the facts of a case). John Adams was an excellent lawyer and would one day become the second President of the United States. As a result of the trial, the British captain and six of his men were freed. Two others received what was considered a mild punishment. They were branded on the thumb with a hot iron.

But Samuel Adams kept making speeches about the bloody massacre, and the courage of the dead men. He published pamphlets about the event and sent them to the other colonies. Before long, many people were thinking of Attucks and his friends as heroes and great **patriots** (lovers of their country). And they were thinking of the British as murderers—and enemies.

CHAPTER CHECK

WORD MATCH

1. riots
2. redcoats
3. trial
4. patriots
5. bayonet

a. British soldiers
b. knife attached to the end of a rifle
c. violent disturbances of the peace
d. an examination of the facts of a case
e. people loyal to the colonies

QUICK QUIZ

1. Describe the events that resulted in the Boston Massacre.
2. Why did the people of Boston resent the 4000 soldiers King George III sent to stop the riots?
3. How did Governor Thomas Hutchinson of Massachusetts cause the war to be postponed?

THINK ABOUT IT

1. John Adams believed in the basic principles that everyone is entitled to a fair trial. What information in this chapter confirms this fact?
2. Three individuals, John Adams, Samual Adams, and Governor Hutchinson, played significant roles in the events surrounding the Boston Massacre. Which of these men do you think was the most significant? Explain.

14 TEA, TAXES, AND TROUBLE

Paul Revere and Samuel Adams were among the Americans who took part in the Boston Tea Party of 1773. They dumped cases of tea off British cargo ships to protest harsh taxes.

Inside Boston's Old South Church, the air was thick with smoke and tension on the evening of December 16, 1773. Hundreds of people listened as one man after another rose to speak against the British government.

Out on the icy water of Boston Harbor, three ships lay quietly at anchor. They had been there for more than two weeks, but no one would unload their cargo of tea.

The crowd in Old South Church showed no signs of breaking up. They complained that Massachusetts' Governor Hutchinson should send the ships back to England. But Hutchinson was loyal to the British Parliament.

Before anyone could speak again, Samuel Adams announced that the governor had delivered his final word. "He will not send the ships back," declared Adams. "We have done all we can for the salvation of our country."

Suddenly, there was turmoil at the back of the church, as groups of people pushed their way out.

"The Mohawks!" someone shouted. "Boston Harbor will be a teapot tonight!"

With a rush of excitement the crowds poured out of the church to see what the bustle was about. Nearly a third of Boston was there lining the streets when 60 men, dressed as Mohawk Indians, marched past on their way to the wharf. The men rowed out to the waiting ships, boarded them, and dumped chest after chest of troublesome tea into the dark water.

Boston Closed

What was it about tea that made the people of Boston so angry? Tea was a symbol of the poor relations between Parliament and the colonies. We do not elect representatives to Parliament, said many people. Why should we pay Parliament's taxes? We will not sell our rights for tea leaves!

At a town meeting in Boston, some people organized a group to spread news about the tea tax. This **Committee of Correspondence** sent letters and messengers all over Massachusetts. They tried to persuade people to unite against the unfair taxes. Soon similar committees sprang up in other colonies.

Female patriots formed the Daughters of Liberty to express their opposition to British tyranny. They chose to buy American and boycott British goods.

When the first shipments of British tea began to arrive in other colonies, protest committees went into action. In Philadelphia, they persuaded the ship captain to take his cargo back to England. In Charleston, South Carolina, the tea was quietly unloaded, and later dumped. Only in Boston did the confrontation become so angry and so public.

When the news of Boston's "tea party" reached England, the British government was furious. To punish Boston, the prime minister, Lord Frederick North, ordered the port of Boston closed. He sent British troops to enforce the shutdown. No ships could enter or leave the harbor. Nearly all trade ceased. Shops and businesses throughout the city had to close. Many people were thrown out of work.

Word of the harsh **penalties** (punishments fixed by law) suffered by Boston spread rapidly. Americans were angry. If Lord North could close Boston, the biggest port in North America, what would stop him from closing other ports as well?

The Colonies Respond

What could Americans do to show their anger at the British government? In 1774, few people were ready to go to war with England. Still, they were not willing to sit by quietly and allow their rights to be trampled on.

Deborah Cushing's husband—an official in the colonial government—refused to support the tea boycott. So she took up her own tea caddy [above] and dumped its contents into the harbor herself.

All through the summer of 1774, people gathered in town meetings and political committees to discuss boycott. It was an exciting idea. Patriotism was no longer a matter of making speeches or dumping tea. Now anyone could show loyalty to the American cause by refusing to buy British goods.

John Adams found out how widespread support for the boycott was on a sultry July afternoon. After a long, dusty ride, he stopped at an inn and asked the landlady, Sally Huston, for a cup of tea. She told him they were boycotting tea, but offered him coffee instead.

By refusing to serve tea to her customers, the landlady was taking a political stand. She was showing her dislike for Parliament's treatment of the American colonies. Before the boycott, most people believed only men should be interested in politics. They assumed women were too busy running their households to care about things like trade and taxes. But the events of the last several months were the talk of every street corner and dinner table. Women as well as men knew about the "tea party" and about Lord North's harsh treatment of Boston. And the boycott made even shopping and housework political.

Women who called themselves **Daughters of Liberty** showed their support for the American cause by buying coffee instead of English tea. They used

American honey in place of molasses imported from the British colony of Barbados. They give up fine cloth from British mills. Instead, women organized spinning parties and made thread to be woven into **homespun** (cloth made of yarn at home).

Some women did not limit their actions to supporting the boycott. In October 1774, fifty-one women gathered in Edenton, North Carolina, to form their own political committee. They drafted a **petition** (a written, formal statement) supporting the boycott, and all of the women signed it.

"We cannot be indifferent . . . to the peace and happiness of our country," they wrote, promising to do everything they could to support the American cause.

The idea of women forming a political committee seemed ridiculous to some people. In Britain, a cartoonist even published a drawing poking fun at the women. But the women of Edenton understood that the government affects everyone, not just men. They knew that without women's support, the boycott would fail.

The Boston Tea Party of 1773 was a dramatic moment in the conflict between Britain and the American colonies, but the boycott that followed was just as important. The boycott brought politics right into people's homes. Both women and men answered the call not to buy British goods. It was becoming harder and harder not to take sides.

CHAPTER CHECK

WORD MATCH
1. homespun
2. penalties
3. Daughters of Liberty
4. petition
5. Committee of Correspondence

a. punishments fixed by law
b. cloth made of yarn at home
c. a written, formal statement
d. boycotted British products
e. spread news about the tea tax

QUICK QUIZ
1. (a) Explain why Governor Hutchinson did not send the ships back to England. (b) What impact did the Governor's actions have on the colonists?
2. Describe the reaction of the British government to the Boston Tea Party? What effects did this reaction have on the colonies?
3. Explain how Sally Huston's refusal to serve tea could be considered a political stand.

THINK ABOUT IT
If you had lived in Boston during this time, would you have supported the position taken by (a) Lord North, (b) colonists involved in the Boston Tea Party, (c) Sally Huston, or (d) ladies of Edenton? Explain your choice.

15 PATRIOTS OF LIBERTY

This is "The Midnight Ride of Paul Revere" through the darkness of the Massachusetts countryside, as painted by artist Grant Wood (1891-1942). Revere risked his life to warn patriots of a British advance.

"Quick! Wake up Mr. Adams and Mr. Hancock! The British are coming!"

It was Paul Revere hollering. He had just made his "midnight ride" from Boston to Lexington.

Earlier that evening, young American spies had discovered that General Thomas Gage, the British commander, had issued secret orders for his troops to march on the Massachusetts countryside.

"The British are coming!" Revere, a 40-year-old patriot riding a borrowed horse, had warned the people along the way. Seven hundred armed British soldiers were headed for the towns of Lexington and Concord.

What did the British want? First, they were out to grab the guns and gunpowder stored by the **Minutemen** in Concord. The Minutemen were farmers who were training to fight the British if war came.

AMERICAN ADVENTURES

(They were called Minutemen because they were supposed to be ready to fight within a minute's notice.)

Second, the British wanted to arrest John Hancock and Samuel Adams, who were staying in Lexington. Hancock and Adams had been stirring up the people against British rule. That had not been a hard thing to do after Lord North, the British prime minister, ordered the port of Boston closed.

Soon Hancock and Adams greeted Revere. "You must leave at once for Burlington. You'll be safe there," Revere told them. "The British want to send you to London—to hang you as criminals. Redcoats are on their way here right now."

Patriots Escape

It was dawn when Adams and Hancock drove away in Hancock's carriage. Suddenly shots were heard coming from Lexington. British soldiers and Minutemen were firing at each other. The fighting which both sides had feared had finally broken out. The date was April 18, 1775.

John Hancock was 38. He was a rich **merchant** (a person who buys and sells goods) and had fine clothes and

The fiery intensity of Samuel Adams (1722-1803) helped fan the sparks of anti-British feeling into revolutionary flame.

manners. Samuel Adams was 53, but he was poor and looked older. His head sometimes shook. His voice was sometimes weak. Yet more than any other man, Adams had fanned the flames of rebellion against the British. He was the man the British most wanted to hang.

Samuel Adams was born in Boston in 1722. He was the son of a brewer who had done very well in business. But when Samuel Adams went into business, he failed. He went into debt. His children often wore clothes given to them by friends.

Soon Adams turned from business to politics. At politics he was a master. He was elected to the Massachusetts legislature. He fought hard against British taxes. He was a leader of the Boston men's group called the **Sons of Liberty**. They tarred and feathered tax collectors and stirred up riots against the British.

Adams attacked British rule every chance he got. His speeches and writings whipped up the anger of the people of Boston. Adams formed the first Committee of Correspondence in his city. Later he gave the signal for the "Indian raid" on the tea ships in Boston harbor.

After King George III closed the port of

Boston, the city's trade and shipping came to a stop. Then Adams called a meeting of the leaders from all colonies. The **First Continental Congress** met in Philadelphia in 1774. The angry colonial leaders sent the king a long list of complaints. The king ignored them. Meanwhile, the Minutemen began to train.

Redcoats March

On the night of April 18 and morning of April 19, 1775, the redcoats marched on Lexington and Concord. They burned whatever **ammunition** (bullets or shells that can be fired from guns or other weapons) they could find. But the Americans had hidden most of their supplies. Then the redcoats ran into the Minutemen. On the march back to Boston, the Minutemen fired on them from the cover of trees, walls, and houses. At day's end, 250 British redcoats and 90 Americans had lost their lives.

Warned by Paul Revere, Adams and Hancock had narrowly escaped. Within a few weeks, both were in Philadelphia for the Second Continental Congress. Adams gave fiery speeches before the Congress. He called for liberty for the American colonies. A little more than a year later, the Declaration of Independence was signed calling for American independence from Britain. Adams gave Americans the courage to fight for their rights. Patriots honored him as the "father" of their liberty.

The Battles of Lexington and Concord, 1775

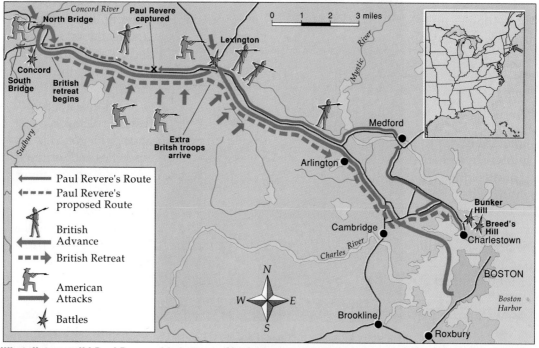

What distance did Paul Revere ride between Charlestown and Lexington? In what direction was he headed when he was captured?

AMERICAN ADVENTURES

This is "A view of the South Part of Lexington" on the morning of April 19, 1775. The "shots heard round the world" that started the American Revolution were fired here.

CHAPTER CHECK

WORD MATCH
1. merchant
2. First Continental Congress
3. Minutemen
4. ammunition
5. Sons of Liberty

a. meeting of leaders from all colonies
b. person who buys and sells goods
c. bullets and shells for weapons
d. stirred up riots against the British
e. farmers trained to fight in case of war

QUICK QUIZ
1. Why did the British want to arrest John Hancock and Samuel Adams? Were they successful? Why or why not?
2. Describe the significance of the First and Second Continental Congresses. What were the dates and locations of these two meetings?
3. List the personal qualities of Samuel Adams that helped him in accomplishing very difficult goals.

THINK ABOUT IT
1. Do you think the United States has leaders today like Samuel Adams who could inspire Americans, in a time of crisis, to rally behind the government? Why or why not?
2. How would American history have been changed if Paul Revere had not made his famous "midnight ride"?

1776

16 "REMEMBER THE LADIES"

The letters of Abigail Adams (1744-1818) provide a vivid glimpse into the upheaval of daily life in Massachusetts during the early days of the American Revolution.

"Remember the ladies, and be more generous and favorable to them then your ancestors," Abigail Adams wrote to her husband John in 1776, as he helped draft the Declaration of Independence.

"Do not put such unlimited power into the hands of the husbands. Remember all men would be tyrants if they could. If particular care and attention is not paid to the ladies we are determined to [promote] a rebellion, and will not hold ourselves bound by any laws in which we have no voice, or representation."

In her most-often quoted letter, Abigail Adams made a plea for women to be treated fairly in the new nation of the United States of America. She believed that women deserved laws of **equality** that, for example, would protect their right to speak as freely as men. She believed that women needed the same education as men to be useful members of society. These were **radical** (extremely different) ideas at the time.

Like almost all women in colonial America, Abigail never went to school. She never held a job outside her home, or voted in an election. Like most, she was expected to be a dedicated wife and mother—no more.

Unlike most of her peers, Abigail grew up among the richest families of colonial Massachusetts. A respected minister's daughter, she was encouraged as a child both to love books and to use her mind. She was intelligent and well-read which made her unusual at that time.

Farm and Business Manager

Abigail learned to express her interests through letters. She wrote long, thoughtful, witty letters to her friends and her husband who was often away. Without formal education, her grammar was irregular and her spelling faulty. Yet she wrote vividly about everyday life in colonial Massachusetts.

She wrote about planting corn, her household budget problems, current politics and values, and the dramatic unfolding of the American Revolution.

In 1774, John Adams was chosen as one of five men to represent Massachusetts in the First Continental Congress in Philadelphia. This meant the start of a long, painful separation for Abigail and John.

John's absence also changed Abigail's role as a wife and mother. Suddenly she had to manage their farm and business affairs, pay bills, hire and fire workers, and settle disputes. Abigail became so skillful at business that she began to buy and sell farm stock and real estate to increase her family's income.

Meanwhile, she had to raise children and protect them from the illnesses of the time, such as **smallpox** (a contagious virus that could cause blindness or death) and **dysentery** (a painful intestinal infection). She had to run her house amidst many demands in a time of upheaval.

The Coming of War

In the rural town of Braintree where she lived, young men were leaving their farms to join the new Continental army. Abigail could see Boston in the distance.

Her neighbors feared that the British in Boston would soon attack their town.

In 1775, the Battle of Lexington erupted only a few miles from the Adams' farm. "Take the spoons. Let's throw them in the kettle here and melt them down into bullets," Abigail insisted of her husband's brother, Elihu Adams.

Soon, her letters described British officials tarred and feathered by Boston mobs, and British troops marching and drilling down city streets.

A Patriot named John Robbins proudly carried this drum into the Battle of Bunker Hill on June 17, 1775. It also was used during the War of 1812.

Children threw snowballs at the soldiers' red uniforms and cried, "Lobster backs, bloody backs!"

On the morning of June 17, 1775, Adams woke up to an explosion. British cannons fired on the harbor town of Charlestown, near Boston. With one hand she grabbed a **spyglass** (small telescope). With the other, she grabbed her son John Quincy. Together they raced to a nearby hill to see what was happening in the distance. "They're burning Charlestown!" she gasped. With John Quincy, she watched fire and smoke light up the morning sky.

Hours later they learned that the British had tried to take Breed's Hill from the American troops. Twice the Americans forced the British to retreat. But the third time the British charge was too much. The Americans gave up Breed's Hill—and then another post, Bunker Hill. Even so, Americans felt proud of the American effort in what is now called the Battle of Bunker Hill.

Abigail wrote to John in Philadelphia, "Figure out to yourself the town in flames all around them, and the heat from the flames so intense as scarcely to be borne. The day was one of the hottest we have had this season. The wind was blowing smoke in their faces. Then consider that we do not count 60 men lost. Every account agrees in 1400 or 1500 slain on their [the British] side."

After this event, life was never the same for the Adamses. They found themselves working harder to break the ties that bound the colonies to England. The American Revolution had begun.

For patriots, the Battle of Bunker Hill was a bittersweet mixture of loss and victory. By day's end, the British had forced them from the hill. But the loss strengthened their resolve to win the war.

This painting shows the Adams' home and farm in the early 18th century. Both John Adams (1735-1826) and his son, John Quincy Adams (1767-1848) were born here.

CHAPTER CHECK

WORD MATCH
1. smallpox   **a.** painful intestinal infection
2. radical   **b.** small telescope
3. equality   **c.** extremely different
4. spyglass   **d.** a contagious disease
5. dysentery   **e.** having the same rights, privileges, and rank

QUICK QUIZ
1. Abigail Adams said, "If particular care and attention is not paid to the ladies we are determined to [promote] a rebellion, and will not hold ourselves bound by any laws in which we have no voice, or representation." Explain what Abigail Adams meant by this statement. Do you agree or disagree?
2. Why were Americans proud of the American effort at the Battle of Bunker Hill?
3. What effects did her husband's absence have on Abigail Adams?

THINK ABOUT IT
1. Name two ways in which Abigail Adams was like most colonial women of her time. Name two ways in which she was very different than her peers. What do you think were some of the personal qualities that made Adams so remarkable?
2. Why do you think no women went to Philadelphia to serve in the Continental Congresses? Do you think women should have been represented in these meetings? Why or why not? Would Abigail Adams have done a good job in representing American women in Philadelphia? Why or why not?

SEARCH FOR FREEDOM

History Detective

1. On the map, the British drew a line down my spine and said to colonists, "Here you'll stop and go no farther." Where am I?

2. Some Virginians, still loyal to the king, called my fiery speeches "treason." I called them "torrents [rushing streams] of freedom." Who am I?

3. My snow-covered streets turned red with blood in what American patriots labeled a massacre. Where am I?

4. My cousin John said I "dipped my pen in acid." I'll "dip it in blood," I replied, "if it keeps the memory of the Boston Massacre alive." Who am I?

5. My passage started boycotts and made drinking coffee a patriotic act. What am I?

6. The opening battles of the Revolution took place here. Where are we?

7. I urged my husband to "remember the ladies," when he wrote a new code of laws. Who am I?

Voices From the Past

In May 1775, Jane Franklin Mecom hastily wrote a letter to her brother Benjamin Franklin as she prepared to flee Boston. After Lexington and Concord, the scent of war was in the air. Read the letter, and then answer the questions that follow.

The storm of anger has risen so high that the British have sent a party to creep out in the night and slaughter our dear brethren at Concord for endeavoring [trying] to defend our property. But God appeared for us and drove the redcoats back with much greater loss than they were willing to admit. They were clearly mistaken about the Minutemen they had to deal with; but the distress the battle has caused is past my description.

1. Who would Mecom say provoked the bloodshed at Lexington and Concord? What evidence supports your answer?

2. Ben Franklin's son William later sided with the British. What side would you expect Jane Mecom to take in the war? Why?

Hands–On History

1. *Expressing a Viewpoint*—Use the library to find out what Benjamin Franklin's stand was during the American Revolution. Then write a letter in reply to his sister Jane.

2. *Debating a Topic*—List arguments for and against the following statement: The Boston Tea Party involved illegal destruction of private property and the colonists should be punished.

YESTERDAY'S NEWS

The American Adventures Newspaper

Colonists Protest Stamp Act

Boston, Mass., August 14, 1765 —King George III's

1.

Parliament has passed the Stamp Act by an overwhelming vote of 205 to 49. British defenders of the tax expected no real trouble from the colonists, but local Sons of Liberty have proved otherwise. Today, some 350 Sons dined in a field just outside Dorchester, a suburb of Boston. The whole company lifted their voices repeatedly to the Liberty Song. Notables, such as James Otis and John Adams, joined in the chorus. The whole occasion, said Adams, "cultivated the sensations of freedom." The purpose of the meeting, continued Adams, was to "tinge [color] the minds of the people . . . with the sentiments of liberty."

3.

Boston, Mass., August 31, 1765—Cries of "buy American" ring throughout Boston as patriots rally to support a boycott against British goods. Loyal Daughters of Liberty weave homespun to take the place of British cotton, satin, and lace. These days, the Daughter's openly sing the following verses:

Young ladies in town, and those that live around
Wear none but your own country linen;
Of economy boast; let your pride be the most
To show clothes of your own make and spinning.

• • • • •

This British cartoon shows patriots as fiends.

Stamp Distributor Hung in Effigy

Boston, Mass., August 15, 1765 —Yesterday morning at daybreak, royal officials discovered a straw effigy (fake figure) of Mr. Andrew Oliver, the stamp distributor, hung in a Liberty Tree. Some officials treated the act as a childish prank; other's took great offense. When the Sheriff ordered the effigy taken down, a crowd gathered.

2.

You Be the Reporter

Match each question with its news item above.

1. What three adjectives would you use to influence readers' opinions about Parliament?

2. What concluding paragraph would you write? Use the following facts: **(a)** That evening a mob marched to Oliver's house. **(b)** Some people threw stones at the windows. **(c)** Oliver feared for his life.

3. What headline would you write for this story?

MAP SKILLS

READING A TRANSPORTATION MAP

The first roads in Colonial America were not roads at all, but dirt trails worn down over time by Indians. As settlers moved in, they widened these roads with use—riding horses or dragging their wagons over them. But as late as 1775, colonial roads were still unpaved, narrow, bumpy, dusty in dry weather, and muddy in wet weather. Few colonial roads had bridges.

The transportation map on the opposite page shows the main roads used by the colonists in 1775. As you can see, few roads went more than 200 miles from the coast. What natural barriers kept people from developing roads farther inland?

Study the map's key. Then note the answers to these questions on a separate sheet of paper.

1. Imagine you are a colonial postman. **(a)** What road would you follow to carry the mail from Trenton, New Jersey, to Wilmington, Delaware? **(b)** What is the southernmost city on this road? **(c)** the northernmost city?

2. Use the scale of miles to check distances along the Main Post Road. **(a)** Approximately how far apart are St. Augustine and Savannah? **(b)** About how many miles apart are most of the other towns along this road: 25 to 50, 50 to 100, 100 to 200?

3. Suppose your horse could carry you at three miles an hour along the typical colonial road. **(a)** About how long would it take you to travel from St. Augustine to Savannah? **(b)** Would travel time from Savannah to Charles Towne be longer or shorter?

4. Find the stage coach route on the map. **(a)** To which of these cities could you travel from New Haven, Connecticut, by stagecoach: Baltimore; Philadelphia; New York; Boston; Portsmouth? **(b)** Was Richmond, Virginia, on this route?

5. The traders of Savannah and Augusta often traveled to Fort Prince George to trade with the Indians. **(a)** What river might they have used to travel from place to place? **(b)** Did a road also connect these three places? **(c)** Could you travel by road between Fort Prince George and Fort Loudoun? Explain.

6. Follow the inland road from Fort Prince George to Charlottesville, Virginia.

(a) Which of these towns does it pass through: Charlotte; Salisbury; Salem; Hillsboro; Lynch's Ferry? **(b)** Is this a north–south road or an east–west one?

7. Follow the road west from Philadelphia to Harris' Ferry. In 1775 how would you have traveled **(a)** between Harris' Ferry and Sunbury? **(b)** between Harris' Ferry and Pittsburgh? **(c)** between Pittsburgh and Fort Sandusky? Explain.

8. Imagine that you lived in Montreal in 1775 and you wanted to get to Fort Niagara. **(a)** Identify two possible routes you could take. **(b)** What kind of transportation would you use along each route? **(c)** Which route would have been the shortest in terms of miles and travel time?

9. With your finger, trace the two routes a traveler could take from Wilmington, North Carolina, to Wilmington, Delaware. **(a)** Which route would you have preferred to travel? **(b)** As you traveled along your chosen route, which towns would you pass through? **(c)** Would you cross or go around the Chesapeake Bay?

10. After British troops burned Charles Town, Massachusetts on June 17, 1775, Abigail Adams wrote about it in a letter to her husband, who was in Philadelphia. **(a)** By what route(s) could the mail courier have carried the letter? **(b)** over how many miles?

AMERICAN ADVENTURES

Colonial America, 1775

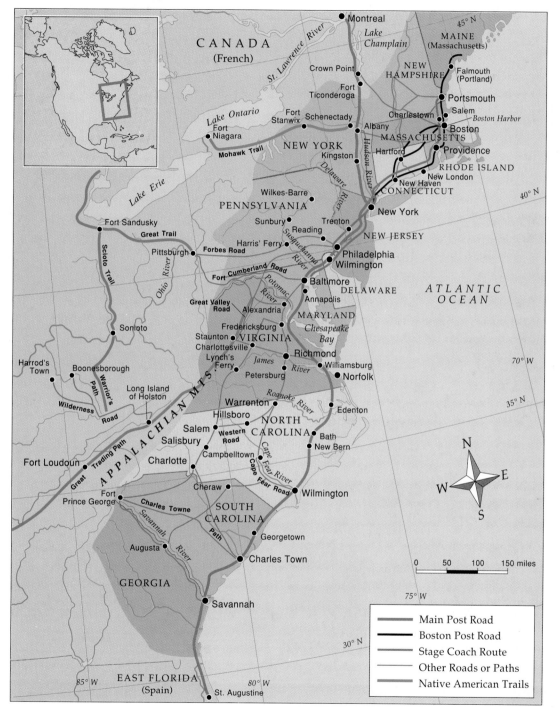

Montreal

CANADA
(French)

Lake Champlain

45° N

MAINE
(Massachusetts)

Crown Point

NEW HAMPSHIRE

Fort Ticonderoga

Falmouth (Portland)

Portsmouth

Schenectady

Charlestown

Salem

St. Lawrence River

Fort Stanwix

Albany

Boston Harbor

Boston

Lake Ontario

Fort Niagara

NEW YORK

MASSACHUSETTS

Mohawk Trail

Kingston

Hartford

Providence

RHODE ISLAND

Hudson River

New London

New Haven

CONNECTICUT

40° N

Lake Erie

Wilkes-Barre

Delaware River

PENNSYLVANIA

New York

Fort Sandusky

Great Trail

Sunbury

Reading

Trenton

NEW JERSEY

Scioto Trail

Pittsburgh

Forbes Road

Harris' Ferry

Philadelphia

Susquehanna River

Wilmington

Ohio River

Fort Cumberland Road

Baltimore

DELAWARE

ATLANTIC OCEAN

Great Valley Road

Potomac River

Annapolis

Alexandria

MARYLAND

Sonioto

Fredericksburg

Chesapeake Bay

Staunton

VIRGINIA

70° W

Charlottesville

Richmond

Harrod's Town

Lynch's Ferry

James River

Williamsburg

Boonesborough

Petersburg

Norfolk

Warrior's Path

Long Island of Holston

Roanoke River

35° N

Wilderness Road

Warrenton

Edenton

Hillsboro

NORTH CAROLINA

Salem

Western Road

Bath

Fort Loudoun

Salisbury

Cape Fear River

New Bern

Great Trading Path

APPALACHIAN MTS.

Charlotte

Campbelltown

Cape Fear Road

Cheraw

Wilmington

Fort Prince George

Charles Towne

SOUTH CAROLINA

N

W   E

S

Savannah River

Path

Georgetown

Augusta

Charles Town

0   50   100   150 miles

GEORGIA

75° W

Savannah

	Main Post Road
	Boston Post Road
	Stage Coach Route
	Other Roads or Paths
	Native American Trails

85° W

EAST FLORIDA
(Spain)

80° W

St. Augustine

30° N

THE FIGHT FOR
INDEPEN

1776

Thomas Paine
publishes
Common Sense.

Continental Congress
approves Declaration of
Independence on July 4.

1777

United States
flag authorized
by Congress.

Americans
defeat British at
Saratoga.

1778

France enters
war on
American side.

1780

Women raise
funds for
American army.

LOOKING AHEAD

One year after fighting broke out between the Americans and British at Lexington and Concord, the American troops were stranded on the western end of Long Island, New York. On the night of August 29, 1776, they climbed into rowboats and barges as quietly as they could. A tall man on a horse signaled for the boats to shove off. If they made any noise, all might be lost.

The British were only a few hundred yards away. Earlier that day they had badly beaten the Americans. They were only waiting until morning when they could attack again and force the Americans to surrender. If they knew

General George Washington and his troops spent a bitter winter at Valley Forge, Pennsylvania, in 1778.

DENCE

1785

1781
Americans defeat British at Yorktown.

1782
Many American loyalists head to Canada and Great Britain.

1783
Treaty of Paris signed.

UNIT 4

Revolutionary War Major Battles

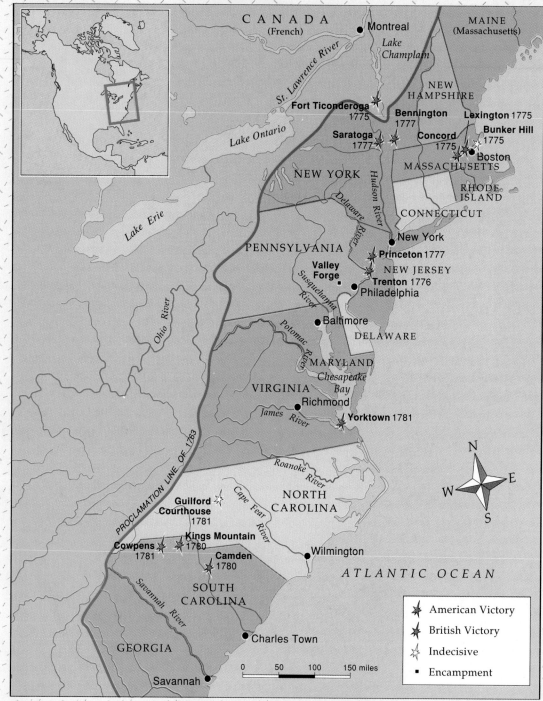

Who won the Battle of Trenton? Which battle took place on Chesapeake Bay?

AMERICAN ADVENTURES

what was happening now, they would surely march on the Americans and crush them.

The Americans' only hope was to secretly cross over the river to the island of Manhattan. Luckily the river was unusually calm and a thick fog concealed any movement. Nine thousand American soldiers made the trip that night across the dark waters of the East River.

When everyone else was safely across, a tall man dismounted from his horse and got into the last boat. He was George Washington, commander of the American army. He was completing one of the most famous retreats in American military history—and narrowly saving his troops from disaster.

Washington's Army

Washington had been commander of the American army for more than a year. He had taken charge on July 3, 1775, two weeks after the Battle of Bunker Hill.

In Washington's first year as commander, there had not been much fighting. The biggest event in the first year of war did not involve armies. It was a decision of the American leaders who attended the Second Continental Congress. Early in July 1776, they declared that they were no longer British subjects. Instead they announced that the 13 colonies were now "free and independent states."

After this declaration, Washington's job was to win American independence on the battlefield. He just barely succeeded. Many times the British had chances to crush Washington's army. Few people thought the colonies stood much of a chance of winning a war against Great Britain. After all, the British seemed to have most of the advantages.

For one thing, the British had a much bigger army. The men in it were professional soldiers. They knew how to march together in perfect order. They were trained to load and fire their guns together. This army was assisted by another strong force at sea. The British had the largest navy in the world.

The colonies had no warships. Their army, the Continental Army, started out with part-time fighters. Most of the men and boys who fought and died were poorly trained for battle. They had a lot of courage but not as much experience as their British counterparts. Many of them did not understand how to use bayonets. They were not used to obeying orders. The captains who tried to lead them often did not know what they were doing.

American soldiers provided a further problem for Washington. They would sign up for a few months of service, then quit and leave for home. By the winter of 1777, most of Washington's army had gone home. He had only 3000 men left, while the British had 20,000.

A stack of money from the American Revolution was not worth much to citizens. States issued their own forms of currency.

It cost a lot of money to feed and equip an army. Here, too, the British had a big advantage. They had enough money to hire thousands of German soldiers to fight with them in America. Washington, on the other hand, had a very hard time raising money. The Continental Congress had practically no power to collect taxes. State governments could raise taxes, but they rarely raised enough. The paper money that Washington used to pay his soldiers was almost worthless.

Without enough men or money, Americans could not defend their cities. They had trouble in Boston in 1775. They lost New York in 1776 and Philadelphia in 1777. They had to give up Savannah, Georgia, in 1778 and Charleston, South Carolina, in 1780.

And yet the Americans finally defeated a superior British army. How did they do this? There were many reasons for the Americans' victory.

American Advantages

Unlike the British soldiers, Americans were struggling for their own freedom. This provided the Americans with special inspiration. Great words and ideas can move people to keep fighting even when all seems lost. Powerful words came easily to two American writers, Thomas Paine and Thomas Jefferson. In 1776, Paine and Jefferson convinced thousands of people that they were fighting for liber-

This painting of the Battle of New York depicts the redcoats sailing on the Hudson River.

ty and the right to establish a republic (a representative form of government).

The Americans were also fighting on their own home ground. They knew the land and the people. North America was a vast continent. The British could not be everywhere at once. American troops lost more battles than they won. But they always managed to slip away from final defeat. They wore the British out.

The Americans had more dedicated leadership than the British. Some British generals were less enthusiastic and made careless mistakes. After winning a battle, they often relaxed, allowing the Americans to escape. But the American leader, George Washington, stayed with his job through victory and defeat. He knew when to attack the enemy and when to retreat. Even more important, he worked day and night with his soldiers. He won their respect and admiration. He was able to keep an army together even in the cold winter months when everyone wanted to quit.

The Americans also had help from England's old enemy, France. After declaring independence, the Americans sent Benjamin Franklin to Paris. He persuaded the French to support the Americans in their struggle against Britain.

In 1777, American victories at Trenton and Saratoga convinced the French that the Americans had a chance of winning. They decided to give ships and money. They also sent many soldiers, including the remarkable Marquis de Lafayette (mar-KEE duh laf-EE-et). This young man was inspired by the ideals of the American cause. He offered his services to Washington and fought bravely with the Americans. The help given by Lafayette and other French people gave the Americans new hope.

The Americans were lucky. For example, fog covered Washington's troops as they retreated from the Battle of Long Island. On a clear night, the British might have seen what was happening. And that probably would have been the end of Washington and his army.

Americans finally had the courage and determination to win. They faced a much superior opponent. Everyone needed to pitch in and help with the war effort. Farmers put down their plows and joined the militia. Women served as nurses, seamstresses, laundresses, and cooks for the army. In addition, as the war raged on, they made war supplies and went door-to-door raising funds. Women and children kept up farms and businesses and protected family property.

Their courage and determination helped Americans overcome obstacles. The colonists needed to overcome great divisions amongst themselves. Only about one-third of the population strongly supported the revolutionary cause. Another third remained loyal to the king. And the remaining third chose neither side. They just wanted to be left alone.

The result was much fighting among the American people. In many ways the American Revolution was a civil war. Brother battled brother and neighbor killed neighbor.

After seven years of tough fighting the American colonists finally defeated the British at Yorktown. In 1783, the treaty of peace was signed in Paris, France, ending the war. And the former British colonies became 13 "free and independent states."

17 LIBERTY'S AUTHORS

Through the summer of 1776, representatives of the 13 American colonies met in Philadelphia, behind locked doors. On July 4, they finally agreed to sign Thomas Jefferson's Declaration of Independence.

"I hold that a little rebellion now and then is a good thing, and as necessary in the political world as storms in the physical," wrote Thomas Jefferson, the author of the Declaration of Independence.

Jefferson wrote many fiery letters about political **liberty** (freedom) during the Revolution. The importance of his words in the American struggle made him a target for the British. In June 1781, British soldiers galloped toward his home, Monticello, near Charlottesville, Virginia. Their orders were to arrest the patriot leader and take him prisoner.

Word of the plot came from a Virginia militia captain. So Jefferson quickly sent his wife Martha, and their two young daughters, Patsy and Polly, to a neighbor's house. Jefferson had just enough time to burn papers that he did not want to fall into the hands of the British before he escaped.

After the Revolution, Jefferson

became the new nation's first secretary of state, then vice-president, and finally president (1801 to 1809). Yet his fame would be endless if he had done no more than write the Declaration of Independence. With it he became one of the greatest champions of liberty. Even today his words inspire people who are struggling for freedom.

Young Tom

Thomas Jefferson was born April 13, 1743, on a tobacco plantation near Charlottesville. His father, Peter Jefferson, was a strong, tough **frontiersman** (a man who lives on the farthest part of a settled country). Like most farmers, he had to chop down woods to build his farm. Tom's mother, Jane Randolph, came from one of Virginia's richest families.

Tom's education was the best that money could buy in those days. He had private tutors until he was almost 17. Then he entered William and Mary College at Williamsburg, the colonial capital of Virginia. Jefferson was unlike most of the fun-loving students there. He thirsted for knowledge and studied 15 hours a day. After college, he studied law and became a successful attorney. In one case, he tried to win freedom for a slave, even though he himself owned several slaves. Jefferson

Calling for freedom from Britain, patriots pulled down a statue of King George III in New York City in 1776.

told the court that "under the law of nature all men are born free." Though Jefferson lost the case, he was torn over the issue of slavery, never freeing his own slaves.

As a young man, Jefferson was strongly influenced by the bold, new ideas of **democracy** (government run by the people) that were beginning to spread in Europe. Until then, it was widely believed that men and women were unfit to rule themselves. They needed powerful monarchs to rule them and to keep order. To think otherwise was dangerous.

During a period called the **Enlightenment**, a few brave men and women in France and England began to question this notion. People, they said, were born good and equal. Citizens were gifted with intelligence and the ability to reason. They could rule themselves better than any monarch and his court of nobles.

Property owners, it was believed, had a better interest in public affairs than those who did not own property. Women were left out of the political picture.

These ideas spread to the American colonies, especially after the government of King George III began to levy taxes that the colonists resented. But most Americans directed their anger against Parliament and the king's ministers, not the king himself. Outwardly, at least, they remained loyal to the king. This was true even after the first battles of the Revolution were fought.

The Declaration

In January 1776, however, a pamphlet was published that produced a wave of feeling against the king and for independence. Called *Common Sense,* it was written by Thomas Paine, an Englishman who had been in America only a short time. With great daring, Paine attacked the king as "the Royal Brute." It was time for Americans to rely on "nothing more than the simple facts, plain argument, and common sense." America would show the whole world how a people could rule themselves and be free of the tyranny of kings.

"Everything that is right or natural pleads for separation [from Great Britain]," argued Paine. "The blood of the slain, the weeping voice of nature cries, 'TIS TIME TO PART." Jefferson read *Common Sense* and agreed with it completely.

Common Sense sold more than 100,000 copies, and by the spring of 1776, public opinion was leaning toward cutting ties with Great Britain. In Philadelphia, the Continental Congress appointed a committee to write a formal declaration of independence. Its leading members were

COMMON SENSE:
ADDRESSED TO THE
INHABITANTS
OF
AMERICA.
On the following interesting
SUBJECTS.

I. Of the Origin and Design of Government in general, with concise Remarks on the English Constitution.

II. Of Monarchy and Hereditary Succession.

III. Thoughts on the present State of American Affairs.

IV. Of the present Ability of America, with some miscellaneous Reflections.

Written by an ENGLISHMAN.
By Thomas Paine

Man knows no Master save creating HEAVEN,
Or those whom choice and common good ordain.
THOMSON.

PHILADELPHIA, Printed
And Sold by R. BELL, in Third-Street, 1776.

Thomas Paine (1737-1809), son of an English Quaker, came to America in 1774. He quickly became a voice for revolution when he published *Common Sense.*

Jefferson, John Adams of Massachusetts, and Benjamin Franklin of Pennsylvania. Yet the job of writing the declaration fell on Jefferson, who was only 33 years old. Jefferson thought that Adams, an older man, should write the declaration and told him so. Adams replied, "You can write ten times better than I." Jefferson's answer was, "I will do as well as I can."

Jefferson's words are as moving today as they were then. "We hold these truths to be self-evident," he wrote, "that all men are created equal, that they are endowed by their Creator with certain . . . rights, among these are life, liberty, and the pursuit of happiness." Yet, Jefferson did nothing to include the idea that women were equal to men and should receive the same rights.

He then accused King George III of many crimes against the American colonists. The king, he said, was a tyrant "unfit to be the ruler of a free people." As a result, the colonies had the right "to be free and independent states."

Jefferson presented the **document** (something written or printed that gives information) to the Continental Congress on June 28 to read and study. Some members were still against declaring independence. They said it was too soon to cut the ties to Great Britain. "It would be like

AMERICAN ADVENTURES

destroying our house in winter," one said, "before we have gotten another." But John Adams and others made strong speeches in favor of independence.

For two days, July 2 and 3, the members made a number of changes in Jefferson's Declaration of Independence. They took out, for example, a statement attacking George III for promoting the slave trade in America. This was done to win the support of some southern members. But most of the document was left as Jefferson had written it.

The fourth of July was a hot day. The members of the Congress wiped their foreheads with their handkerchiefs. One by one they voted "yes" to Jefferson's Declaration. Ever since, July 4 has been celebrated as Independence Day in the United States.

Soon the Declaration appeared in all the newspapers. The United Colonies of America had become the United States of America. And Americans were no longer the subjects of a far-away king, but free citizens of their own nation.

This is Independence Hall in Philadelphia, Pennsylvania.

CHAPTER CHECK

WORD MATCH
1. democracy
2. the Enlightenment
3. frontiersman
4. document
5. liberty

a. period of political questioning
b. government of the people
c. lives on farthest part of settled country
d. freedom
e. printed piece of information

QUICK QUIZ
1. What impact did the pamphlet, *Common Sense*, have on the colonists?
2. Explain the bold new ideas of a democracy that started to spread in Europe. How did these ideas impact on the men and women of France and England and then spread to America?

THINK ABOUT IT
In the Declaration of Independence Jefferson wrote, "We hold these truths to be self evident, that all men are created equal, that they are endowed by their creator with certain . . . rights, among these are life, liberty, and the pursuit of happiness." In your own words, explain what Jefferson meant by this statement.

18 A NEEDED VICTORY

Through brilliant planning and force of personality, George Washington was able to turn a ragtag, poorly disciplined army into a victorious military force.

It looked like the end for General George Washington's army. Unless he got more men, he said, "the game will be pretty near up."

Washington and his army had been driven off Long Island and out of New York into New Jersey. Then the British had chased the Americans across the Delaware River into Pennsylvania. It was now December 1776. Washington had fewer than 3000 men left out of about 20,000. The rest either had been killed, had been taken prisoner, or had **deserted** (run away from duty).

Many American soldiers had no shoes, shirts, or coats. Winter was closing in, and the men were freezing. At the end of the year, their terms of service would be up. Then most of them would leave the army and go home. Washington badly needed a victory just to keep up the fighting spirit of his restless troops.

Across the Delaware River, in Trenton, New Jersey, were 1500 enemy soldiers. They had come from the small German state of Hesse, and they were called **Hessians** (HESH-unz). They had been hired by the British. The Hessians had chased Washington's army across New Jersey. Now they were enjoying their victory and the coming of Christmas.

Washington planted a spy, John Honeyman, among the Hessians. Honeyman told Washington that the Hessians were planning a big party on Christmas. There would be lots of eating—and drinking. The Hessians would be in no condition to fight.

Crossing the Delaware

This was the chance Washington needed. He planned an attack on the Hessians. If the attack succeeded, he might be able to make a dash to nearby New Brunswick. New Brunswick was where the British were keeping their supplies.

On the night of December 25, Washington's men prepared to cross the Delaware. Washington ordered the words of Thomas Paine's *American Crisis* to be read to his troops:

"THESE ARE THE TIMES that try men's souls. The summer soldier and the sunshine patriot will, in this crisis, shrink from the service of the country; but he that stands it now, deserves the love and thanks of man and woman."

Inspired by these words, the men crossed the river in 40-foot rowboats. Huge chunks of ice crashed against the boats. But nevertheless 3000 men rowed across. The men split into two columns and headed for Trenton, nine miles away. One **column** (line of soldiers) took the river road. The other took an inland road. Snow, sleet, and hail fell upon the soldiers.

Both roads to Trenton were covered with ice and snow. Men slipped and fell along the way. Men in bare feet or torn shoes made a trail of blood on the snowy roads.

Early in the morning, a sleepy Hessian guard thought he saw men moving on the inland road. He called out a warning—too late. Shots rang out; men ran and shouted. Down by the river, the second column of Americans was charging with bayonets. Cannons opened fire.

Defeating the Hessians

Colonel Johann Rall, the Hessian

Christmas night, 1776: Inspired by the words of Thomas Paine, hundreds of American soldiers crossed the icy Delaware River to stage a sneak attack on allies of British forces.

The Battle of Trenton, 1776-1777

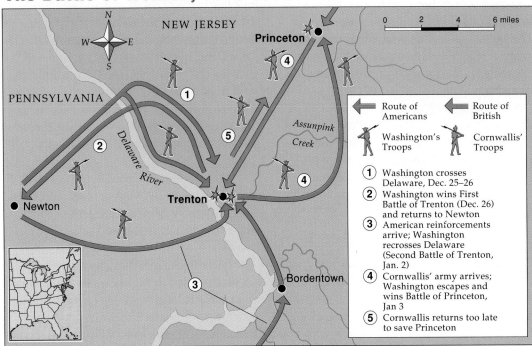

How many miles did Washington and his troops have to march to reach Trenton after crossing the Delaware? How many miles did they march between Trenton and Princeton?

commander, was awakened by the noise. He was still dazed and exhausted from the Christmas party. But he dashed bravely into the streets between the stone **barracks** (buildings for soldiers to live in). He cursed and called his sleepy, tired men out to fight. Most of them couldn't even get into action. The American rifle and cannon fire was too heavy.

Finally, Colonel Rall was hit by a bullet and fell wounded. The frightened Hessians threw down their rifles and surrendered. Rall died after giving up to Washington. More than 900 of the enemy were taken prisoner. About 100 Hessians were killed or wounded. Only two of Washington's men were killed and three were wounded.

After the battle, Washington retreated back across the Delaware. A few days later he set out again, this time doing battle with British troops. At Princeton, Washington's army put some of these troops to flight. Again the Americans were victorious. At the Battle of Princeton, 100 British troops were killed or wounded.

Washington decided against attacking the British at New Brunswick. His troops were too weary to attempt it. Instead he moved his **command** (soldiers or region over which an officer has authority) to Morristown in the hilly area of northern New Jersey. There he spent the next six months.

The Americans were amazed by their

AMERICAN ADVENTURES

victories at Trenton and Princeton. They wore rags—but they had beaten a tough, well-trained army. As a result, many Americans signed up for more service.

The British gave up all hope of ending the war in the winter of 1776 to 1777. Washington's army was saved. It would fight on until help came from France.

This drawing shows the course taken by General Washington's army after crossing the Delaware River (bottom left) from Pennsylvania to New Jersey. There, the Americans won surprising victories against the Hessians at Trenton and the British at Princeton.

CHAPTER CHECK

WORD MATCH
1. Hessians   **a.** ran away from duty
2. deserted   **b.** soldiers or area under officer's authority
3. column   **c.** German troops hired by the British
4. barracks   **d.** line of soldiers
5. command   **e.** buildings soldiers live in

QUICK QUIZ
1. Describe the condition of General George Washington's army in December 1776.
2. Why were the American victories at Trenton and Princeton so important?

THINK ABOUT IT
How might the course of American history have changed if Washington's army had not won the battles at Trenton and Princeton? Explain.

19 THE DEFEAT OF GENTLEMAN JOHNNY

In this 20th century painting, the British General Burgoyne surrenders to the American General Gates after the Battle of Saratoga.

"**G**entleman Johnny" Burgoyne (burr-GOIN) did not have much use for American soldiers. He believed that his own British troops were better fighters on the battlefield. They fought like Europeans. American troops fought like people from the backwoods. They pretended to surrender and then fired on the enemy. They **sniped** at the British from behind trees. They surprised their foes and caught them in **ambushes** (traps). At least the British knew how to stand up and fight like gentlemen, General Sir John Burgoyne thought.

Burgoyne knew that the Americans were troublesome. They could be as annoying as a swarm of buzzing flies. But Burgoyne was very sure of himself. He had no doubt that he could defeat the Americans—no doubt at all.

His faith in himself was clear to British leaders. Early in 1777, it won him a leading role in the war. His job was to cut off New England from the rest of the colonies. New England had given the colonies many of their soldiers. It had given the Continental Army much of its meat. Without help from New England, the Continental Army would be greatly weakened. Then, the British believed, the war could be brought to a speedy end.

The plan to cut off New England had been made before the Battle of Trenton. It involved British forces under three commands. Burgoyne was to lead his soldiers down from Canada and southward across Lake Champlain. Lieutenant Colonel Bar St. Leger was to move another force from Fort Oswego (ah-SWEE-go) on Lake Ontario to the Hudson River. General Sir William Howe was to lead a third force up the Hudson River from New York. All three forces would come together at Albany. They would defeat any enemy troops in the area. They could then take firm control of the Hudson River valley. Without a crossing point along the Hudson, Americans would not be able to get supplies from New England (*see map on page 112*).

British Blunders

To British leaders in London, the plan looked almost ideal. But when their generals tried to follow it, they **blundered**

Benedict Arnold (1741-1801), whose name later came to mean traitor, was an honored hero in earlier American campaigns against British troops.

(made foolish mistakes) all along the way. St. Leger ran into fighting in the Mohawk valley. Finally, he fell back to his starting point, Fort Oswego. Howe, meanwhile, never took part in the plan at all. Instead of going to Albany, Howe gathered his troops in New York City and sailed southward toward Chesapeake Bay.

At first, Burgoyne did make some headway. He set out from Canada in June 1777, with more than 7000 men. His army easily captured Fort Ticonderoga (tie-kon-deh-ROE-guh) on the southern edge of Lake Champlain. But soon Burgoyne ran into trouble. His army had to cut its way through thick forests. It had to cross swamps and streams. It had to build some 40 bridges along the way. Burgoyne's men became weak and sick.

To add to his troubles, Burgoyne made a serious mistake. He sent about 700 Hessian soldiers to Vermont (then still part of New York) to get food and horses for his men. At Bennington, they were attacked by untrained American soldiers. These soldiers called themselves the Green Mountain Boys. Almost all of the Hessians were killed or captured. Many of the soldiers sent to help them were also lost. In all, Burgoyne lost about 900 men.

Battle of Saratoga

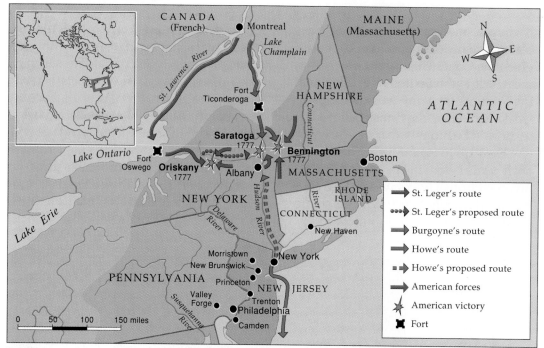

Which general was supposed to travel north up the Hudson River? In what direction did he travel instead? Why do you think the British generals chose to travel over water instead of over land?

On September 19, Burgoyne's army met a larger American army near Saratoga, New York. The British marched out of a forest into an open field. Up ahead, men with fur caps and long rifles lay in wait, hidden among the trees. Suddenly there was the crack of American rifles. Their main targets were British officers. Many were killed. British gunners were picked off before they could load their cannons.

The British fled back to the woods. When the Americans charged them, the British drove them back. For three hours the two armies fought back and forth across a field. The Americans finally pulled back, but the British had lost more than 600 men.

Final Retreat

Burgoyne waited for help but none came. Then, on October 7, the two armies fought it out again. This time, an American general named Benedict Arnold was the hero of the day. Riding horseback, he led three charges against the British lines. On one charge, British troops under young General Simon Fraser held their own. "Get him and the day is won!" Arnold shouted. A moment later he aimed his rifle and fired. Fraser fell from his horse, badly wounded. His troops fell back. Soon Arnold also fell from his horse with a bullet wound in his leg. He was carried from the field.

But the Americans won the day. Burgoyne's troops retreated toward Saratoga. Soon his entire force was surrounded. He had never figured that "soldiers from the backwoods" would defeat him on the battlefield. The Americans had proved him wrong. On October 17,

AMERICAN ADVENTURES

Burgoyne surrendered his army of more than 5000 British and Hessian troops.

The victory at Saratoga was the most important the Americans had won so far. When news reached Europe, it led to a victory of another sort. For several months, Americans had been trying to win France over to their side. Now they finally succeeded. In February 1778, the French signed a treaty with America. The treaty gave America a powerful ally in its struggle for independence.

Yet the tide of war did not turn overnight. That winter, Washington and about 11,000 men camped at Valley Forge in Pennsylvania. His aim was to keep watch on the British in nearby Philadelphia. After Saratoga, the winter at Valley Forge was a low point for the American army. There was not much food. Soap was as scarce as meat. Soldiers stood in the snow in bare feet. About 3000 men died.

At Valley Forge, Washington did get some unexpected help. It came with the arrival of a tough **drillmaster** (military drill teacher), Baron Friedrich von Steuben (FREED-rick vahn STOO-bun). Von Steuben came from Prussia, a powerful German kingdom. He was put in charge of training Washington's men. He taught them to use bayonets and to march in perfect order. Washington's men respected him and worked hard.

In June, they marched away from Valley Forge. With von Steuben's help, the American army had been reborn. It became a tough, well-trained body of soldiers. It was ready now for the hard fighting ahead.

CHAPTER CHECK

WORD MATCH
1. Benedict Arnold
2. sniped
3. blundered
4. ambushes
5. drillmaster

a. shot from a hidden position
b. traps
c. American general who led the charge
d. made foolish mistakes
e. instructor in military drill

QUICK QUIZ
1. Explain why General Sir John Burgoyne became known as "Gentleman Johnny."
2. Why was it said that the American army was reborn when it left Valley Forge in June?

THINK ABOUT IT
1. Why do you think the British wanted to cut New England off from the rest of the colonies? Describe this military plan.
2. Explain the significance of the American victory at the Battle of Saratoga. What effect did this battle have on American relations with France?

20 RAISING FUNDS FOR THE REVOLUTION

The women of Philadelphia did their part to aid the struggling American army by raising money. With the proceeds, they bought linen and sewed thousands of shirts for the poor and ill-clad soldiers.

"Charleston, [South Carolina] has fallen!" The grim news sped through the workshops and markets of Philadelphia. Outside a printer's shop, a crowd of tradesmen and **apprentices** (persons learning trades) eager for the latest news gathered to read a **broadside** (a poster featuring news). In the open-air markets, women talked of little else as they shopped under the bright May sun in 1780.

Esther Reed noticed none of these things as she made her way through the streets to the home of her friend, Sarah Bache. Reed had recently gathered her children and fled into the countryside when the British had attacked Philadelphia.

Over coffee (not the boycotted tea), the women talked about ways to help the army. They knew that some women marched behind supply wagons with the army. The women scrubbed kettles full of laundry in exchange for army **rations**

114

(fixed amounts of food.) What else could they do? Reed's husband was General Washington's aide. She knew what the soldiers needed most: stockings, shoes, better food, new guns—and encouragement.

Perhaps we could take up a collection among the women we know and buy something for the soldiers, suggested Bache. It would not be much, but it would be a way to show appreciation for their sacrifices.

Sarah Bache was one of the women of who set up a fund-raising network to help General Washington's men.

of being very successful."

Thirty-nine women took to the streets of Philadelphia and nearby Germantown, Pennsylvania, visiting their neighbors to explain the plan and ask for donations. It seemed ridiculous to some people. Respectable women were not supposed to walk through the streets of the city, begging for money.

Anne Rawle opposed American independence. "Of all the absurdities, the ladies going about for money exceeded everything," she complained in a letter. "They were so extremely [insistent] that people were obliged to give them something to get rid of them."

Tour of Duty

Reed and Bache called a meeting of their friends to discuss the idea. The response was enthusiastic. Many of these women had fled with their families or suffered during the British occupation of Philadelphia. They were eager to show their support for American independence.

Mary Morris, one of the women who took part, explained it in a letter to a friend. "Instead of waiting for the **donations** [contributions] being sent, the ladies . . . go from door to door to collect them," she wrote. "I am one of those honored with this business. Yesterday we began our tour of duty and had the satisfaction

"Born for Liberty"

Esther Reed, Sarah Bache, and the other patriot women knew their project was unusual. When Americans organized boycotts of tea and other British goods, people began to understand that women could play an important political role. But fund-raising was something entirely new. In a broadside of their own, the women proclaimed themselves "born for liberty." They explained that they wanted to offer more than sympathy in support of the war.

This is a street scene of Philadelphia as it was during the days of the American Revolution. This picture shows the intersection of Second Street and Market Street, not far from where the First Continental Congress met. The spire in the center belongs to Christ Church.

"The women of America . . . aspire to render themselves more really useful; and this sentiment is universal from the north to the south of the thirteen United States," they wrote. "If opinion and manners did not forbid us to march to glory by the same paths as the men, we [may] at least equal, and sometimes surpass them in our love for the public good."

The women worked diligently, calling on hundreds of homes. By July 4, 1780, Reed was able to write to her friend, General Washington, with news of their success. About 1650 people had donated more than $300,000.

When Washington wrote back to thank Reed and the other women for their work, he suggested that the money be deposited directly in the Bank of the United States to be part of the army's general fund.

Reed took this suggestion to the women who had done the work, but the women would have no part of it. We raised this money as a special gift for the soldiers, they said, to show them that the women of Philadelphia are grateful. We want them to know who has sent this.

The women then proposed that the money be divided among all the soldiers, with each one getting a share. This time Washington refused outright. They will only use the money to get drunk, he argued. Finally, Reed and Washington agreed on a way to spend the money. The women would buy linen cloth and sew shirts for the American army.

2000 Shirts

Reed had guided the women's fundraising effort from the beginning. But in September 1780, she fell suddenly ill and died at the age of 33. The work which had meant so much to her continued without her. Women who had been inspired by patriotism to begin the project, now sought to complete it.

They met regularly at Bache's house to cut and sew the shirts. Each shirt took hours of careful hand sewing to make it sturdy enough for army use. For months the women worked, and by December, they had each made about 40 shirts, 2000 in all. On December 26, Bache sent the shirts to General Washington to be distributed. We hope they will "be worn with as much pleasure as they were made," she wrote.

News of the Philadelphia project spread throughout the states. Many people praised the women for their patriotic efforts, but only a few tried to imitate them. Women in New Jersey raised more than $15,000. A smaller donation came from women in Maryland. Elsewhere, women who might have organized such a drive were instead busy running farms, businesses, and households while their husbands were at war.

Like Esther Reed, many American women found their lives deeply affected by the war. Some were forced to flee their homes to escape the British. Others chose to stay, but found themselves unwilling hosts to British soldiers quartered in their homes. Women who had no other means of support when their husbands joined the army often traveled along, earning rations by washing, cooking, and nursing for the soldiers. And some unfortunate women were the victims of war—brutalized, raped, or killed by soldiers battling over questions of loyalty. Like the men who fought on the battlefields, women took heroic risks for liberty.

CHAPTER CHECK

WORD MATCH
1. broadside
2. rations
3. quartered
4. donations
5. apprentices

a. persons learning a trade
b. poster featuring news
c. gifts or contributions
d. supplies of food
e. living in assigned housing

QUICK QUIZ
1. In what ways did American women participate in the war?
2. Describe some of the problems women faced at home during the war.

THINK ABOUT IT
In the broadside explaining their actions, the women of Philadelphia wrote that "Opinion and manners ... forbid us to march to glory by the same paths as men." What did they mean by opinion and manners?

21 "I WOULD HAVE HANGED MY BROTHER"

This portrait shows a loyalist family living in Canada. On the back of the portrait, someone had written, "The Eight portraits cost Ten pounds each, the dog Brador was added without cost."

Six hungry men walked up to a log cabin in the woods of Georgia. They found a turkey and shot it. Then they pointed their rifles at a woman in the house. "Cook it for us," they said. The woman took the dead bird and began to pluck it.

The men found some whiskey in the house and began to drink it. They talked and laughed about the man they had killed a few hours before. He had been an officer in the Georgia militia. They had

shot him in his bed.

The woman told her daughter to fetch some water. She also managed to whisper another message into her ear. "Call your father," she said. The girl left the house.

The men were careless. They did not know the woman they were dealing with. Her name was Nancy Hart and she knew about guns. She waited for her chance to grab one of the men's guns. Finally she reached out and took it. The man leaped at her. She killed him with one shot.

AMERICAN ADVENTURES

Another came at her. She shot him too. The others she held as prisoners.

Soon her husband entered with a group of friends. They wanted to shoot the invaders on the spot. But Nancy Hart said that would be too good for them. Hanging them would be better, she said. That is how her enemies died, hanging from a tree outside her cabin door.

Nancy Hart and her husband were farmers, not soldiers. The men they killed were not really soldiers either. These men were Americans who supported the British king. Scenes like this that took place in the woods of Georgia were fairly common. For the American Revolution was much more than just a soldiers' war.

During the Revolution, Joseph Brant, a Mohawk chief, convinced many Native Americans to fight on the side of British troops and American loyalists. Brant's true name was Thayendangea, or Two-Sticks-of-Wood-Bound-Together, a name that means strength.

"Enemy Country"

The fact was that Americans were badly divided among themselves. Many of them believed as Nancy Hart did. They wanted independence even if it took a war to win it. But perhaps as many as a third of all American colonists remained loyal to the British king. The people in this second group were called **loyalists**.

Which colonists were loyalists?

Generally loyalists were those who thought they had the most to gain by siding with the British. Many were merchants, large landowners, and other wealthy people who feared great change. But not all loyalists were wealthy—not by any means. On the southern frontier, for example, the group included many poor farmers and hunters. These people looked to Britain for protection (safety). They opposed the Revolution because it was being led by the very people they most disliked. These leaders were the wealthy planters and merchants along the east coast.

Loyalists lived in all 13 colonies. But they were perhaps most common in five— New York, Pennsylvania, Maryland, Delaware, and Georgia. In

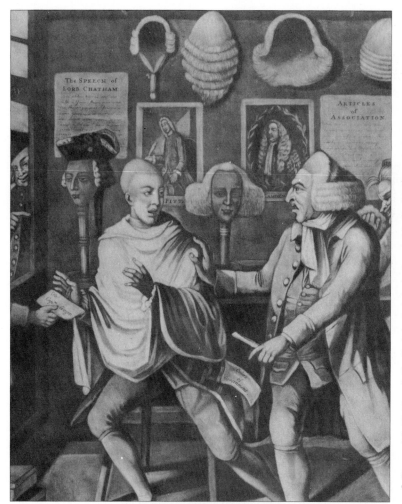

British friends. They could be punished for traveling in stagecoaches without identification cards. It was even risky to drink to the health of the British king. One loyalist who tried this was pushed into a large barrel (curved container with a flat top and bottom). There he was forced to dance all night to the tune of "Yankee Doodle."

The homes of loyalists were raided. Their property was stolen. Sometimes

New York, loyalists may have made up more than half of all the colonists. In Pennsylvania, many Quakers were suspected of being loyalist because they refused to fight. Patriots from New England and Virginia were aware of loyalist strength in the middle colonies. They sometimes spoke of this area as "the enemy's country."

Most patriots hated loyalists more bitterly than they hated the British. They blamed loyalists for persuading (convincing) the British to fight. Loyalists were treated as traitors and outlaws. They could be arrested for writing letters to

they were put to death. Patriot leaders such as John Adams raged against Americans who sided with the British. "I would have hanged my brother," said Adams, "if he took part with our enemy in this country." (Luckily for Adams' brother, he, too, was a patriot.)

Loyalists were no friendlier to patriots—at least not in areas where they had control. One of these was New York City, held by the British for most of the war. The British used New York churches as prisons for "rebels." They often let prisoners starve to death. Bodies were then piled in carts and hauled through the streets. Loyalists laughed and hooted as they saw these carts go by. "There goes another load of rebels," they would say.

Making Choices

Thousands of Americans did not care who won the war. They were neither loyalists nor patriots. They just wanted to be left alone. James Moody, for example, was a New Jersey farmer. His neighbors tried to make him sign a paper swearing loyalty to the new American government. He refused to do it, explaining that he just wanted to be left in peace. But his neighbors kept threatening him. One day they even shot at him while he was out farming. That made Moody so angry he decided to leave his farm and fight for the British.

The war brought suffering and fear to many. It brought hope to some. In Virginia, the royal governor made a promise to those slaves owned by rebel planters. He promised them freedom if they ran away from their masters and served the British army. Hundreds of slaves in Virginia and other states joined the British. But few were set free. Instead they became the property of British officers. They were made to do the heavy labor of building forts and hauling cannons and supplies.

The war also raised the old question of whether a woman could take part in politics. Only in New Jersey were women allowed to vote. In most places, women could not hold office or attend town meetings. It would be years before the new code of laws that resulted from the Revolution would "remember the ladies."

CHAPTER CHECK

WORD MATCH
1. loyalists
2. hauling
3. protection
4. barrel
5. persuading

a. curved container with a flat top and bottom
b. convincing
c. supporters of the Crown
d. safety, security
e. carrying by force

QUICK QUIZ
1. List the five colonies where most loyalists lived. What significant reason can you give for loyalists living there?
2. How did the wealthy merchants' and landowners' reasons for remaining loyal to Great Britain differ from those of the poor farmers and hunters?

THINK ABOUT IT
Patriots and loyalists were sharply and bitterly divided over the issue of separation from the mother country. What evidence in the chapter supports this statement?

22 SURRENDER AT YORKTOWN

General George Washington led his troops to victory at the Battle of Yorktown as shown in this 1780s painting by John Trumbull.

The British drummer boy hammered at his drum as hard as he could. But the noise of the cannons drowned out his message. Gunsmoke curled around his legs. Finally, the Americans and French let up on their firing for a moment, and the drum beat could be heard. The message was clear: The British were asking for a meeting.

A British officer stepped out, waving a white cloth. Soon he was blindfolded and taken to General Washington's head-quarters. The British officer had a message for Washington. **Lord Cornwallis**, the British commander at Yorktown, Virginia, wanted to surrender. It was a great victory for the Americans and their French allies. Cornwallis' surrender would end the Revolutionary War.

How was the victory won? When the French entered the war in 1778, they gave the British cause for great alarm. France was one of the most powerful countries of Europe. Its aid to the Americans was sure to lengthen the war. Now the British decided on a new course. British commanders turned much of their attention to the area south of the Potomac River. There they expected to find many loyalists who might aid their cause.

Southern Campaign

In December 1778, the British took Savannah, Georgia. A year-and-a-half later they seized Charleston, South Carolina. There they took 5000 American troops prisoner. That was nearly all of the Continental Army south of the Potomac.

Yet the British found themselves in trouble in the Carolinas. They suffered stinging defeats at King's Mountain in 1780, and at Cowpens in South Carolina

the next year. In 1781, they decided to leave the Carolinas and move north. They built up an army of 7200 men in Virginia. Lord Cornwallis took charge of this army and camped it at Yorktown on the coast. Facing the British Army was a much smaller one made up of French and American troops. These troops were led by the Marquis de Lafayette, Baron von Steuben, and General Anthony Wayne of Pennsylvania.

George Washington had a much larger American army outside New York City at this time. And Washington had a crucial decision to make. Should he attack the British in New York? Or should he march south and strike against Cornwallis in Virginia? Washington favored

A French engraving shows the seige of Yorktown and the surrender of the British leader Lord Cornwallis in 1781. Without the help of the French fleet, the Americans might not have won the battle. What are the French doing in this engraving to help the Americans?

Southern Campaigns

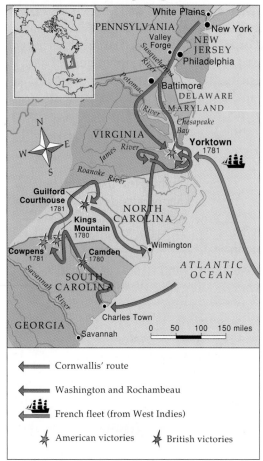

**Which states did Cornwallis's troops pass through?
Which states did Washington's troops pass through?**

attacking New York. If it were captured, the war might be ended.

Washington had a meeting with **Count Rochambeau** (roe-sham-BOH), the French commander. Rochambeau had an army of 5000 men, but he was against an attack on New York. "The British are too strong in New York," he said. "It would be much better to attack Cornwallis in Virginia."

By Land and by Sea

Washington and Rochambeau knew that their armies alone could not defeat Cornwallis in Virginia. They would have to have sea power as well. What if the armies trapped Cornwallis at Yorktown, and then Cornwallis sailed away in British ships? Cornwallis would have to be blocked at sea as well as on land.

Washington and Rochambeau sent a message to French Admiral de Grasse in the West Indies. They asked for the help of his fleet. It was the middle of August before they got their answer. De Grasse was sailing for Yorktown to block a British escape by sea. He would also land extra troops.

Washington and Rochambeau began racing south to Yorktown with their troops. By the middle of September, they had joined the small French and American army that was already there. And in the meantime, de Grasse had won a victory at sea. He had beaten a British **fleet** (group of ships under one's command) sent from New York to help Cornwallis. Now Cornwallis was **hemmed in** (confined) by land at Yorktown—and blockaded at sea by the ships of Admiral de Grasse.

The Americans and their French allies had 16,000 men at Yorktown. Cornwallis had less than half that many. Soon the allied cannons were pounding the British defenses day and night. Then, on October 14, French and American troops attacked. They struck swiftly after dark. They captured two British outposts.

Allied cannons pushed closer to the front. Soon 100 of them were blasting the British lines. Now the British position was hopeless. Their defenses were smashed. Finally, on October 17, a British drummer boy began hammering out a message. Cornwallis was finished.

After the fighting, British **fifes** (small instruments like flutes) and drums struck up an old tune. It was called "The World Turned Upside Down." The song was a fitting end to the Revolutionary War. For the British, the world had indeed been turned upside down. They had lost a war they had expected to win. They had lost their 13 American colonies as well. The peace treaty ending the war was not to be signed until September 1783. But Yorktown was the last major battle. Already it was becoming clear that the 13 British colonies were to be 13 "free and independent states."

Many black women and men supported the patriot cause in the American Revolution. This portrait shows an unidentified sailor in 1779.

CHAPTER CHECK

WORD MATCH
1. fleet
2. Count Rochambeau
3. hemmed in
4. Cornwallis
5. fifes

a. confined
b. British leader who surrendered at Yorktown
c. flute-like instruments
d. French commander
e. ships under one's command

QUICK QUIZ
1. Why did the British forces find themselves in trouble in South Carolina? Do you think this caused the British to move their forces to Virginia? Explain.
2. Explain Washington's and Rochambeau's position on attacking either New York City or General Cornwallis in Virginia.

THINK ABOUT IT
Why did England change its war plan from separating New England from the rest of the colonies to controlling all the area south of the Potomac? Do you think it would have been better for the British to have stayed with their original plan? Explain.

23 A MOST LOVED MAN

During his long and full life, Benjamin Franklin (1706-90) was an author, scientist, inventor, diplomat—and "a most loved man."

In 1781, everywhere people went in Paris, France, the same face seemed to stare out at them. His portraits hung over the fireplaces of French homes. His picture was painted on clocks and pocket watches. He was one of the most famous people in France. He was not a French king or count, but plain old Benjamin Franklin from America.

Franklin wore a simple fur hat on his head and plain spectacles on his nose. In France, anyone who was at all important wore a fancy powdered wig. But not Franklin. He simply let his gray hair hang down over his shoulders.

Ben Franklin was a charming and witty man. He knew how to use his charm and wit to help the American cause. Without his work in Paris, Americans could not have won the **Battle of Yorktown**. After all, the Yorktown victory depended on a combined attack by French and American troops and French ships. Why were the French helping the Americans? Partly because Ben Franklin had talked them into it.

Franklin had a way with words and an understanding of complex ideas. He was also willing to try anything new. Franklin had been this way ever since he first left home in 1723.

Franklin was only 17 years old then. He had become tired of working in his older brother's Boston print shop. So Franklin ran off to seek his fortune. He had only a dollar in his pocket when he finally reached Philadelphia. But he soon found a good job working for a German printer. After a while he was able to open his own printing shop.

Soon Franklin was printing a newspaper. It sold more copies than any other paper in the American colonies. In 1732, Ben printed *Poor Richard's Almanac*. This **almanac** had news of the weather, holidays, and the best time to plant seeds or pick grapes. It also had many wise and funny sayings that Franklin made up. Some of these were:

"God helps those who help themselves."

"Lost time is never found again."

"Half the truth is often a great lie."

People loved Poor Richard's sayings. They bought many copies of the *Almanac*, and Ben became rich. He also became a leading citizen of Philadelphia. He did many things to make

These are Benjamin Franklin's bifocals and almanac.

Philadelphia a good town to live in. He became its **postmaster** (in charge of all mail) and sped up the mail service. He started a fire department and a police department. He began the town's first library and first hospital. He also started the school that later became the University of Pennsylvania.

At the age of 42, Franklin had made enough money to retire from business. He liked science and wanted to learn more about electricity. Soon after, Franklin invented the **lightning rod**. This kept houses from catching fire when struck by lightning. Franklin won many honors for his work.

As time went on, Franklin became more and more active in public affairs. He went to England to try to make the British government deal fairly with the colonies. When the Revolutionary War broke out, he helped Thomas Jefferson write the Declaration of Independence. Soon after that, in 1776, he sailed for France to try to get some help for Washington's struggling army.

Winning over France

Franklin said he represented a nation called the United States. But no government in Europe thought this nation even existed. The United States then was only an idea in the heads of a few colonial rebels. Franklin now had to persuade the French king to recognize

Among Ben Franklin's many contributions was the development of volunteer fire companies trained to put out fires and rescue people and property from other dangers.

the new government as the true one for America.

France wanted to strike back at its old enemy, England. But the young French king, Louis XVI, was afraid of losing another costly war. He would help the Americans secretly, but would not yet dare to recognize their government. Then came news of the Americans' surprising victory at Saratoga in 1777. Franklin wept with joy when he heard of it.

Yet, even now, the French king hesitated about getting mixed up with the Americans. So Franklin came up with another scheme. He met secretly with a representative of the English government. This Englishman said George III was ready to make peace. England would now give Americans almost complete freedom to govern themselves. But they would still have to be part of the British Empire.

Franklin probably did not take this meeting seriously. He just wanted to scare the French king into thinking that the Americans might make peace. Suddenly King Louis decided he would have to act. He signed a treaty of alliance with the United States. The final result of this alliance was the victory at Yorktown.

Reaching Terms with Britain

Later, in 1781, one more treaty had to be worked out in Paris. That was the treaty of peace with England. Franklin worked on its terms with John Adams of Massachusetts and a New York lawyer, John Jay. Again, Franklin helped give

Americans the best bargain they could hope for. Britain said the western border of the United States should be the Allegheny (aluh-GAY-nee) Mountains. The U.S. Congress said it should be much farther west—along the Mississippi River.

In Paris, Franklin suggested that Britain pay the United States for all the houses and property its armies had destroyed. Perhaps Britain should pay for this damage by giving Americans all of Canada. Franklin knew that the English would never agree to give up Canada. But he proposed the idea anyway. In the end, the British found a way to avoid a showdown over Canada. They agreed to make the Mississippi River the western border of the United States.

The **Treaty of Paris** was signed in September 1783. In the treaty, Britain rec-ognized the independence of its former colonies. It gave the new nation all the land westward to the Mississippi from the Great Lakes in the north to Florida in the south. It also gave Americans the right to fish off the shores of what is now Canada.

Benjamin Franklin was 70 years old when he first arrived in Paris. He was almost 80 when he left for home in 1785. He was so sick and lame that he could not walk. He had to be carried out of Paris on a seat strapped between two mules. People who lined the streets wept to see him go. They knew they would never see anyone quite like him again.

CHAPTER CHECK

WORD MATCH
1. postmaster
2. lightning rod
3. almanac
4. Treaty of Paris
5. Battle of Yorktown

a. Britain recognizing the independence of the colonies
b. a book published annually
c. combined attack by French and Americans
d. in charge of all mail
e. protects buildings in a storm

QUICK QUIZ
1. Why was Benjamin Franklin so loved by the French?
2. What were some of Benjamin Franklin's major achievements?
3. How did Benjamin Franklin convince the French king to help the new American nation?

THINK ABOUT IT
1. What strategies used by Franklin indicate he was a skilled negotiator?
2. Compare the contributions of Thomas Jefferson to those of Benjamin Franklin.

THE FIGHT FOR INDEPENDENCE

History Detective

1. "Government of the people, for the people, by the people" These words describe my form of government. What am I?

2. Drafted by a 33-year-old Virginian, John Adams called my Fourth of July passage America's Day of Deliverance. What am I?

3. The British spent the winter of 1777 to 1778 in Philadelphia, while ragged patriots kept watch in frigid huts on my snow-covered fields. Where am I?

4. When my brother asked why Sarah Bache and I sewed shirts, I said, "Every heart and every hand . . . must help in this glorious contest." Who am I?

5. Although we were Americans, patriots called us enemies and traitors. Who are we?

6. I counted on British relief by sea and instead found myself hemmed in by the French navy on a peninsula in Virginia. Who am I?

7. Inventor, statesman, and author, I was one of the first Americans to win international fame in the royal courts of Europe. Who am I?

Voices From the Past

Read the two quotes below. The first was delivered by an Iroquois chief to the British in 1776, the second by an Iroquois chief to George Washington in 1790. Then answer the questions that follow.

You tell me the Americans, with whom you are at War, are all mad. I now tell you that the Americans are the wise people. . . . They tell us your quarrel is between yourselves and desire us to sit still. . . . But you want us to assist you which we cannot do—for suppose the Americans conquer you; what would they then do to us?

• • •

When your army entered the country of the Six Nations, we called you Town Destroyer; and to this day when that name is heard our women look behind them and our children cling to their mothers.

1. At the outbreak of war, how did the Iroquois respond to British pleas for support? Why?

2. What message is the Iroquois chief trying to give George Washington?

Hands–On History

1. *Thinking Historically* —The Continental Congress has approved a document stating that *All men are created equal.* Write a dialogue about this news, between any two of the following people: a free black, a Daughter of Liberty, a French volunteer in the American army, a loyalist.

2. *Writing Creatively* —Write a short pamphlet to rally American spirits during the dark days of the war. Keep in mind the kind of words used in Thomas Paine's *Common Sense.*

YESTERDAY'S NEWS

The American Adventures Newspaper

1.

Cambridge, Mass., March, 1776—Talented poet and slave Phillis Wheatley, visited with Commander-in-Chief Washington for several hours at his Cambridge headquarters. In October 1775, Wheatley had sent the general a poem entitled "His Excellency General Washington." In the poem, Wheatley described Washington as "first in peace and honours."

Washington was so touched by the poem that he sent Wheatley a letter. Wrote Washington: "The elegant Lines you enclosed . . . exhibit a striking proof of your great poetical Talents."

Wheatley's owner granted Washington's request to meet personally with the young black writer.

2.

This unidentified sailer was one of many black men who supported the patriot cause.

Slaves Petition for Their Freedom

Boston, Mass., January 13, 1777— **3.**

The petition presented to the Massachusetts Legislature read: *Every principle from which America has acted in the course of their unhappy difficulties with Great Britain pleads . . . in favor of your petitioners [the slaves who signed the petition]. They humbly beseech [ask] to . . . be restored to the enjoyments of that which is the natural rights of all men.*

Passage on Slavery Dropped from Declaration

Philadelphia, Penn., July 2, 1776—After much debate, delegates to the Continental Congress voted to drop a controversial passage from Thomas Jefferson's draft of the Declaration of Independence. The passage blamed the king for the "evil" slave trade. Jefferson, quoted here, had charged that the king carried out a *cruel war against human nature itself, violating its most sacred rights of life and liberty in the persons of a distant people [Africans] . . . captivating [capturing] and carrying them into slavery.* Some delegates feared the passage might anger both Northern slave traders and Southern slave owners.

Observers have found it interesting that Jefferson, a Virginia planter *and* slave owner, would speak out so strongly against slavery.

> *You Be the Reporter*
> Match each question with its news item above.
> **1.** What headline would you write for this news story?
> **2.** Research some facts about Wheatley. Write several sentences that describe what her meeting with Washington may have been like.
> **3.** What lead sentence would you write for this article?

THINKING ABOUT REGIONS ON A MAP

Under the Treaty of 1783, the United States officially won its independence from Britain. The new nation also won a considerable piece of land. Under the terms of the treaty, the United States gained all the land westward to the Mississippi River, and from the Great Lakes in the north to Florida in the south. In effect, this was an increase of about a third of the area of the original 13 colonies. What did the nation look like in 1783?

Study the map and its key. Then note the answers to these questions on a separate sheet of paper.

1. Britain had wanted to establish the Alleghany mountains as the western boundary of the United States. **(a)** What area did the United States gain when the boundary was set at the Mississippi River? **(b)** What states now make up this area? (see map on page 812.)

2. Locate the northern boundary of the United States. Under the treaty, did the U.S., Britian, or both nations have possession of the Great Lakes? Explain.

3. The United States made up only one part of the North American continent in 1783. Who controlled **(a)** the land west of the Mississippi River? **(b)** the land north of the Great Lakes? **(c)** Florida?

4. Compare the regions of North America shown on the map. **(a)** What areas(s) did Russia and France control in 1783? **(b)** What two colonial powers controlled the largest areas? **(c)** Had all of North America been explored by 1783? Explain.

5. The Treaty of 1783 did not settle all land questions in North America. **(a)** In 1783, along which coast was a large area in dispute? **(b)** What other land in North America was in dispute at that time? Explain.

6. Think about the political boundaries on the map. **(a)** Which countries could you predict that the United States might fight with over land in the years ahead? Why? **(b)** How could you find out for sure?

A **region** is made up of places that are unified by some characteristic. Regions can be defined by facts of physical geography, such as river valleys or mountains. Sometimes regions are based on economic, political, social, or other characteristics.

Answer the following questions about regions on this map.

7. Look at the area of the United States included in the Treaty Line of 1783. **(a)** What three major regions made up this area? **(b)** Were these regions based on physical or political characteristics?

8. Look at the entire area of North America. **(a)** What six major regions of the continent are shown on this map? **(b)** What historical or political factor is used to define these regional boundaries?

9. If you wanted to describe the geographic regions of North America, **(a)** what physical features might you use to define them? **(b)** what specific geographic regions could you identify? (Refer to the Physical Map of North America on page 810 if you need help.)

10. Look at a modern political map of North America. What are the major political regions of North America today?

For Extra Credit: Find places on a map of North America today whose names are clues to their British, Spanish, Russian, or French origins.

North America, 1783

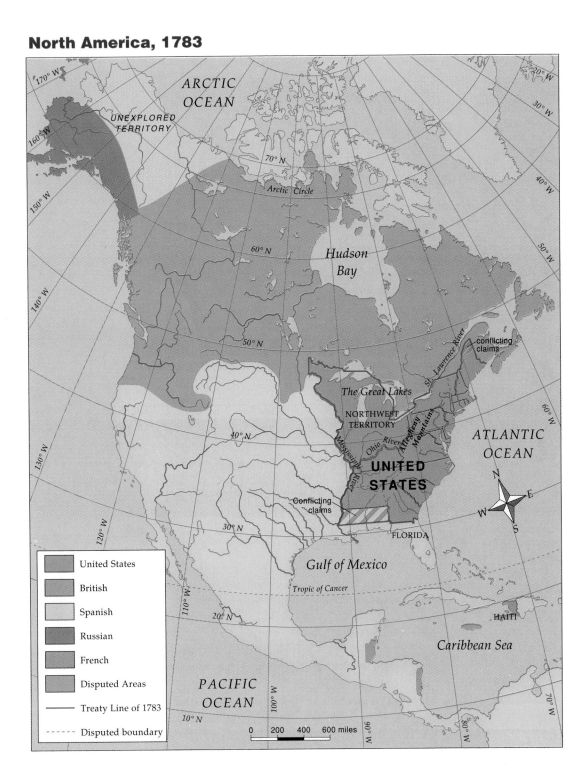

Legend:
- United States
- British
- Spanish
- Russian
- French
- Disputed Areas
- Treaty Line of 1783
- Disputed boundary

ARCTIC OCEAN

UNEXPLORED TERRITORY

170° W
160° W
150° W
140° W
130° W
120° W
110° W
100° W
90° W
80° W
70° W

70° N
60° N
50° N
40° N
30° N
20° N
10° N

Arctic Circle

Hudson Bay

conflicting claims

The Great Lakes

NORTHWEST TERRITORY

St. Lawrence River

Mississippi River

Ohio River

Allegheny Mountains

UNITED STATES

ATLANTIC OCEAN

Conflicting claims

FLORIDA

Gulf of Mexico

Tropic of Cancer

HAITI

Caribbean Sea

PACIFIC OCEAN

20° W
30° W
40° W
50° W
60° W
70° W

0 200 400 600 miles

LOOKING AHEAD

On the last day of the convention, an old man rose to make a closing statement. He said there were some things he did not like about the new constitution (plan of government). But, for the good of the nation, he was going to support it. He urged the other delegates to join him. The man told them to forget about their differences. They all had to be in agreement if the new constitution was to be approved.

The other delegates listened to the man. He was Benjamin Franklin, the oldest representative of the convention. He had served his

In the meeting room of Independence Hall, Philadelphia, Pennsylvania, both the Declaration of Independence and the Constitution were signed.

A MORE
PERFECT

1787		1788	1789		1790
1787	**1787**	**1788**	**1789**	**1789**	**1790**
Daniel Shays leads revolt against high taxes.	Constitutional Convention meets in Philadelphia, Pennsylvania	U.S. Constitution becomes law of the land.	George Washington inaugurated as first President.	First Congress meets in New York City, New York.	Quakers petition Congress to end slavery.

UNION

UNIT 5

During America's early days as a nation, New York City's Tontine Coffee House was a popular meeting spot for politicians and businessmen. Places like this were where many people heard and discussed the latest news.

country for many years and was well-respected.

Franklin had gathered with other concerned Americans to write a new constitution. They were worried about the fate of their nation. They believed that the government needed to be changed. If not, all they had fought for might soon be lost.

During the struggle for independence, the American states were united in their opposition to Great Britain. But after the war, many disagreements arose. The most important was how to govern the new country. What exactly did they mean by the term United States? How united should the new states be?

The First National Government

Some people wanted the nation to be a loose organization of states. They believed that citizens in each state should govern themselves. These people feared a strong national government. Why? They had just fought a war against the powerful British government.

Others argued that a strong national government was needed to solve the problems of the new country. Each state had to give up some of its power so that the nation could be stronger. Otherwise, the states would never be united as one country.

The first national government was created during the Revolutionary War. The rules for this government were listed in a document called the Articles of Confederation. For seven years, from 1781 to 1788, the United States was governed by this plan.

The Articles of Confederation established a national Congress (lawmaking body consisting of a Senate and House of Representatives). There was no president or chief executive. This was similar to most state governments of the time. They either had no governor, or governors with little power. They feared having another very powerful leader like the British king.

At first, most Americans wanted a weak national government. The powerful British government was still fresh in their minds. The Articles gave Congress authority to handle national issues such as declaring war, establishing an army and navy, and issuing and borrowing money. But most problems would be dealt with by the state governments.

The Articles gave most power to the states. Each of the 13 states could cast only one vote in Congress. A law could be passed only if nine of the 13 states voted for it. And Congress had no way to enforce its laws if the states refused to obey. This type of government sounded fair, but it did not work well in practice.

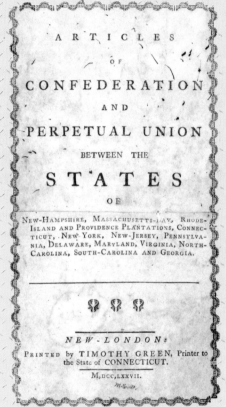

ARTICLES

OF

CONFEDERATION

AND

PERPETUAL UNION

BETWEEN THE

STATES

OF

NEW-HAMPSHIRE, MASSACHUSETTS-BAY, RHODE-ISLAND AND PROVIDENCE PLANTATIONS, CONNECTICUT, NEW YORK, NEW-JERSEY, PENNSYLVANIA, DELAWARE, MARYLAND, VIRGINIA, NORTH-CAROLINA, SOUTH-CAROLINA AND GEORGIA.

NEW-LONDON:

PRINTED by TIMOTHY GREEN, Printer to the State of CONNECTICUT.

M,DCC,LXXVII.

The Articles of Confederation tied the 13 colonies only loosely together. In time, a new plan of government was needed.

The main problem was that the states had too much power. Each of the 13 states acted as if it were a separate nation. A state could coin its own money, arm its own soldiers, and build its own navy. Each could, and sometimes did make laws that hurt neighboring states.

Because of these differences, Americans often suffered. Among their troubles was the confusion over money. Some Americans traded with coins minted by the states. Others used foreign coins. Still others traded with goods. Some people in New York used salt pork. Others in North Carolina used whiskey.

There was also trouble over trade. The 13 states competed with each other for business. They hated to see their own merchants and farmers losing business to people in other states.

The merchants of New York, for example, complained about people buying firewood from Connecticut merchants. To stop this, the New York state legislature placed a high tax on firewood from out of state. Connecticut merchants tried to get even. They refused to sell anything to New York for one year. Business was hurt everywhere because of this competition between states. And the United States

Congress was helpless to do anything about it.

One of the biggest problems concerned foreign policy. Like any nation, the United States needed to make treaties with other countries. But in 1785, most European nations did not respect American power. They knew how weak Congress was. Congress could not even collect enough taxes to equip a strong army.

This left American diplomats helpless. Dealings with the Spanish, for example, posed difficult problems. Spain controlled the city of New Orleans and the lower Mississippi River. Spanish officials stopped Americans from using New Orleans for their trade. Americans complained bitterly. But the king of Spain only ignored them. He knew that the U.S. Congress was too weak to do anything about it.

The Northwest Ordinance

The only successful act of Congress under the Articles was the Northwest Ordinance passed in 1787. This act presented a far-sighted plan for dealing with western lands north of the Ohio River (see map below). It allowed settlers in this area to form new states. Eventually, these states would be equal with the 13 original states. The Northwest Ordinance became the model for creating new states.

Settlers in the area could become self-

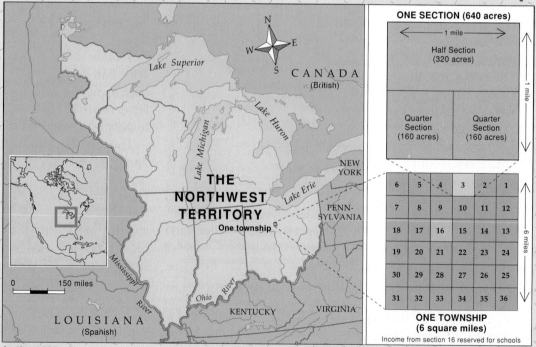

The Northwest Territory, 1781 and the Land Ordinance Township

In the 1780s Congress divided the Northwest Territory into townships. What was the size of each township? What was the size of each section? How many sections were in each township?

AMERICAN ADVENTURES

governing in two steps. First, when an area had 5000 eligible voters, the people of the territory could elect a legislature. Second, when an area had 60,000 settlers, it could become a state.

America was one nation not yet united fully, as shown here by its different flags. Some of the many early U.S. flags were the Stars and Stripes [left], and a 1775 Gadsden flag [bottom].

DON'T TREAD ON ME

The Northwest Ordinance promised settlers in the western land freedom of worship. It encouraged public support of schools. And it barred slavery in the territories.

Even the success of the Northwest Ordinance, however, could not make the Articles of Confederation work. In the fall of 1786, a group of unhappy Massachusetts farmers led by Daniel Shays, rebelled against their state government. They wanted reforms to cut taxes. Although Shays' Rebellion failed, it scared many people. The Articles were not strong enough.

How could the government be strengthened? One way was to throw out the Articles and start over again. In 1787, a group of 55 men met in Philadelphia to write a new plan of government.

This group included some of the most important leaders in America. Among them were George Washington, Benjamin Franklin, and James Madison. They drew upon many sources for creating their new constitution. They studied ancient Greek and Roman history. They looked at the Iroquois League of Five Nations. And they read political theories by John Locke and Jean Jacques Rousseau (rhu-SO).

Many compromises were made before they all agreed upon a plan. Eventually they gave a new Congress far more power than the old Congress had. They also created the office of president and a national court called the Supreme Court.

Not all Americans approved of the new Constitution. People debated whether or not to give the national government so much power. However, the promise of a bill of rights convinced most voters to support the new Constitution.

George Washington was easily elected as the first American President. He chose able people to help him run the government. And his actions helped guarantee the success of the new government.

24 SHAYS' REBELLION

The Revolution was won, but for Captain Daniel Shays, the struggle continued. He and other poor farmers had to fight to keep their land. This 1787 woodcut shows Shays [left] with fellow rebel Job Shattuck.

After the Revolution, hard times fell on the farmers of Massachusetts. They talked openly of rebellion. Violence finally broke out in the fall of 1786. Mobs armed with guns, swords, and clubs stormed courthouses and shut them down. In one town, a mob went further. It broke open the jail and freed the prisoners. When officials tried to stop the mob, they were treated roughly.

How did this rebellion come about? When the Revolutionary War ended in 1783, the newly independent states plunged into debt. This was caused mainly by the loss of trade with Great Britain. They had to borrow money to fight the war. To pay their debts, each state began printing its own paper money. The money soon became worthless, and the prices of goods went sky-high.

In the spring of 1786, the Massachusetts legislature placed unusually high taxes on land to raise money. These taxes hit farmers the hardest. Many

AMERICAN ADVENTURES

The Massachusetts state militia rode against Shays and his men. Early U.S. militiamen were often disorganized, as this painting shows.

of them were not able to pay the new taxes or repay their personal debts.

When the state began to seize their farms to pay these debts, some farmers who were Revolutionary War **veterans** (people who served in the armed forces) were especially angry. They had left their farms to fight the British, and now their farms were being taken from them. Often farms were sold at auctions for much less than their true value. Farmers and others who could not pay their debts were thrown into jail. They had to stay there until friends or relatives bailed them out.

Farmers Protest

During the summer of 1786, the farmers protested peacefully. They met in several counties and asked the legislature for

reforms (changes). They wanted lower taxes and cuts in state officials' salaries and in lawyers' fees.

When the legislature did nothing to help them, the farmers rebelled. The primary leader of the rebellion was Daniel Shays of Pelham, Massachusetts. He had fought bravely at Saratoga and other battles. After the war, he faced the same problems as other returning veterans. He was sued for debt, and had to sell the handsome sword given to him in honor of the victory at Saratoga. Normally a law-abiding man, he was driven to take up arms against the state.

County courthouses were the first targets. If these courts were closed down, the judges could not order farms to be seized, or people put in jail for debts. Governor James Bowdoin (BOH-duhn) denounced the rebels for stirring up "riot, anarchy and confusion."

As the violence continued, many American leaders became alarmed. What if the rebellion spread to other states? George Washington, who was then living peacefully at Mount Vernon, lost his calm. To a friend in Massachusetts he wrote, "For God's sake tell me what is the cause of all these commotions? . . . Commotions of this sort, like snow-balls, gather strength as they roll, if there is no opposition in the way to divide and crumble them."

The State Fights Back

To fight the rebellion, the Massachusetts government called for 4400 volunteer soldiers. The cost of a military campaign was estimated at $20,000. But the state treasury was almost empty. The state had to borrow money from wealthy citizens in Boston.

Command of the state **militia** (army of nonprofessional soldiers) was given to General Benjamin Lincoln, a veteran of the Revolution. In 1779, he had surrendered Charleston, South Carolina, and his army of 5400 men to the British. Some people accused Lincoln of being a coward. Now he was eager to prove his courage by quickly crushing the rebellion.

In January 1787, Shays decided to attack Springfield. He wanted to prevent the county court from meeting and hoped to get much-needed weapons from the U.S. **arsenal.** The arsenal was surrounded by Shays' men. The plan was for Shays to attack from one side with 1200 men. Another force of 400 men led by Luke Day would attack from the other side. The arsenal was defended by about 1100 militia under the command of General William Shepard. Meanwhile, General Lincoln was rushing toward Springfield with a large force to help Shepard.

The attack was set for January 25. Unfortunately for the farmers, Day decided to wait until the 26th to attack. He sent a note to tell Shays of the change, but the messenger was captured by Shepard's men. So when Shays advanced on the 25th, he had to face the full force of the defenders alone.

Shepard ordered his cannons to fire three times. The first two shots were fired high into the air as a warning. When the rebels kept advancing, another volley was fired directly at them. Four rebels fell dead in the snow, and 20 others were wounded. The rebels fled until they were rallied by Shays. Then he led them on an orderly retreat to Petersham, a rebel center.

It was the middle of winter and deep snow covered the ground. Shays hoped that the militia would not follow him. But he misjudged General Lincoln. Marching his force through a blinding snowstorm, Lincoln arrived at Petersham and launched an attack. Taken by surprise, the rebels were routed (defeated army made to flee) and many were taken prisoner. Within a short time, the rebellion was crushed, and Daniel Shays fled to Vermont.

The rebels lost their battle. They went home to fight on the political front. The next spring they elected a sympathetic new governor, John Hancock. A signer of the Declaration of Independence, Hancock pardoned the rebels. The new legislature passed laws to help the state's farmers. Peace and prosperity soon returned to Massachusetts.

A Stronger Federal Government

The rebellion had frightened many Americans, particularly those who were wealthy or not in debt. They feared total collapse of the government. Under the Articles of Confederation, the federal government had no power to help the states preserve law and order. Shays and his rebels had to be put down by the state militia paid with borrowed money.

Leaders like George Washington, Alexander Hamilton, and James Madison wanted to make the federal government stronger. In February 1787, Congress invited the states to send delegates to a convention in Philadelphia. The purpose of the convention, which met in May, was to revise the Articles of Confederation. But the convention went even further. Instead of patching up the Articles, it drew up an entirely new U.S. Constitution.

CHAPTER CHECK

WORD MATCH

1. arsenal
2. veterans
3. reforms
4. militia
5. routed

a. emergency army of citizens
b. store of arms
c. defeated army made to flee
d. changes
e. served in time of war

QUICK QUIZ

1. What caused a distinguished war veteran, Daniel Shays, to take up arms against the state of Massachusetts?
2. Explain Shays' plan of attack against the U.S. arsenal at Springfield.

THINK ABOUT IT

1. Why was Shays' Rebellion so frightening for many Americans?
2. Do you agree with George Washington, Alexander Hamilton, and James Madison that the United States needed a stronger federal government? Why or why not?

CHAPTER 25 ORIGINS OF THE CONSTITUTION

James Madison (1751-1836) used his broad knowledge of governments and some new political ideas when he sat down to help write a new constitution for his young and troubled nation.

James Madison was uncomfortable. Philadelphia's hot, humid streets were infested with bugs in May of 1787. But the steamy weather did not deter him from the work ahead. Madison was about to prove his brilliance by writing a constitution for his country.

Madison, 36 years old, was one of Virginia's seven delegates to the Constitutional Convention. He had tried to improve himself both physically and mentally for the task. He had gone horseback riding and hiking. And he had read and read.

Sleeping only about four hours a night, Madison spent the remaining hours of darkness reading or taking notes by the flickering light of a candle. He had two thin notebooks. In one, he listed the problems of the existing United States government under the Articles of Confederation. In the other, he wrote about foreign alliances.

The books he read dealt mainly with the relationships of people and their governments. Among those whose words inspired him was Aristotle, a Greek **philosopher** (one who searches for wisdom or knowledge) who lived from 384 to 322 B.C. Ancient Greece is considered the birthplace of democracy. Aristotle believed that governments must be responsible to their people.

Locke and Rousseau

Madison also read the works of philosophers John Locke and Jean Jacques Rousseau. These men wrote in the period called the Enlightenment. From the 1600s to the late-1700s, European philosophers formed new ideas about human worth and the relationship between people and their governments. Locke, who lived from 1632 to 1704 was at various times a medical doctor, a politician, a writer, and a political philosopher. His life spanned a turbulent time in England when popular forces challenged the absolute rule of the kings and people tried to make Parliament more democratic and representative. In 1689, he witnessed the peaceful Glorious Revolution, which resulted in a short written constitution. It said that the king and queen would now answer to Parliament.

Associated with a proposed plot to kill Britain's King Charles II, Locke spent six years of **exile** in Holland. At the time, that nation was the home of many European political and religious **refugees** (people who fled country during a conflict). Locke was impressed by the freedom Holland offered. He came to believe all nations should be that free.

In 1690, Locke wrote *Two Treatises of Government*. In this book, he argued that natural laws give people the right to life, liberty, and property. The purpose of a government, he wrote, is to protect these natural rights. If a government fails to do that, said Locke, the people have a right to rebel against it. He also rejected the long-held belief that the power of kings came directly from God. Political power, he said, comes only from the people. Thus a government can only exist with the consent of the people.

Rousseau was another great thinker whose writings inspired Madison. Rousseau, who was born in Switzerland and spent much of his life wandering in France, lived from 1712 to 1778. Rousseau also believed in natural rights—but he believed they belonged to all people at birth, not just the wealthy and powerful. In his book, *The Social Contract,* he wrote that all citizens must take part in their government all the time. The English people, he pointed out, were really only free on the

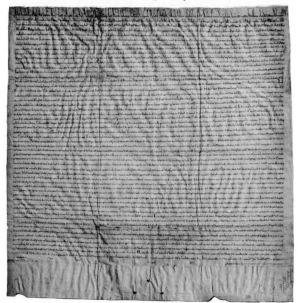

In 1215, rebellious barons forced Britain's King John (1167-1216) to accept the Magna Carta [above]. It listed rights and freedoms that the government could not deny its people.

Although American leaders opposed being ruled by Britain's king, they respected certain British traditions, such as Parliament. This painting shows one part of Parliament, the House of Lords.

days they elected their government.

Other Influences

James Madison spent night after muggy night in his Philadelphia rooming house thinking about the writings of Locke, Rousseau, and others. But it was an old British document signed long ago in 1215 that may have influenced Madison most. The **Magna Carta,** sealed (rulers put seals on documents instead of signing them) by King John, ruler of England, was the first important written, rather than oral, contract between a ruler and his subjects.

The Magna Carta was significant to Madison because it contained an important idea—those who govern are subject to the law of the land as well as those who are governed. It also said that ordinary people have basic liberties. One of the most famous sections says, in part, that "no freeman shall be taken or imprisoned . . . except by the lawful judgement of his peers and the law of the land." The principles of the Magna Carta were not enforced at the time it was written, but it influenced the lives of future generations.

James Madison was inspired by the Magna Carta and the writings of Enlightenment thinkers. Their new ideas about the relationship between citizens and their government would be put to use. The time had come to write a constitution that would create a strong central government for the 13 states. James Madison was ready to do what had to be done.

The U.S. Congress, composed of two counter-balancing chambers, the House of Representatives and the Senate, was inspired partly by Britain's House of Commons [above] and House of Lords.

CHAPTER CHECK

WORD MATCH

1. Aristotle
2. refugees
3. exile
4. Magna Carta
5. philosopher

a. Greek philosopher
b. long period living away from one's own country
c. great charter sealed by King John
d. fled country during time of conflict
e. searches for wisdom and knowledge

QUICK QUIZ

1. How did James Madison prepare himself for the difficult task of writing the Constitution for his country?
2. What is the significance of the Magna Carta?
3. What political ideas of Locke and Rousseau did James Madison include in his writing of the Constitution?

THINK ABOUT IT

In what way was Jefferson's task of writing the Declaration of Independence similar to Madison's task of writing the Constitution?

26 SUMMER IN PHILLY

This 1790 engraving shows Philadelphia's State House. Delegates to the 1787 Constitutional Convention spent four steamy months here, behind closed doors and shuttered windows.

Philadelphia in 1787 was a bustling, prosperous place. With 54,000 people, it was the largest city in America. It was a center for both business and education. According to one French visitor, Philadelphia was "the most beautiful and best built city in the nation." The same visitor said, "Here you will find more knowledge of politics and literature . . . than anywhere else in the United States."

In the spring of 1787, Philadelphia was preparing for an extraordinary event. Twelve of the 13 states had agreed to send **delegates** (formal representatives) to a special convention there. The convention's purpose? The purpose was to revise—or perhaps scrap entirely—the nation's government.

Under the Articles of Confederation, the 13 states acted more like separate countries than part of one nation. The Congress had no power to enforce rules on the states. The men who gathered at

Travelers to the Philadelphia convention faced mud-clogged roads and washed-out river crossings. A trip that takes only one-half hour today took 24 hours or longer in 1787.

the Constitutional Convention would argue and debate, and finally, write a new Constitution for the U.S. This constitution would include a much stronger federal government.

The Great Convention

The convention was scheduled to begin on May 14. Around the country, there was a growing feeling of anticipation. Newspapers ran articles about the upcoming meeting. Some of them called it The Great Convention of the States. People wondered what the delegates would do once they traveled to Philadelphia.

James Madison, a delegate from Virginia, was the first to arrive. He was 11 days early. Madison went straight to Mary House's boardinghouse on Market Street, where he had reserved a room. The red brick building was a popular stopping place, and Madison had stayed there many times before.

In the days before the convention began, Madison closeted himself at House's boardinghouse. He went over the books and papers that he had brought with him. As the other Virginia delegates began to arrive, he conferred (met for discussion) with them. He wanted Virginia to be the first to put forward a plan for the convention to follow.

Poor traveling conditions delayed many delegates. Spring rains turned already-questionable roads into mud. Rivers became flooded and difficult to cross. Some delegates had a hard time raising the money to make the trip. It was the middle of July before the New Hampshire delegates could manage it.

A Hero's Return

Washington's arrival on May 13th created much excitement in Philadelphia. As his carriage entered the city, cannons boomed and church bells rang. Crowds

The Heart of Philadelphia, 1787

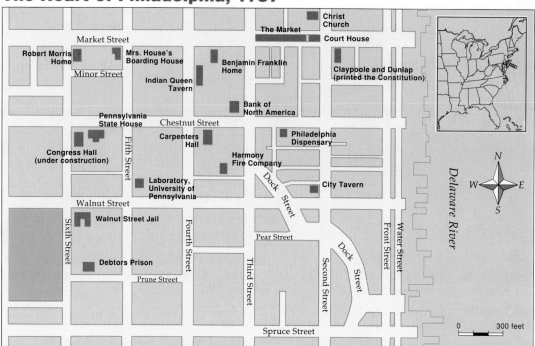

What might have been George Washington's route from the home of Robert Morris to Carpenters Hall? How would you direct the delegates to get from Carpenters Hall to the market?

lined the streets, cheering and hoping to get a glimpse of the nation's hero. Washington was greatly respected and admired by virtually all Americans. His presence would make the whole idea of the convention more acceptable to many people.

But the general had misgivings (doubts) about coming to Philadelphia. For one thing, he had announced in 1783 that he was retiring from public life forever. For another, he wasn't sure that this convention was the best way to work out the nation's problems.

He was also worried about recent events, particularly Shays' Rebellion. In the end, he reluctantly left his farm and his wife Martha to join the delegates in Philadelphia.

The wealthy families of Philadelphia went out of their way to entertain the visitors. Washington, unlike the scholarly Madison, enjoyed socializing. He happily attended the teas, dinners, and outings to which he was invited.

The Oldest Delegate

One of the more important delegates lived right in Philadelphia. At 81, Benjamin Franklin was the oldest representative at the convention.

Franklin had given years of public service to American politics. He was an inventor, a scientist, and a philosopher. His home was filled with useful or curious items he had invented.

Franklin didn't speak much at the

AMERICAN ADVENTURES

convention. Sometimes he had others speak for him. He was old and ill, and often in pain. In fact, walking or riding in a carriage was too uncomfortable for him. He traveled to the meetings in a special sedan chair carried by four prisoners from the local jail.

When Franklin did speak, often it was to share an amusing or comforting story. Sometimes he tried to smooth over differences or calm excited tempers during the debates.

By May 25th, enough delegates had arrived for the convention to begin its work. In all, there would be 55 delegates, although seldom more than 30 were present at one time.

The Delegates Assemble

Thomas Jefferson, the U.S. minister to France at the time, was very impressed by the delegates as a group. He would later refer to them as "an assembly of demigods [god–like persons]."

Many of the delegates were well-known national leaders. All were experienced with politics in some form. Twenty-six of them were college graduates. This was unusual in a time when very few people went to college. Many of the delegates were either wealthy or comfortably well-off.

Whatever similarities there were among the group, there were also many differences. Some were planters, some were businessmen, some were lawyers. Some represented small states, while others represented large states.

It would take four months of hard, frustrating work before these 55 men could agree on a new plan. But their work paid off. The gift they gave us, the U.S. Constitution, continues to serve us well after more than 200 years.

CHAPTER CHECK

WORD MATCH

1. delegates
2. Madison
3. demigods
4. conferred
5. misgivings

a. met for discussion
b. god-like people
c. doubts
d. formal representatives
e. delegate from Virginia

QUICK QUIZ

1. (a) Describe the conditions that delayed the opening of the Great Convention.(b) Would these same conditions have an effect on a constitutional convention today? Explain.
2. (a) Why do you think James Madison wanted Virginia to have a plan ready when the convention opened?

THINK ABOUT IT

Imagine that you are a citizen of Philadelphia in 1787. Describe how you would feel as you watched the delegates arrive in your city. What would you want them to accomplish?

27 THE GREAT COMPROMISE

In 1856, Junius Brutus Stearns painted this scene of the 1787 Constitutional Convention. All eyes are on the most respected man at the convention, and in the nation, George Washington.

In the State House in Philadelphia where the delegates met, it was often unbearably stuffy. Yet the delegates kept the windows and doors firmly closed. Why? One reason was to keep out the flies. In the summer of 1787, these buzzing, biting creatures seemed to be everywhere in Philadelphia. The main reason, though, was to keep the proceedings secret. The delegates decided right away that they did not want people eavesdropping on them. They did not want misleading rumors to be spread

about their work before it was complete.

If everything was so secret, how do we even know what happened at the convention? Several of the delegates kept notes. The most detailed ones were kept by James Madison.

Madison took a seat near the front of the room, and dutifully wrote down everything. He attended every single session. In addition to taking notes, he got up to speak a total of 161 times. Madison's record tells us a lot about the convention's debates—which weren't always friendly.

The delegates had different ideas about the convention's purpose. Some felt that they had come there merely to improve the Articles of Confederation. Others wanted to do away with the Articles completely.

The Virginia Plan

On May 29, Edmund Randolph, Virginia's governor, introduced a plan worked out by Madison and the other Virginia delegates before the convention started. The Virginia Plan suggested a central government that would have three branches: the **legislature** (makes the nation's laws), the **executive** (carries the laws out), and the **judiciary** (makes sure the laws are constitutional).

This plan was very different from the government set up by the Articles of Confederation. Under the Articles, Congress just had one house. Its members were chosen by the state legislatures. There was no separate executive branch.

The Virginia Plan said that Congress should have two houses instead of just one. Members of the "first" house would be elected directly by the people of each state. Members of the "second" house would be elected by the representatives of the first house.

Under Randolph's plan, however, the states would have **proportional representation** in both houses of Congress. That is, the larger states in population would have more votes in each house than the smaller states.

The Virginia Plan would make the central, or federal, government stronger, and the states weaker. Congress would have the power to **veto** (reject) any state laws that did not go along with the national constitution.

For the next two weeks or so, the delegates discussed the Virginia Plan. Not all of them were happy with it. Delegates from the small states—Delaware, Connecticut, New Jersey, Maryland — didn't want to give up equal representation in Congress. They feared that the large states would control Congress and thus the nation's laws.

Some delegates believed that a strong central government would be distant and uncaring—almost like the royal government of England. Roger Sherman of Connecticut, a publisher of almanacs, was a leader of this "localist" group.

The New Jersey Plan

On June 15, William Paterson, former attorney general of New Jersey, presented another plan. The New Jersey Plan was not very different from the Articles of Confederation. It suggested keeping the one-house legislature, with each state having an equal vote. This plan gave Congress a little more power than the Articles did, but not much.

Leaders of the big states attacked the New Jersey Plan. James Wilson, a lawyer from Pennsylvania, was one of these leaders. "Why should a National Government be unpopular?" Wilson asked. "Has it less dignity? Will each Citizen enjoy under it less liberty or protection? Will a Citizen of Delaware be degraded by becoming a citizen of the United States?"

Madison joined the attack. Under Paterson's plan, Madison said, Congress would not be able stop the states from doing whatever they wanted. The states would be free to make treaties with each other or with foreign nations. Each state would be able to print its own paper money.

The Great Compromise

On June 19, the convention voted to return to the Virginia Plan. The nationalists had won, for the time being. But the small states and the localist leaders would not accept the plan unless they got at least some of their demands.

One of their important demands was for each state to have an equal vote in Congress. The nationalists insisted, however, on proportional representation.

Finally, the convention went back to a suggestion Roger Sherman of Connecticut had made early on. Let the first house have proportional representation, he had said, but let each state have an equal vote in the second house.

There was another problem, however. How should the number of representatives for the first house be decided? By population or by wealth? And how did slaves fit into the picture?

The issue of slavery was a difficult one. Some delegates, including some Southern ones, were disgusted and appalled that the U.S. was a slaveholding nation. Although most did not think slaves or blacks could be responsible citizens, they did not want to acknowledge or support slavery in any way. But these same delegates knew that some Southern states would leave the union rather than give up slavery.

Finally, James Wilson came up with

Checks and Balances

PRESIDENT **Initiates Policy and Enforces Laws**	
President to Congress	**President to Supreme Court**
Can veto bills	Appoints Justices
Can call special sessions	
Recommends new laws and federal budget	
Submits treaties and appointees for approval	
CONGRESS: Makes Laws	
Congress to President:	**Congress to Supreme Court**
Can impeach the President	Approves or rejects President's appointees
Can override the President's veto	Can override decisions with new legislation
Can refuse money for President's budget	Can remove a Justice or change the number of Justices
Approves or rejects Presidential appointments	
SUPREME COURT Interprets Laws	
Supreme Court to Congress	**Supreme Court to President**
Can declare laws unconstitutional	Can declare the President's acts unconstitutional

How can Congress set limits on the President's power? What power does the Supreme Court have over Congress?

an idea that both North and South could accept. The delegates decided to count each slave as three-fifths of a person. They said this fraction should be used in determining the number of representatives each state had in the the first house, the House of Representatives.

Roger Sherman's proposal for equal representation in the second house, the Senate, was added to Wilson's suggestions. On July 16, the convention voted and narrowly accepted the whole package.

This Great Compromise, as it would later be called, created the House of Representatives and the Senate, and set the convention on a path to success. But by compromising the question of slavery, it also set the stage for regional conflicts which would ultimately result in civil war.

Slaves, such as those in this watercolor by Benjamin Henry Latrobe, were at the heart of a bitter debate at the convention. How would they be counted under the new system of government?

CHAPTER CHECK

WORD MATCH

1. legislature
2. executive
3. veto
4. proportional representation
5. judiciary

a. a system in which a group (such as a state) is represented according to its size
b. makes sure laws are constitutional
c. a refusal to approve
d. carries laws out
e. makes the nation's laws

QUICK QUIZ

1. What were some of the main differences between the Virginia Plan and the New Jersey Plan?
2. What was the Great Compromise? How did it benefit both small and large states?

THINK ABOUT IT

1. Why did the delegates want to keep the proceeding of the convention secret? Do you agree or disagree with their reasons and actions? Explain.
2. If you had been a delegate at the constitutional convention, would you have voted for a strong central government or for strong states' rights? Defend your position.

28 THE FEDERALIST DEBATE

As word of the new constitution spread across the nation, Americans rejoiced. This float in a Philadelphia parade honored Alexander Hamilton, one of the Constitution's staunchest supporters.

July 4, 1788, was celebrated in many United States towns with more than the usual enthusiasm. This Independence Day was special. Just two weeks earlier, New Hampshire had **ratified** (approved) the new U.S. Constitution. It was the ninth state to do so, enough to make the Constitution the law of the land. Philadelphia held the biggest parade in its history. The crowds laughed as one wagon passed by. It was carrying a broken-down ship called the *Confederation*. This represented the U.S. government under the old Articles of Confederation.

The crowds cheered as another wagon rolled by carrying a sturdy ship called the *Federal Constitution*.

Yet the celebrations could not conceal an important fact. In many states, there was still strong opposition to the Constitution. So far, two of the largest states had not yet ratified the Constitution. These were Virginia and New York. In both states, a majority of people opposed it. Without the support of these important states, it was very unlikely that the new plan of government would succeed. So the fate of the Constitution, and of national government

AMERICAN ADVENTURES

in America, depended on their approval.

Opposing Views

People who supported the new Constitution were called **Federalists**. They believed that the national, or federal, government should have much more power than the individual states. Under the Articles of Confederation, the states acted as though they were independent countries. For example, many of them charged their own taxes on goods coming in from foreign countries. Some even charged taxes on goods brought in from other states. They had the power to tax people, but the U.S. Congress did not. Congress had to ask the states for money to run the national government.

Federalists were alarmed by Shays' Rebellion in Massachusetts. It showed that the U.S. government was too weak to keep law and order. Federalists believed that the U.S. government needed more power, or the new nation would fall apart. They also mistrusted the mass of voters and felt that government leaders could best determine the nation's policies.

Those who opposed the new Constitution were called **Antifederalists**. They believed that people were better off when power was held by state governments, rather than by the national government. They feared that under the Constitution, the president would become as powerful as any king. Congress would have unlimited power to tax people. The burden, they believed, would be heavy. They argued that the country was getting too big to be ruled by a distant, national government. In time, the U.S. government would lose touch with the people and become undemocratic. Antifederalists also had more faith in the ability of ordinary citizens to govern themselves.

Finally, Antifederalists believed that the states were the best defenders of the people's liberties. State constitutions guaranteed personal freedoms such as the right to speak and worship freely. These guarantees were known as a bill of rights.

Before the Constitution could become law, 9 of the 13 states had to approve it. But enforcing it could become difficult if some states opposed it. This cartoon shows two states breaking the needed unity.

THE FEDERALIST DEBATE

THE FEDERALIST DEBATE

THE FEDERALIST DEBATE

But the U.S. Constitution did not have a bill of rights.

The Debate Rages On

The debate between Federalists and Antifederalists raged heatedly in Virginia and New York. The public was bombarded (overwhelmed) with speeches, newspaper articles and pamphlets. And on both sides there were brilliant leaders who argued skillfully for their cause.

In Virginia, the best-known Antifederalist was Patrick Henry, the fiery speechmaker and defender of liberty. He spoke for most of the Antifederalists at the Virginia convention called to ratify the Constitution. Why, he asked, was a bill of rights left out of the Constitution? The powers given to Congress and the president under the Constitution were far too great, Henry said. The president might easily become a tyrant who would keep the people in submission. "I would rather have a king, lords, and commons," Henry declared, "than a government [filled] with such insupportable evils."

The best-known Federalists in Virginia were George Washington and James Madison. Washington preferred to remain in the background and did not attend the Virginia convention. But his views supporting the Constitution were well known to the delegates. In a letter to a friend, he wrote, "I do now most firmly believe that it is the best constitution that can be obtained at this [time] . . . . This, or a [break up] of the Union are the only [choices] before us."

Madison urged the Virginia convention to ratify the Constitution. But he also said that the convention should recom-mend to Congress that it add a bill of rights to the Constitution. This compromise helped the Federalist cause. On June 25, the convention voted 89 to 79 to ratify the Constitution.

In New York, the leader of the Federalists was a young, skillful lawyer, Alexander Hamilton. Hamilton believed that the best way to influence public opinion in favor of the Constitution was to write a series of newspaper articles. But time was getting short and he needed help. So he asked James Madison and John Jay, a diplomat, to join him. In all, the three men wrote 85 articles under the title of *The Federalist*.

The most famous of the Federalist articles was Number 10, written by Madison. In it, he answered the Antifederalist charge that a federal government could not be democratic. The opposite was true, Madison said. In a small country, it was easy for a majority **faction** (group) to gain control of the government. But in a large country like the United States, this could not happen. In the U.S., there were so many different groups competing with each other that none would be able to gain complete control of the government. Many New Yorkers were convinced by this argument and switched to support the Federalists. On July 26, the New York convention voted to ratify the Constitution, 30 to 27.

The approval of Virginia and New York ended all serious opposition to the Constitution. Congress began to put the new plan of government into effect immediately. Under the Constitution, the new nation would grow strong and united.

Federal and State Powers

STATE		FEDERAL
NO	Power to issue money	YES
NO	Power to deprive a citizen of life liberty or property without due process of law	NO
YES	Power to tax personal income	YES
YES	Power to collect a sales tax	YES
NO	Power to grant a title of nobility	YES
NO	Power to collect an import tax	NO
YES	Power to establish a court system	YES
NO	Power to make treaties with other nations	YES
NO	Power to enforce laws	YES
YES	Power to declare war and make peace	YES

Which powers belong solely to the federal government? What powers do the federal government and state governments share?

CHAPTER CHECK

WORD MATCH
1. ratified
2. faction
3. Federalists
4. Antifederalists
5. bombarded

a. believed in strong state government
b. approved
c. group
d. believed in strong federal government
e. overwhelmed

QUICK QUIZ
1. What was the special significance of New Hampshire ratifying the new constitution?
2. Why was it important for Virginia and New York to ratify the Constitution?
3. What events caused New York and Virginia to ratify the Constitution?

THINK ABOUT IT
What were the main arguments of the Federalists and the Antifederalists? Which one of the positions would you have taken? Why?

CHAPTER 29 THE BILL OF RIGHTS

We the People of the Un
insure domestic Tranquility, provide for the common defence, prom
and our Posterity, do ordain and establish this Constitution for the U
Article. I.
Section. 1. All legislative Powers herein granted shall be vested in a Congress of the United States, which shall consist of a Senate and House of Representatives.
Section. 2. The House of Representatives shall be composed of Members chosen every second Year by the People of the several States, and the Electors in each State shall have the Qualifications requisite for Electors of the most numerous Branch of the State Legislature.
No Person shall be a Representative who shall not have attained to the Age of twenty five Years, and been seven Years a Citizen of the United States, and who shall not, when elected, be an Inhabitant of that State in which he shall be chosen.
Representatives and direct Taxes shall be apportioned among the several States which may be included within this Union, according to their respective Numbers, which shall be determined by adding to the whole Number of free Persons, including those bound to Service for a Term of Years, and excluding Indians not taxed, three fifths of all other Persons. The actual Enumeration shall be made within three Years after the first Meeting of the Congress of the United States, and within every subsequent Term of ten Years, in such Manner as they shall by Law direct. The Number of Representatives shall not exceed one for every thirty Thousand, but each State shall have at Least one Representative; and until such enumeration shall be made, the State of New Hampshire shall be entitled to chuse three, Massachusetts eight, Rhode Island and Providence Plantations one, Connecticut five, New York six, New Jersey four, Pennsylvania eight, Delaware one, Maryland six, Virginia ten, North Carolina five, South Carolina five, and Georgia three.
When vacancies happen in the Representation from any State, the Executive Authority thereof shall issue Writs of Election to fill such Vacancies.
The House of Representatives shall chuse their Speaker and other Officers; and shall have the sole Power of Impeachment.
Section. 3. The Senate of the United States shall be composed of two Senators from each State, chosen by the Legislature thereof for six Years; and each Senator shall have one Vote.
Immediately after they shall be assembled in Consequence of the first Election, they shall be divided as equally as may be into three Classes. The Seats of the Senators of the first Class shall be vacated at the Expiration of the second Year, of the second Class at the Expiration of the fourth Year, and of the third Class at the Expiration of the sixth Year, so that one third may be chosen every second Year; and if Vacancies happen by Resignation, or otherwise, during the Recess of the Legislature of any State, the Executive thereof may make temporary Appointments until the next Meeting of the Legislature, which shall then fill such Vacancies.

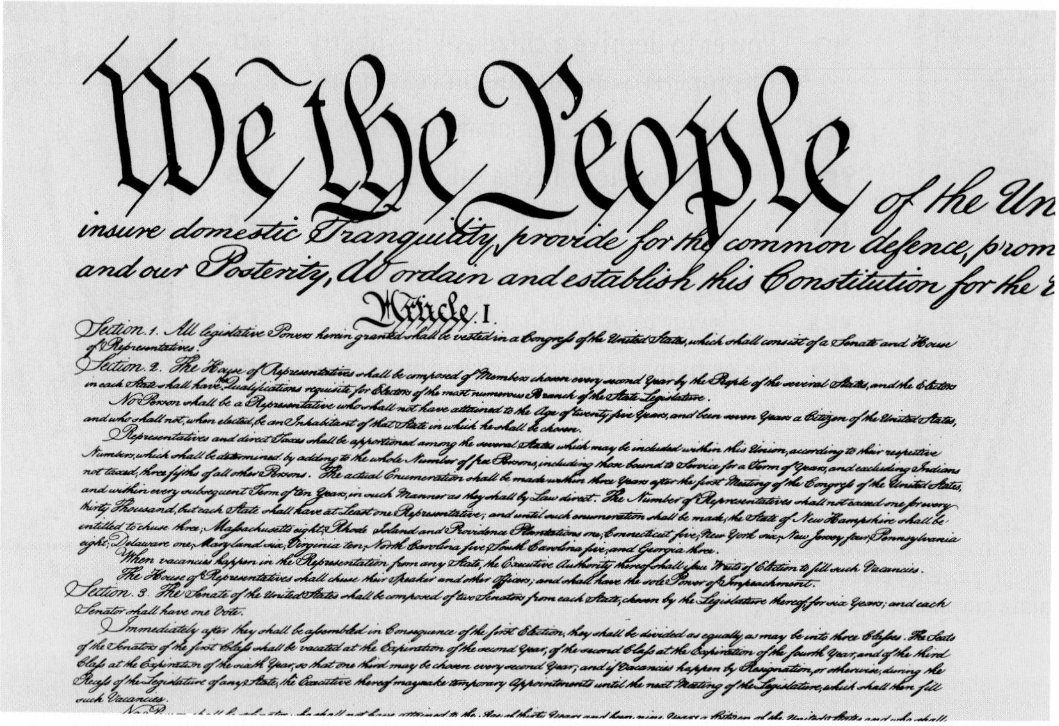

Added in 1791 to the Constitution, the Bill of Rights contained 10 amendments which guaranteed individual liberties for all Americans. Its first page and opening words are shown above.

At the close of the 18th century, when men often settled disputes with deadly duels, Thomas Jefferson's sharpest weapon was his mind. In 1787, the year the United States Constitution was completed by the Convention in Philadelphia, Jefferson was an American diplomat in France. Still he remained interested in the goings-on back home. When his friend James Madison, a delegate to the Convention, sent Jefferson a copy of the new Constitution, he eagerly read it. He didn't keep his opinion of its shortcomings to himself. He was surprised and angered that it did not have a bill of rights spelling out the rights of Americans.

"A bill of rights," wrote Jefferson from France, "is what the people are entitled to . . . and what no just government should refuse."

Jefferson's words became public. And the people—the butchers, the bakers, the candlestick makers, all the people whose support was needed to ratify the Constitution—agreed. How could their Constitution not contain words specifically protecting the rights of all people?

Debate Over Rights

Why didn't the original Constitution contain a bill of rights? One reason: It fell victim to some delegates' fears of the amendment process. Some delegates from southern states, for example, feared that an **amendment** (change or addition to the U.S. Constitution) could be used to wipe out slavery. And some delegates from small states feared that an amendment might take away their equal representation in the Senate. Most delegates—especially those from the eight states with their own bills of rights—felt the inclusion (being a part) of such a document in a federal constitution was not necessary.

Alexander Hamilton of New York, reasoned that no bill of rights was needed because the Constitution did not give Congress the right to interfere with citizens' rights. He also felt that the **preamble** (introduction) of the Constitution, "We the People of the United States," spoke more of individual rights than did even state bills of rights.

Some delegates disagreed. One such delegate, George Mason of Virginia, had helped write the Virginia Declaration of Rights, which inspired Thomas Jefferson when he wrote the Declaration of Independence. "I wish that the plan had been prefaced with a bill of rights," Mason said of the Constitution.

The delegates voted on the matter of a bill of rights. The 10 states present, even Virginia, voted against a bill of rights. Mason left the Convention without signing the Constitution. He was a disappointed man. But he must have been pleased by the outcry that greeted the Constitution when it was published after the Convention **adjourned** (closed for a time) in September 1787. Newspapers were filled with letters by irate citizens demanding a bill of rights—and by replies from delegates justifying their opinions.

Noah Webster, a master of words, was wickedly sarcastic when he wrote newspaper letters making fun of the very idea of a bill of rights. He suggested a list of rights that would include sleeping on the left side, eating and drinking, and fishing in public rivers.

Bill of Rights

By 1788, six states were still needed to ratify the Constitution. To get more support for the

The Bill of Rights promised individual freedoms to many people—but not to women, blacks, and Native Americans. This early 19th-century painting on a tray shows Reverend Lemuel Haynes in the pulpit.

Constitution, Madison helped to write a bill of rights. As a member of the House of Representatives from Virginia, Madison guided the passage of 12 amendments. The rules for amending the Constitution were written into the Constitution itself. One way to amend the Constitution was for two-thirds of the states to propose an amendment. Then a nationwide convention would have to approve their work. A second way, was to have two-thirds of each house of Congress approve an amendment. Then

three-quarters of the state legislatures would have to ratify it. Madison chose this second method as the quicker way.

In 1789, Congress proposed the amendments to the state legislatures for ratification. Ten were finally approved. They became part of the Constitution on December 15, 1791.

These 10 amendments make up the Bill of Rights. Some of them do not seem as important today as they once did. For example, the Third Amendment says that soldiers cannot be put up in a private

In the 18th century, the anti-slavery movement was strong in both Britain and the United States. This 1782 painting shows the symbolic figure, Liberty, promising education and prosperity to all freed blacks.

AMERICAN ADVENTURES

home without the owner's consent—except in wartime. Hardly anyone pays much attention to this amendment anymore. But other amendments seem just as important now as they were in 1789.

One of the most important amendments today is the First Amendment. It says that Congress cannot make laws to work for or against any religion. It says that the government cannot inferfere with the freedom of speech, of the the press, or of the right of the people to meet when and how they choose. This Amendment also gives citizens the right to ask the government to correct wrongs. (Turn to page 820 to learn more about the other amendments.)

What the Bill of Rights left out was as important as what it included. There was still no mention of the right to vote for women, blacks, or Indians. Blacks were still sold into slavery. Women were not allowed to serve on juries. It would be many years before these groups were entitled to the same rights that white males had as spelled out in the U.S. Constitution.

The Constitution created in 1787 told the United States government what it could do. The first 10 amendments—or Bill of Rights—said what the government could not do. At first, these amendments protected people only from unfair actions of the federal government. But in recent years, the Supreme Court has told state governments that they too must uphold the U.S. Bill of Rights. Without the Bill of Rights, we the people, might be citizens of a land that is neither free nor democratic.

CHAPTER CHECK

WORD MATCH

1. preamble
2. consent
3. adjourned
4. inclusion
5. amendment

a. closed session, for a time
b. change or addition to the U.S. Constitution
c. being a part of the whole
d. introduction
e. agreement

QUICK QUIZ

1. Why do you think James Madison agreed to a bill of rights?
2. Describe Thomas Jefferson's reaction to the new U.S. Constitution.
3. Explain why Alexander Hamilton felt that the new constitution did not need a bill of rights.

THINK ABOUT IT

Suppose you are giving a welcoming speech to a group of new American immigrants. How would you explain the Bill of Rights to them? What would you tell them about the effects it may have on their lives?

30 THE FIRST PRESIDENT

An American painting shows George Washington on his way to his inauguration in Trenton, New Jersey. He is crossing under one of the many arches which were erected to celebrate his journey.

In Virginia, George Washington was easygoing. But in New York City, the United States capital at that time, he found it hard to relax with callers. As President, he opened his home to casual visitors only one hour a week–on Tuesdays. These social hours were usually stiff and formal.

Though Washington seemed uncomfortable, he kept on with the Tuesday custom. He was, after all, his country's first President. Everything he did was important. Every move that he made might set an example for future presidents.

The Constitution described a president's duties in a general way. But it said nothing about how to receive visitors. It did not tell Washington exactly how to deal with Congress. It did not tell him how to work with a **cabinet** (officially chosen group) of advisers. In fact, it did not even tell him he had to have such a cabinet. Washington had to figure out what was best to do from day to day. He often had doubts about his own ability and wisdom. And yet, because he cared so much about the Constitution, he held the country together for eight difficult years.

How did he do this? Why do many scholars still think that America's first President was also its best? Here are three reasons for Washington's success.

Washington's Success

First, Washington chose able people to help him. The President heads the Executive branch of the United States government. It is his job to see that laws passed by Congress are properly enforced throughout the country. He cannot do this alone. Instead he must seek the help of the most able people he can find.

Washington surrounded himself with talented people. He chose Thomas Jefferson to take charge of foreign affairs as Secretary of State. He selected Alexander Hamilton to raise and spend government money as Secretary of the Treasury. He named Henry Knox to take charge of the nation's military needs as Secretary of War. And he chose Edmund Randolph to enforce federal laws as Attorney General. These four men formed the President's Cabinet.

Two members of the Cabinet were already well-known. Jefferson, now 46, had written the Declaration of Independence. Alexander Hamilton, now 34, had worked hard to get the Constitution ratified. These two men had little in common. Jefferson thought

This cartoon shows a government agent collecting the new whiskey tax.

Hamilton cared too much about the problems of wealthy businessmen. He accused Hamilton of favoring a government ruled by kings. For his part, Hamilton thought Jefferson much too eager to stay popular with the people. He believed that Jefferson's ideas would ruin the national government. But these two men did share one view. They both admired George Washington and worked hard to serve him.

Second, Washington gave leadership to Congress. Washington did not sit back and wait for Congress to pass laws. He told Congress what laws he thought were necessary. The country needed strong leadership. It owed millions of dollars to foreign countries. How was it going to pay these debts? Leadership could only come from one place—the President and his Cabinet.

Actually, it was Hamilton who came up with most of the ideas. He wanted the federal government to create a national bank, the Bank of the United States. He wanted the national government to pay off all the debts owed by the state governments. To raise money for this and other purposes, he recommended a **tariff** (import tax). This tax would be placed on those foreign-made goods that competed with goods made in the U.S. In addition, he thought certain other goods, like whiskey sold in the U.S., should also be taxed.

A 19th-century painting shows Pennsylvania farmers protesting against the new tax on whiskey. Farmers could make whiskey out of their corn and rye crops.

Once they had decided on these policies, Hamilton and Washington persuaded Congress to pass the bills they recommended. Partly because of these laws, business improved. The nation paid off most of its debts. The American people gained confidence in their new government.

Third, Washington had the courage to make hard decisions. Many times, Washington acted in ways that were certain to make people angry. In 1794, for example, a group of farmers in western Pennsylvania refused to pay the new tax on whiskey. The law allowed tax officials to enter homes to collect the money. Some farmers attacked the house of one of the tax officials. They tarred and feathered officers of the law. In turn, several farmers were arrested.

Washington decided that the **Whiskey Rebellion,** as it was called, had to be crushed. He called together 15,000 troops to march across Pennsylvania. Washington himself put on a uniform and led the army at the beginning of the march. The farmers surrendered without a fight. Washington's actions angered some people. These people accused him of acting like a bully and a tyrant.

Washington Retires

As his second presidential term wore on, Washington became eager to

AMERICAN ADVENTURES

retire to private life. He had never wanted to be president. He did not have the same confidence in himself that other people had. Now he had also grown weary of the arguments between Hamilton and Jefferson and their followers. In 1796, a third election for president was due to take place. Twice before, Washington had been elected by a **unanimous** vote. But now Washington announced that he would not again be a **candidate** for president.

Like many things that Washington did, this decision also set an example for future presidents. It became the custom after that for presidents to retire after two terms. The custom lasted until 1940, when President Franklin Roosevelt ran for a third term.

"Friends, and Fellow-Citizens," began Washington in his 1796 farewell address. He asked that people forgive his mistakes and remember the good that he tried to do. Washington urged Americans to remain steadfast in support of the Union. He tried to discourage the growth of political parties, because he thought such parties would divide the nation. He also warned against forming "permanent alliances" with foreign powers. He feared that such alliances would keep the nation from acting in its own best interests.

The President looked forward to his retirement from public office and life "under a free Government,–the ever favourite object of my heart, and the happy reward, as I trust of our mutual cares, labours, and dangers."

CHAPTER CHECK

WORD MATCH
1. Cabinet
2. Whiskey Rebellion
3. candidate
4. tariff
5. unanimous

a. import tax
b. officially chosen group of advisors
c. when Pennsylvannia refused to pay new tax
d. person seeking office
e. agreeing completely

QUICK QUIZ
1. List three reasons why many scholars still think that America's first president was also its best?
2. Compare and contrast the backgrounds of Thomas Jefferson and Alexander Hamilton.

THINK ABOUT IT
1. Explain the term "legal precedent". How did George Washington set legal precedents for future presidents?
2. Explain Hamilton's ideas for a national bank. If you had lived in colonial times would you have supported the concept of a national bank?

A MORE PERFECT UNION

History Detective

1. Normally a law abiding man, I gathered farmers and used force to try and have our new government lower taxes. Who am I?

2. I was passed by Congress in 1787 to settle how future states would be formed. What am I?

3. Although my work kept me overseas, I was able to influence people to adopt the idea of a bill of rights. Who am I?

4. Known already for my beauty, I am the city that housed the convention that formed our Constitution. Where am I?

5. Proposed by the delegates from one state, my idea was to divide the central government into three branches. What am I?

6. I set out to make sure the Constitution was based on the same idea as the Magna Carta: Both leaders and citizens must live within the same laws. Who am I?

Voices From the Past

In 1913, Charles Beard published *An Economic Interpretation to the Constitution of The United States*. Why? Beard felt that Americans knew little about the Constitution. One of his concerns was the first words of the Constitution: "We the people of the United States of America. . . ." Here is part of his discussion:

How many favored the adoption of the Constitution, and how many opposed it? Voters took part in the selection of delegates to the Convention. But a considerable number of the adult white male population was kept from participating in the elections of delegates. Philadelphia had a population of 28,000 but a total of 1450 votes were cast in the election—about 5 percent of the population. It seems a safe guess to say that not more than 5 percent of the population in general, expressed an opinion one way or another on the Constitution.

1. Does Beard believe it is fair for the Constitution to speak for all people? Why or why not?

2. White males who did not own enough property were not allowed to vote. Can you think of other groups that may not have been allowed to vote?

Hands–On History

Speech Writing—Imagine that you are a delegate to the Constitutional Convention. You are from a very small state and oppose the Virginia Plan (page 153). Write a speech defending your view.

YESTERDAY'S NEWS

The American Adventures Newspaper

Constitution Amended

New York, N.Y., December 15, 1791— Following years of planning and voting, today 10 amendments were added to the Constitution. These 10 amendments were selected from the original 12 amendments Congress offered to the states two years ago. Officially called the Bill of Rights, this document is said to be the people's Constitution. Whereas the Constitution explains what the government can do, politicians say the Bill of Rights explains what people can do and what the government can not do. The first amendment states this clearly. It ensures a person's freedom to express his or her opinions about anything—including the government.

Each new amendment to the Constitution was carefully discussed.

1.

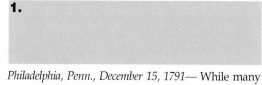

Philadelphia, Penn., December 15, 1791— While many people celebrate the passage of the long-awaited Bill of Rights, others are disappointed by what they feel is missing from the document.

The Constitution was criticized most for its three fifths clause. It states that the number of representatives each state has in the House of Representatives will be decided by its population. When measuring this population, each state can only count non-free persons (slaves) as three fifths, instead of one. Many slave owners fought against this measure so they could gain more representation for their state; other people felt it was unfair to say anyone was less than a complete person. The Bill of Rights does not settle this issue, and many people hoped it would.

Also women were not specifically added to the Constitution by the Bill of Rights. Many women feel the government has ignored them. Some women complain that they have been denied the right to have a trial by jury that all Americans are entitled to by the Constitution. However, by far, women's greatest complaint concerns suffrage. Although women can own land and property, they still are not given **2.**

Yesterday's News received a copy of a letter to the famous politician John Adams from his wife, Abigail. Mrs Adams writes: "... If particular care and attention is not paid to the Laidies we are determined to [begin] a rebellion and will not hold ourselves bound by any Laws in which we have no voice, or Representation." Many women throughout the country share Mrs. Adams' sentiments. This sort of outlook leaves concerns such as women's suffrage open for future debate and changes. For now, women look at the Bill of Rights and find little to rejoice in.

You Be the Reporter

Match each question with its news item above.

1. Write a headline for this story that would get people's attention.

2. The writer forgot to finish this sentence! How would you complete the thought?

USING GRAPH INFORMATION

How should states be represented in the U.S. Congress? That question stirred up much controversy in 1787 when delegates from the 13 states met at the Constitutional Convention. The question was resolved only through compromise. In 1787, no one was sure exactly how many people lived where. Therefore, the delegates decided that a national **census** (counting of the population) would be held every 10 years to ensure that each state was fairly represented. The bar graph below shows some of the results of the first census taken in 1790. Information on this graph helps explain the controversy over representation.

Bars on this type of graph are drawn in different lengths to stand for different amounts. Answer the questions on a separate piece of paper.

1. Study the graph's title, labels, and key. **(a)** What do the bars represent? **(b)** What do segments of each bar stand for?

2. Compare the lengths of the bars in the graph. **(a)** Which state had the largest total population in 1790? **(b)** Which had the smallest?

3. According to the Virginia Plan, states with larger populations would have had more votes in Congress than smaller states. **(a)** Which states would have most liked this plan? Why? **(b)** Which states would have opposed it? Why?

4. According to the New Jersey Plan, all states—large and small—would have had an equal number of votes in Congress. Which states would have preferred this plan to the Virginia Plan?

Total Slave and Free Populations of the States (1790 Census)

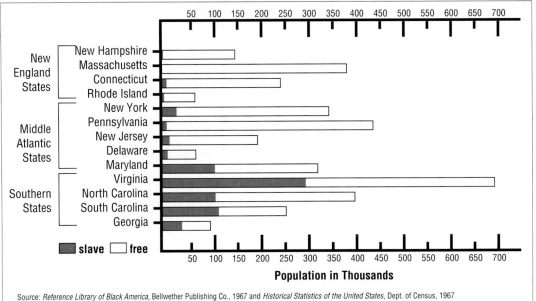

Source: *Reference Library of Black America*, Bellwether Publishing Co., 1967 and *Historical Statistics of the United States*, Dept. of Census, 1967

The Great Compromise determined that all states would be equally represented in the U.S. Senate. But they would be represented by the sizes of their population in the House of Representatives. This led to the controversy over whether slaves should be counted for representation or not.

5. Look at each bar's segment of slave population. **(a)** Which state had the most slaves? **(b)** Which had the least?

6. Compare each state's slave and free populations. **(a)** Which two states had the highest proportion of slaves? **(b)** Which states had a smaller total population than the slave population of Virginia?

7. If slaves had not been counted at all, which state would have had the largest delegation in the House of Representatives?

8. Which states do you think would have wanted representation in Congress according to **(a)** total population? **(b)** free population only?

9. The delegates compromised again by deciding to count each slave as three-fifths of a person. Which states would have gained the most votes in the House of Representatives by this decision?

A pie graph shows how the total amount of something is made up of different sized parts. The pie graph below, for example, represents the total slave population of the United States in 1790. Each section of the pie stands for a region of the country.

10. Compare sections of the pie graph. **(a)** Which region had the most slaves? Which had the fewest? **(b)** Which region do you think was most in favor of the three-fifths compromise?

Distribution of Slaves by Region, 1790

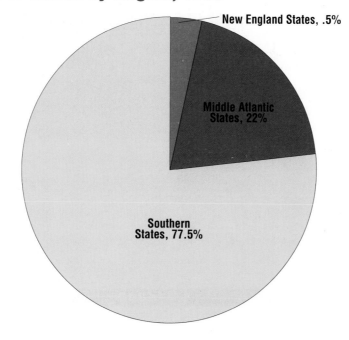

New England States, .5%

Middle Atlantic States, 22%

Southern States, 77.5%

A NEW NATION

1790	1795	1800	1805

1790
Census shows four million people living in U.S.

1793
France declares war against England.

1793 *(Eli Whitney invents cotton gin.)*

Eli Whitney invents cotton gin.

1803
U.S. buys Louisiana Territory from France.

1805
Lewis and Clark reach Pacific Ocean.

1806
Noah Webster publishes first English-language dictionary.

In 1782, a French immigrant to the United States described his new country in a book called *Letters from an American Farmer*. Jean de Crevecœur (krev-koor) wrote about the "unknown bounds of North America." Crevecœur praised his new land as "this smiling country." He claimed it was "the most perfect society now existing in the world. Here [one] is free."

Crevecœur's feelings were typical of many Americans at that time. People started thinking of themselves as citizens of a vast nation, and began taking pride in being Americans.

After the War of 1812, U.S. ships again sailed the seas freely, expanding international trade. Here, the ship *Grand Turk* sails into Marseilles, France, in 1815.

ALISM

6

UNIT

1810   1815   1820   1825

1807
Robert Fulton invents the steamboat.

1812
U.S. goes to war against Britain.

1823
Monroe Doctrine issued.

When James Hoban designed this official home for U.S. presidents, he called it the Palace. But George Washington wanted a more modest name, and his wishes won out. The White House cornerstone was laid in 1792.

After the American Revolution, the United States truly was a large country. The peace treaty, signed in 1783, gave the United States all of Great Britain's land from the Appalachian Mountains to the Mississippi River. The new nation contained an area more than twice the size of the original 13 colonies.

Real Estate Bargains

Then, in 1803, the United States signed another treaty—one that has been called "the greatest real estate bargain in history." The United States bought a huge piece of land from France. The territory became known as the the Louisiana Purchase.

Stretching from the Mississippi River to the Rocky Mountains, this chunk of land nearly doubled the size of the United States. It was about 828,000 square miles and included some of the world's most fertile land. At a price of $15 million, the U.S. paid three cents an acre for it.

Although they were uncertain what lay ahead, many people began pushing farther westward. Led by early settlers such as Daniel Boone, they cleared some land, farmed it for a few years, and then moved on. Slowly, the land east of the Mississippi River began to become settled and developed by **European Americans** (Americans of European descent).

Few settlers knew much about this new land that their government had purchased. Hundreds of thousands of Native Americans lived there, but whites thought this vast land should be their own. Even the government was not sure where some of the borders were. Explorers such as Meriwether Lewis and William Clark tried to learn more about it.

The movement west created problems between Native Americans and settlers. Almost all of the land that the settlers moved onto was already occupied by Indian peoples. Sometimes the Americans bought this land outright. But most often, it was taken by force. Most whites believed that Native Americans were primitive and that European settlement could only help their lot.

Native American leaders such as Tecumseh (tih-KUM-seh), the great Shawnee chief, tried to stop the expansion of American settlers. But the forces the Indians faced were too strong. Before long, most tribes were forced to move west of the Mississippi River.

Population Boom

The availability of good, cheap land drew pioneering Americans westward. The invention of two new machines also encouraged westward expansion. The first was the cotton gin, invented by Eli Whitney in 1793. Previously, it had taken a slave a whole day to pick seeds from one pound of cotton. But by using the cotton gin, one slave could produce 50 pounds of seedless cotton fiber a day.

Suddenly, farmers in the South could make a handsome profit growing cotton. All they needed was land on which to grow it—and slaves to pick it and bale it. In a short time, cotton plantations spread westward from the Carolinas to Mississippi.

Sadly, the invention of the cotton gin was a disaster for blacks. The high profits from cotton tempted white Southerners to acquire even more slaves. Many slaves were sold and forced to leave their families and friends to work in the new western plantations.

Another important invention was the steam-powered riverboat. It had as great an effect on the West as the cotton gin had on the South. Before the steamboat, western farmers shipped their prod-

ucts on flatboats, which could only go in one direction—downstream. Since flatboats could not go upstream, goods had to be hauled over land in this direction. It took weeks, even months, to get goods to market this way. Steamboats, which could move in both directions, greatly speeded up transportation.

The first successful steamboat was produced by Robert Fulton in 1807. In a short time, steamboats were moving up and down rivers in many parts of the country. Aboard them, farmers' goods could travel to market in a week's time. The steamboat helped America grow with greater speed toward the West.

The United States flag showed how fast America was growing. In 1790, there were only 13 stars on the flag, representing the 13 original states. But as people moved west, they set up new state governments. By 1821, the U.S. flag had 24 stars. These stars represented almost as many new Western states as old Eastern ones.

The U.S. population also grew rapidly between 1790 and 1820. In 1790, government officials took a **census** (count) of the American population. They recorded

In these notebooks, Lewis and Clark—fearless explorers of the new Louisiana Purchase territory —recorded their observations and discoveries.

almost four million people. Every 10 years, another census was taken. The census of 1820 showed a population of 9,638,000. During 30 years, the population had increased about two-and-one-half times.

Growing Pains

Because of rapid growth, the country began to show signs of "growing pains." The nation divided its loyalties and its votes between two main **political parties** (groups set up for the purpose of directing the policies of a government).

There were no political parties in the United States in 1790. Only 10 years later, however, two parties were clearly compet-

The Louisiana Purchase, 1803

What river formed the eastern boundary of the Louisiana Purchase? What body of water formed the southernmost boundary? What other natural feature formed the western border?

AMERICAN ADVENTURES

ing with each other for power. One was the Federalist party, led by John Adams and Alexander Hamilton. The other was the Democratic–Republican party, headed by Hamilton's old rival, Thomas Jefferson.

The great clash between these two parties occurred during the election of 1800. Jefferson and the Democratic–Republicans won control. Never again would the Federalists elect a president. But many Federalists, such as John Marshall, chief justice of the U.S. Supreme Court, still held positions of power.

Foreign Affairs Troubles

Another problem was in the area of foreign affairs. A war broke out in Europe because of a revolution in France. The French people rose up against their government in 1789. They overthrew their king and established a republic. The new French government declared war against England. That war lasted off and on for more than 20 years. Americans watched this war closely. Starting with George Washington, each American president tried to keep the United States from getting involved.

Then the British navy began seizing American ships that traded with France. (The French also seized American ships, but their navy did not have the power of the British fleet. Still, the U.S. fought an undeclared naval war with France from 1798 to 1800.) Sometimes the British dragged American sailors from their ships and forced them to serve in the British navy.

Americans had other grievances against Great Britain. On the nation's western frontier, many settlers feared that the British were secretly arming Tecumseh's Indian confederation against them. Some Americans saw a war with Britain as a

Thomas Jefferson's bold ideas and intellectual curiosity led to tremendous U.S. expansion.

chance to gain more territory. These people, called the War Hawks, hoped to take over Canada. Because Spain was then an ally of Great Britain, the War Hawks hoped to take over Spanish Florida. Forced to defend its borders on land and sea, the United States declared war on Great Britain, and the War of 1812 began. After both sides suffered setbacks, the war finally ended in 1814.

In 1823, President James Monroe issued his Monroe Doctrine. This warned Europeans to stay out of affairs in the western hemisphere. This eventually led to U.S. dominance in the western hemisphere. It also strengthened people's pride and patriotism. Speakers at the Fourth of July celebrations talked of the glory of their young country. Americans had come to believe that the United States was the greatest country in the world.

This painting shows trailblazer Daniel Boone leading a band of settlers westward. They risked hardship, danger, and loneliness in their quest for new homes in wilderness territories.

Daniel Boone heard the war cries of the Ottawa (AHT-uh-wah) Indians coming closer. The air was filled with smoke and the screams of dying men. An army of British regulars and American colonials, commanded by General Edward Braddock, had walked into an ambush. Minutes before, they had been advancing confidently on Fort Duquesne (doo-KANE), near present-day Pittsburgh. Suddenly, French and Ottawa troops began firing from behind trees. The British panicked. Many of them were killed as they tried to flee.

Boone, a wagon driver hauling supplies for Braddock's army, had no gun. Quickly he cut the harness from his wagon. Then he jumped onto one of his horses and rode away as fast as he could.

In 1755, when this early battle of the French and Indian War (1755 to 1763) took place, Boone was only 21. During his service with Braddock's army, he fell in love with the western country. Another wagon driver, John Finley, had been to Kentucky. At that time, Kentucky was used by the Cherokee and Shawnee tribes as a hunting ground. Finley told Boone that it was filled with great herds of buffalo, deer, and other animals. A man could get rich by killing the animals and selling their hides. Boone decided that one day he would go to Kentucky.

In time, Boone did go there to hunt and explore. He led the way for settlers who wanted to build homes and farm the land in Kentucky. It was the beginning of the westward movement of Americans across the Appalachian Mountains.

Growing Up

Daniel Boone was born November 2, 1734, to Quaker parents on a farm in Pennsylvania. He was the sixth child in a family of 11 boys and girls. Daniel liked hunting better than farming. Once, after killing a bear, he carved these words on a tree:

D. Boone cilled a bar on tree
in the year 1760.

When Daniel was 15, the Boone family moved to the North Carolina frontier. There he became famous as a sharpshooter and a hunter. There he met Rebecca Bryan, who also came from a family of Pennsylvania Quakers. Daniel married her soon after he returned from the bloody battle near Fort Duquesne. Rebecca could make bullets, use a gun, and hunt while Daniel was away.

For the next ten years, Daniel divided his time between farming and hunting. By the time he was 34, he and Rebecca already had seven children.

In Boone's day, rifles had to be reloaded with powder—carried in powder horns like this—after each firing.

Boone wondered if he would ever be able to get out of debt.

Going West

One day in 1766 he found the answer. A peddler (seller of small items) who came to his door turned out to be the John Finley he had met earlier. Once again, Finley talked about getting rich by hunting for hides in Kentucky. Boone jumped at the chance. In the spring of 1769, he, Finley, and four other men set out for the rich, rolling land that the Indians called Ken-ta-ke. It meant "place of fields."

For two years, Boone wandered all over Kentucky. Once he was taken prisoner by a group of Shawnee men. They took all his animal skins and then let him go with a warning. "Don't come here any more," their leader told him, "this is the Indians' hunting ground, and all the animals are ours." Boone, like other settlers, disregarded the wishes of Native Americans.

Boone could not rest until he actually lived in Kentucky. When he got home, he talked to his neighbors about settling there. In September 1773, the Boones and a number of other families headed for Kentucky. The trail was too narrow for wagons, so their goods were carried on packhorses. Young children rode, but all the others walked in single file.

Near the Cumberland Gap, one group was attacked by Cherokees. Three men were killed instantly. Two wounded people were tortured until they died. One of them was Boone's 16-year-old son,

James. Boone later said that it was the darkest hour of his life. He still wanted to go to Kentucky, but the others had no heart for it. Filled with despair, they turned back.

Boone never gave up his dream of settling Kentucky. In March 1775, he started out again with 28 companions. Together they hacked out a new trail called the Wilderness Road. At the Kentucky River, they stopped and built a settlement surrounded by heavy log walls. The men named it Boonesborough in honor of their leader. Soon they brought their families to live there.

In the winter of 1776, when the American colonies were at war with Great Britain, Boone and a group of men set out for a distant salt spring to collect salt. One day, Boone went off alone to hunt buffalo. Suddenly, four Shawnees captured him. Boone promised their chief, Blackfish, that he would surrender his men if the Shawnees would spare their lives. Blackfish agreed and Boone did as he promised.

The prisoners were taken to the Shawnee's main village in present-day Ohio. Some were turned over to the British in return for money. The others, including Boone, were taken into the tribe. Blackfish adopted Boone as his own son. For a time, Boone was content to hunt and fish with his Shawnee "brothers."

Then one day Boone learned that

Roads Leading Westward, Early 1800s

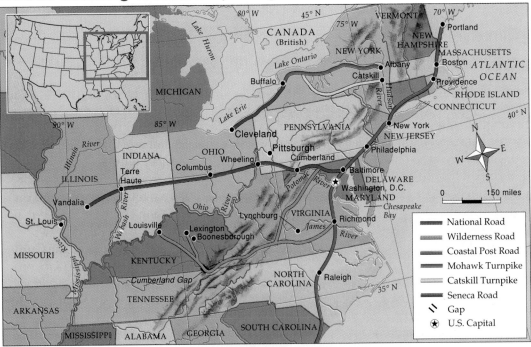

Where did the National Road begin? Through which states did it pass? Which western route looks the most mountainous?

AMERICAN ADVENTURES

Blackfish was planning to attack Boonesborough. He knew that he would have to warn the settlement. That morning he grabbed a fast horse and rode away. Arriving at Boonesborough, he quickly prepared the fort for an attack.

There were not more than 50 men and boys to defend the fort. Blackfish's war party numbered more than 400 men. They fired rapidly, but the thick walls of the fort protected the settlers. Soon the Shawnees began digging a tunnel to undermine the fort. Each day the settlers could hear the click of their shovels getting nearer. The Shawnees also began to shoot flaming arrows into the fort. They started many fires, but the women and children beat them out.

The settlers were getting very tired, and they wondered how much longer they could hold out. Then a heavy rain began to fall. The next day the settlers saw a welcome sight. The rain had made the Shawnees' tunnel fall in. The fort was soon abandoned after the **siege** (surrounding of a fort by an army trying to capture it).

After the Revolution, Kentucky was peaceful, but Boone was not a happy man. The place was getting too crowded for him. "Too many people," he said. "I want more elbow room." When he was nearly 65, Boone and his family moved farther west to Missouri. There, Boone hunted to his heart's content. On September 26, 1820, when he was almost 86 years old, Boone died peacefully in his sleep. He was buried next to Rebecca near the Missouri River.

Years later, they were reburied in Kentucky with great ceremony. Daniel and Rebecca Boone had come home for good. However, many Indian lives were lost as people like the Boones moved west and settled on what was Indian land. It was a story that would be retold again and again.

CHAPTER CHECK

WORD MATCH

1. Blackfish
2. peddler
3. salt spring
4. siege
5. John Finley

a. source of an important mineral
b. one who sells small items door to door
c. a man who treated Boone like a son
d. a man who encouraged Boone to go to Kentucky
e. surrounding of a fort by an army trying to capture it

QUICK QUIZ

1. What idea was planted in Daniel Boone's mind when he served under General Edward Braddock?
2. Do you think the life of the Boone family was different from any other North Carolina or Kentucky frontier family? Explain.

THINK ABOUT IT

1. What setback did Daniel Boone suffer on his first trip to Kentucky with his neighbors?
2. Did Boone ever accomplish his goal of settling in Kentucky?

32 ALL THE WAY TO THE PACIFIC

Sacajawea proved to be an invaluable member of Lewis and Clark's exploration team (1804–1805). In this painting, she embraces her Shoshone relatives while Captain Meriwether Lewis looks on.

Captain Meriwether Lewis was in a tight spot. Near the Great Falls of the Missouri River, he had come upon a herd of at least 1000 buffalo. Lewis was far from his camp and needed food. He shot one of the buffalo and waited for it to fall. Suddenly he became aware that a huge grizzly bear was creeping up on him. Lewis raised his rifle to shoot. Then he remembered that he had not reloaded! Now the bear was coming at him rapidly and there was no time to reload.

Lewis made a run for it, but the bear kept gaining on him. He ran into a nearby river, turned around and faced the bear. Suddenly the grizzly ran away as fast as it had chased Lewis moments before. Lewis breathed a sigh of relief.

Grizzly bears, buffalo, and rattlesnakes were just a few of the dangers that Lewis faced every day. At that time, European Americans knew very little about the land beyond the Mississippi River. A few fur trappers and traders lived there among Native Americans. Some returned east with stories of a great prairie on which there were endless herds of buffalo. President Thomas Jefferson wanted much more exact information. He wanted maps made. He wanted to know all about the Indian tribes who lived there. He was curious about its plants and animals. Above all, he wanted to know whether there were rivers that lead directly to the Pacific Coast. His goal was to open up the West to American settlers and trade.

Jefferson decided to send a team of explorers into the Louisiana Territory and beyond to the Pacific Ocean. He chose his own private secretary, Meriwether Lewis, to lead the expedition. A 29-year-old Virginian, Lewis had served with the army. For his partner, Lewis chose a 33-year-old Kentuckian, Lieutenant William Clark, who worked well with Indians.

Lewis and Clark chose 23 soldiers, three **interpreters** (translators of foreign languages), one slave, and supplies for the expedition. Their plan was to travel up the Missouri River in three small boats. If no rivers flowed through the Rockies, they would cross them on horseback. Then they would look for other rivers that flowed into the Pacific.

The Trip Begins

On May 14, 1804, the explorers started up the Missouri River from St. Louis.

Snow began to fall in October, and the days turned colder. Soon the river would freeze over. Lewis and Clark decided to camp for the winter among the Mandan Indians in what is present-day North Dakota.

One day the captains were visited by a French Canadian and his young wife, Sacajawea

(sack-ah-jah-WEE-ah), a member of the Shoshone (shuh-SHOW-nee) tribe who lived near the Rockies. The trader said they wanted to join the expedition. He told Lewis and Clark that he could speak with many Indian tribes in sign language and would be useful to them. The explorers hired him, but they were fearful about taking a girl of 17 on a long and dangerous trip. But some Indians advised Lewis and Clark to take Sacajawea with them because she could help them get horses from the Shoshones. They needed horses to cross the mountains, so they invited Sacajawea to join them.

When spring arrived, the expedition started west again. It now had a new member, Sacajawea's baby boy Pomp. The explorers continued up the Missouri River. They had to tow their boats against the strong current.

"The fatigue which we encounter is incredible. The men are in the water from morning to night hauling the boats. They walk on sharp rocks which cut their feet, or on round stones which make them fall down," Clark wrote in his diary. "Add to these difficulties the rattlesnakes, which require great caution to prevent being bitten."

It took a long time for the explorers to find the Shoshones. Then one day in August, Lewis went searching on foot for Indian trails. Suddenly he came upon two Indian women and a little girl. He knew from the way they were

One of the objects that Lewis and Clark collected was this dress, made by the Cree Indians. The decorations came from the Cree's trade with Europeans.

The Route of Lewis and Clark, 1804–1805

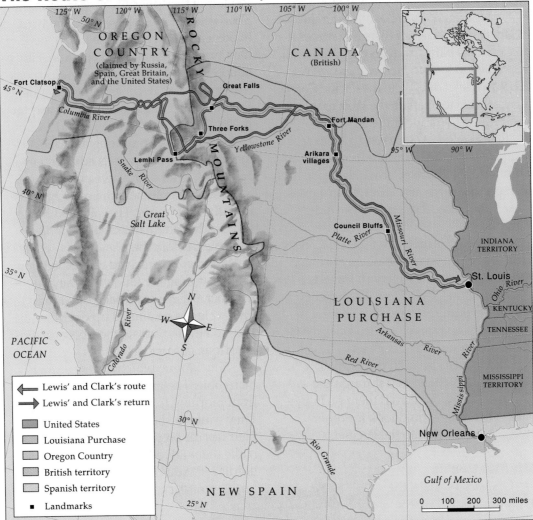

When Lewis and Clark left St. Louis, in which direction did they travel? Which direction did they travel when they followed the Columbia River to the Pacific? Besides traveling on foot, what other forms of transportation might they have used? Base your answers on specific features of this map.

dressed that they were Shoshones. One woman fled when she saw him. The other woman and the little girl sat with their heads bowed. They expected to be killed. Instead, Lewis gave them presents and smeared their cheeks with a red paint. To the Shoshones, this was a sign of peace. The woman then led Lewis to the

Shoshones' camp. She told the chief, Cumeahwait (gah-ME-ut), that the white man was a friend. Soon Lewis was welcomed by the Shoshones.

Later Clark arrived at the Shoshone village with the others. Sacajawea was asked to help the captains speak to Cumeahwait. As soon as Sacajawea saw the chief, she

AMERICAN ADVENTURES

burst into tears. He was her brother whom she had not seen in years. Cumeahwait was also moved at seeing his sister. Cumeahwait told Lewis and Clark that there were no passable rivers flowing through the Rockies. They would have to cross the mountains by horseback on Indian trails.

Crossing the Rockies

The expedition suffered terribly crossing the Rockies. On September 3, snow began to fall steadily. Packhorses slipped on the narrow, icy trails and plunged to their deaths in the canyons below. Food was scarce—sometimes the men had to shoot horses to keep from starving. Sacajawea wrapped Pomp tightly in his blanket and held him close to her body all the time.

Finally, the half-starved explorers reached the other side of the Rockies. There they set up camp among the Nez Percé Indians. The Nez Percé gave them food until they got back their strength. Then the men built dugout canoes to make the trip by river to the Pacific Ocean. On the Columbia River, their canoes were almost smashed going over rough rapids. But on November 15, 1805, the expedition saw the Pacific Ocean at last. Clark wrote in his diary, "Ocean in view! Oh, the joy!"

Lewis and Clark had traveled 18 months and thousands of miles to reach their goal. They had made many maps and kept careful records of trails, plants, animals, and Indian tribes. They had proven that the continent could be crossed, even if there was no direct water route to the Pacific. In so doing, they opened up the West to generations of Americans who would follow in their path. When Lewis and Clark got back to St. Louis in September 1806, they were welcomed as national heroes.

CHAPTER CHECK

WORD MATCH
1. interpreters
2. peace pipe
3. territory
4. fur trappers
5. continent

a. one of the main bodies of land in the world
b. symbol of friendship
c. those who sell animal skins for profit
d. translate a foreign language
e. tract of land

QUICK QUIZ
1. President Thomas Jefferson wanted accurate information about the Great Prairie. List the four things he wanted to know.
2. Describe Lewis and Clark's trip, from the western side of the Rockies to the Pacific Ocean. Do you think this was a significant event in American history? Why or why not?

THINK ABOUT IT
Imagine an American president suggesting that you and one of your friends help develop the first American space station. Do you think you would be willing to accept the challenge as Lewis and Clark did over 150 years ago? Why or why not?

33 TECUMSEH AND THE PROPHET

The great Shawnee chief, Tecumseh (1768?–1813), believed that Indian lands belonged to the Indian peoples—all Indian peoples. No one group, he said, had the right to buy or sell those lands.

The great Shawnee chief, Tecumseh, was furious. The Shawnees and other Indian nations were being forced from their homelands. Tecumseh traveled thousands of miles to speak to Indian tribes from the Great Lakes to the Gulf of Mexico. They must unite to defend their country, he warned them, or they would lose it to the advancing European American settlers.

"They have driven us from the great salt water [the Atlantic Ocean], forced us over the mountains [the Appalachians], and would push us into the lakes [Great Lakes]," said Tecumseh. "We are deter-mined to go no further."

Tecumseh was a dramatic speaker and the tribes listened to him. Many of them agreed to join together to fight for their lands. Tecumseh was forging the most powerful confederation of tribes in Indian history.

But when he returned to his homeland in the Indiana Territory late in 1809, he was shocked by what he found. While he was away, the territorial Governor William Henry Harrison, who later became the ninth president of the United States, had pressured other chiefs to give up more of their land. Three million acres in Indiana were sold by the chiefs for a few thousand dollars.

Tecumseh made it clear that he and his allies would not accept this treaty. Indian country, he said, was the common property of all the tribes and could not be sold.

"Sell a country?" he asked. "Why not sell the air, the clouds and the great sea, as well as the earth?"

Tecumseh's Crusade

Tecumseh's attitude toward European Americans was shaped by two events that took place during his childhood in the Old Northwest. The first was when settlers murdered his father. The second was later when settlers killed a Shawnee chief named Cornstalk, who had become the boy's idol.

As a young man, Tecumseh fought bravely against an American army sent to protect settlers in the area that is present-day Ohio. The Indian tribes were defeated in 1794, and forced to give up most of their land. But Tecumseh was a persuasive speaker and won the respect of most of the Indians in the region.

Many Shawnees believed that the Prophet possessed supernatural powers. Like his brother, Tecumseh, Tenskwatawa was a compelling leader.

"Where today are the Mohawks . . . and many other once-powerful tribes of our people?" asked Tecumseh. "They have vanished before the [greed] and oppression of the white man, as snow before the summer sun." Soon he united the Indian tribes in defense of their lands.

Tecumseh was joined in this **crusade** (vigorous action for a cause) by his younger brother, Tenskwatawa (tens-QUA-ta-wa). Tenskwatawa was a medicine man who was called the Prophet by whites. Once a heavy drinker, the Prophet became deeply religious and gave up alcohol. He preached against the use of liquor by the Shawnees. He also urged them to end wars between the tribes. The Prophet won many followers among the Indians and this alarmed Governor Harrison. The governor denounced the Prophet as a fake. If he was truly a prophet sent by the Great Spirit, challenged Harrison, why didn't the Prophet prove it by performing a miracle?

The Prophet predicted that an **eclipse** of the sun would take place on June 16, 1806. A huge crowd came to the Prophet's village in Ohio to see what would happen. At 11:32 A.M., the Prophet raised his hands, pointed to the sun, and commanded it to darken. Just then, the moon moved across the sun and darkness followed. The crowd was awed by this "miracle." Many Indians now swore loyalty to the Prophet and Tecumseh.

Uniting Indians

In the next few years, Tecumseh and the Prophet stepped up their efforts to unite the Indians. Governor Harrison feared that the Shawnee leaders were becoming too powerful and decided to strike a blow against them. The Prophet had moved his village westward to the Tippecanoe (tip-EE-ca-noo) River in Indiana. On November 6, 1811, while Tecumseh was away, Harrison led an army of almost 1000 men to the edge of the Tippecanoe village.

Finally, the Prophet ordered the Shawnees to attack. At dawn the next day, about 450 Shawnees charged Harrison's camp. They were met with a hail of deadly fire and driven back. By dawn, the Indians were defeated and withdrew. Harrison then burned the Prophet's village to the ground.

When Tecumseh saw what had happened, he turned his anger on his brother. He blamed the Prophet for ordering a foolish attack that was bound to fail. As a punishment for causing the death of many Shawnees, Tecumseh banished him from the tribe.

War on the Americans

Meanwhile, the United States was moving closer to a war with its old enemy, Britain. Many Americans believed that the British were agitating the Indians and giving them arms to attack the settlers. When the War of 1812 began, Tecumseh saw a chance to strike back at the Americans. It was a chance, he said, "for the Indians of North America to form ourselves into one great combination." Tecumseh allied himself with the British

Area of the Tecumseh Confederation, 1812

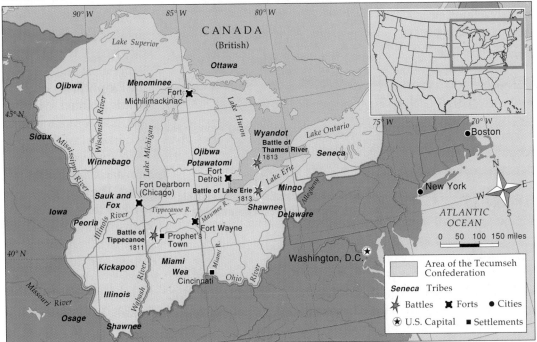

What tribes formed the Tecumseh Confederation? How many forts were located in their territory?

and declared war on the Americans.

Tecumseh had success early in the war. At that time, an American army launched an invasion of Canada from Detroit, in the Territory of Michigan. The attack was driven back by Tecumseh's Indians and some British soldiers. Then Tecumseh captured the American fort at Detroit. Tecumseh treated the American prisoners with dignity and won their respect. As a reward for his dramatic victory, the British made Tecumseh a brigadier general in their army.

But a year later, disaster struck the Indian–British alliance. On September 10, 1813, U.S. warships commanded by Oliver Perry defeated a British fleet on Lake Erie. The victory gave the United States control of the lake and cut off the British forces in Detroit from their supply bases in Canada.

British Commander Henry Proctor decided to abandon Detroit and retreat eastward into Canada.

Tecumseh did not have enough men to fight the Americans alone. He followed the British in retreat. Tecumseh was filled with gloom. One night, he told his chiefs that he expected to die.

At the Thames (tehmz) River in Canada, a large U.S. army caught up with the retreating British and Indians. It was led by Tecumseh's old enemy, William Henry Harrison. When the Americans attacked, the British troops surrendered.

Tecumseh's men were left alone to fight the American army. It was a furious battle. Tecumseh was wounded again and again. By nightfall, he was dead.

So ended Tecumseh's dream of creating a strong and united Indian nation. Before long, one tribe after another would be removed from its homeland and forced onto reservations west of the Mississippi River.

CHAPTER CHECK

WORD MATCH
1. William Henry Harrison
2. Oliver Perry
3. crusade
4. eclipse
5. agitating

a. commanded U.S. warships in fight against British
b. stirring up feelings
c. when the moon moves between the Sun and Earth
d. fought against Indians in effort to gain land in Indiana Territory
e. vigorous action for a cause

QUICK QUIZ
1. Why did Tecumseh travel thousands of miles to speak to Indian tribes?
2. Name two events that affected Tecumseh's attitude toward the European Americans. Do you think his attitude was justifiable? Explain.

THINK ABOUT IT
Why was Tecumseh able to make an alliance with the British? Describe the military operation that earned him the title of brigadier general in the Army. What ruined the good relationship between Britain and Tecumseh? Explain.

CHAPTER 34 WASHINGTON IN DANGER

In August 1814, British troops marched into the nation's capital as the citizens of Washington fled. The troops set fire to many public buildings, and flames lit the skies over the city well into the night.

P anic was spreading in Washington, D.C. Everyone was trying to leave the nation's capital at once. Families piled their possessions into wagons and carts. They clogged the road to safety in Maryland for eight miles.

What caused the panic? On August 18, 1814, a War Department messenger on horseback rushed into the town of 8000 people with some startling news. A British fleet had entered Chesapeake Bay and their army of 4000 men was only 40 miles from the capital.

The city was completely unprepared for an attack. Although the United States had been at war with Great Britain since June 1812, the fighting had centered around the Great Lakes and Canada. Few Americans believed that the British would threaten Washington. President James Madison expressed fears about it, but Secretary of War John Armstrong scoffed.

"Washington in danger!" he said. "It's absurd. The British will never come here." So nothing was done to prepare a defense for the city. Now the untrained militia force hastily called up to oppose the British did not seem to have a chance.

The British Advance

One person in Washington clearly was in no rush to leave. She was Dolley Madison, the President's wife. On August 22, President Madison left the city to plan its defense. But first he asked Dolley whether she had the courage, or firmness, to remain in the White House until his return. Dolley assured him that she had no fear "but for him and the success of our army."

The next day, the First Lady received a message from her husband which warned her to be ready to leave the city at a moment's notice. She had already filled several trunks with her husband's papers and had loaded them into a carriage. Still she waited for his return.

Battle of Bladensburg

The British army advancing on Washington collided with a larger force of American militia at Bladensburg (BLAY-dinz-burg), Maryland, on August 24. There was a brief fight before a new weapon, a rocket gun, turned the tide for the British. Rocket guns were not very accurate, but they made a terrifying noise. Soon most of the defenders fled.

There was only one bright spot for the Americans at Bladensburg. A few hundred gallant U.S. sailors, most of whom were free blacks, held their ground. They were led by a tough old navy captain, Joshua Barney, who had fought in the Revolutionary War. After Barney was wounded and taken prisoner, the British prepared to enter the capital of the United States.

Torching the Capital

That afternoon, Dolley Madison received three messages from her husband warning her that British troops

Dolley Madison (1768–1849) braved a British attack long enough to save a portrait of the nation's first president.

might appear at any moment, and urging her to flee. By this time, she had sent his papers and some valuable White House silverware to safety. Now, hearing of the outcome at Bladensburg, she fled to safety in Virginia. But first, she insisted on removing a famous portrait of George Washington that hung in the White House dining room.

That evening, 200 British redcoats led by General Robert Ross entered the city. The streets were empty, and the houses dark. What would Ross do in the deserted city? He remembered an incident that took place the year before in Canada. American militiamen had burned the Parliament building in York (present-day Toronto), the capital of British Canada. So Ross ordered his soldiers to torch government buildings in Washington.

The first to be set afire was the Capitol. A gunpowder explosion was set off, and soon the entire building was in flames. Within an hour, the Capitol was an empty shell.

To prevent the British from capturing supplies, the commander of the U.S. Navy Yard ordered it to be burned. All during the night, docks, ships, and warehouses burned fiercely while ammunition exploded.

While the Capitol and Navy Yard burned, other British soldiers led by Ross broke into the deserted White House. Within minutes, flames roared through the roof of the White House.

The British **arson** (crime of purposely setting fire to property) attack on Washington was meant to harass Americans and gain **revenge** (harm done in return for a wrong) for the burning at York. There was no way the small British army could hold the city once the Americans organized for an attack. Twenty-four hours after entering Washington, the British returned to their ships in Chesapeake Bay.

British Rockets Over Fort McHenry

The British fleet now sailed to attack

The War of 1812

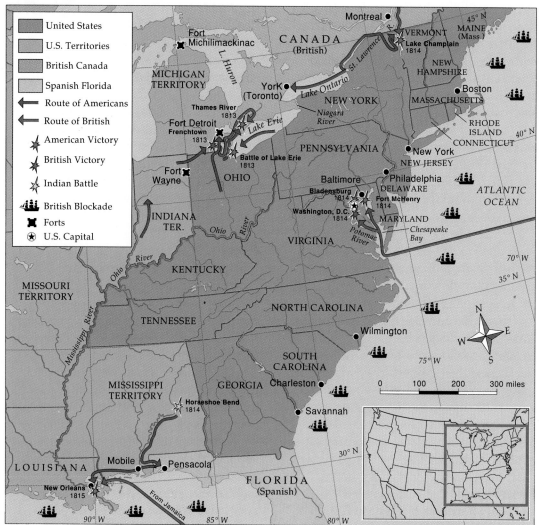

Which forts were located on the Great Lakes? Which were beside rivers? How many miles of coast did the British blockade?

AMERICAN ADVENTURES

Baltimore, a port used by **privateers** (privately-owned armed ships hired by a government). On September 12, the British army landed about 14 miles from the city. British soldiers marched overland, opposed by 3200 American troops who inflicted severe casualties on the British. The next day, the British fleet sailed toward the city's harbor which was guarded by Fort McHenry.

The British were surprised to find a large, well-trained U.S. army waiting for them outside the city. They decided not to attack such a strong force without help from their fleet. Soon British ships pounded away at Fort McHenry with rockets and shells.

On one of the ships was an American lawyer named Francis Scott Key. He had gone aboard earlier to ask the British to free an American prisoner. Occasionally, the glare of the British rockets showed the huge American flag waving over the fort.

Key was so proud of the way Fort McHenry held out that he wrote a poem about it. Later set to music, the poem became the American national anthem, "The Star-Spangled Banner."

Unable to capture Fort McHenry, the British gave up the attack on Baltimore. The next morning the British fleet departed. The city was safe.

The attacks on Washington and Baltimore gained nothing for Britain. But the burning of Washington made Americans angry, and the defense of Baltimore filled them with pride. These feelings united them in the war against Britain.

By the summer of 1814, both sides were tired of fighting. Peace talks began in Ghent, Belgium. On December 24, 1814, a peace treaty was signed. Neither side gained or lost any land in the War of 1812. But the United States did gain a new feeling of pride as a nation.

CHAPTER CHECK

WORD MATCH
1. Fort McHenry
2. arson
3. Bladensburg, Maryland
4. revenge
5. privateers

a. harm done in return for a wrong
b. privately-owned armed ships hired by a government
c. crime of purposely setting fire to property
d. where a U.S. army held out against British
e. where British advancing on Washington beat the Americans

QUICK QUIZ
1. What was one of the last things Dolley Madison did as she fled from the invading British?
2. What was the significance of the Battle of Bladensburg? Explain.

THINK ABOUT IT
Do you think General Ross was justified in burning several government buildings in Washington in retaliation for the American burning of the Parliament Building in Toronto? Are the actions of both countries justifiable?

CHAPTER 35 STRENGTHENING THE SUPREME COURT

John Marshall (1755-1835) was the fourth chief justice of the U.S. Supreme Court. During his 34 years in that office, Marshall changed the Court's influence on American government forever.

He was tall and a bit clumsy. He was so forgetful that he often lost his hat or coat. He had a lot of hair which he seldom combed. He wore dirty boots and old clothes. Yet he was perhaps the most important judge in United States history. His name was John Marshall.

Marshall had much in common with another powerful person in government—Thomas Jefferson. Like Jefferson, he came from Virginia. Both men wore plain clothes that never quite fit. Jefferson and Marshall even belonged to the same family; they were cousins. Yet they were hardly close friends.

In fact, they despised each other. Marshall, a Federalist, believed that the national government should be much stronger than state governments. Jefferson, a Democratic–Republican, thought that states' rights should be carefully preserved.

The two cousins did not trust each other for another reason. They belonged to different branches of the federal government. As president, Jefferson led the executive branch. As chief justice of the Supreme Court, Marshall headed the judicial branch. He was named chief justice in 1801 by the last Federalist president, John Adams. Soon after, Jefferson became president. Because of the system of checks and balances, Jefferson and Marshall tried to block each other's policies.

The result was the first great tug of war between a president and the Supreme Court. President Jefferson hated to see Federalists such as Marshall in the judicial branch. Jefferson and his secretary of state, James Madison, did what they could to prevent this. Among other things, they tried to stop a Federalist, William Marbury, from becoming **justice of the peace** (judge who tries minor cases) in the District of Columbia.

This picture of a Philadelphia jail was printed on currency during Marshall's term as chief justice. The money helped finance the jail—and kept the court system strong.

Requesting a Writ

President Adams had **appointed** (named for an office or position) Marbury just before leaving office. He had signed a **commission** giving Marbury the right to hold the office. But Marbury had not yet received the commission when Jefferson became president. Jefferson ordered Madison not to deliver the commission to Marbury. After waiting two years for the commission, Marbury became angry. He asked Marshall's Court to force the President to give him his commission. He tried to persuade the Court to issue an order known as a *writ of mandamus* (man-DAY-mus). This document orders a public official or a lower court to take legal action.

Marshall would have liked to help Marbury. But in 1803 the Supreme Court was weak. If Marshall had ordered Jefferson to deliver the commission to Marbury, Jefferson would have laughed at him. Marshall and the Court would have looked silly.

Marshall came up with a very clever solution. He announced it in his decision in the case of *Marbury* v. *Madison*. He first said that Marbury had a right to be a justice of the peace, and that Jefferson was wrong in not giving him his commission. But then Marshall said that there was nothing the Supreme Court could do about it. The right to issue a writ of mandamus had been granted by Congress in 1789, not by the Constitution. Because that right went beyond the Constitution, Marshall declared it was unconstitutional. The Supreme Court therefore did not have the right to issue a writ of mandamus at all.

It was a brilliant decision for several reasons. First, it gave Marshall a chance to scold President Jefferson and tell him he was wrong. Second, it limited the power

Port cities could be very profitable for traders and shippers—especially if they could eliminate competition. One of Marshall's landmark decisions enforced fairer trade practices between states.

of the Supreme Court by stating that the Court could do nothing about Marbury's appointment. But at the same time, the decision showed how powerful the Court could be. Marshall showed that the Court had the power to declare a law of Congress unconstitutional.

Marbury never did get his job as justice of the peace. Jefferson withheld the appointment. The real victors in this case were Marshall and his Supreme Court. Ever since this decision, the Supreme Court has had the final say on laws of Congress. The Court's power to decide if acts of Congress are constitutional is called **judicial review.**

John Marshall continued to make bold decisions. One of Marshall's greatest involved the Bank of the United States. Another involved steamboats. Both decisions had the same effect. They gave more power to the national government and took power away from the states.

Taxing a Bank

Marshall's decision on the Bank of the United States came in 1819 in the case of *McCulloch* v. *Maryland*. The case arose from an attempt by the state of Maryland

to tax the bank heavily and therefore destroy it. For 28 years, people had wondered whether the Bank of the United States was legal. The bank had been the pet idea of Alexander Hamilton. Hamilton had wanted Congress to create a bank that would serve the goals of the United States government. He said a national bank would help the economy to run smoothly. But did the Constitution give Congress the power to create such a bank? No, said many Republicans. Yes, said most Federalists.

Who was right? John Marshall agreed with Hamilton. Congress, he said, did have the power to charter a bank. True, in the list of powers granted to Congress, the Constitution said nothing about banks. But it did say this: "The Congress shall have power . . . to make all laws which shall be necessary and proper" for carrying out its other powers.

Two of these specific powers listed in the Constitution are Congress's power to collect taxes, and Congress's power to pay off debts. Could a bank help the government to collect taxes and pay off debts? Yes, said Marshall, speaking for the Court. Therefore, the bank law was "necessary and proper." The Bank of the United States was constitutional. The state of Maryland did not have the right to tax it.

Controlling Commerce

Steamboats gave Marshall another chance to increase the power of the national government. A New York law said that only one company could operate steamboats on the Hudson River. But what if a steamboat company in the neighboring state of New Jersey wanted to carry passengers across the river to New York? The judges of New York said this was against the law. Not so, said John Marshall in 1824. In a case called *Gibbons* v. *Ogden*, he said Congress alone could control commerce between the states. The New York law was judged unconstitutional. A New Jersey steamboat company could do business in New York.

John Marshall spent 34 years—half his life—on the Supreme Court. He served as chief justice during the administrations of five presidents. He did as much as any president to strengthen the federal authority. When he died in 1835, Americans honored him by ringing the Liberty Bell in Philadelphia.

CHAPTER CHECK

WORD MATCH
1. judicial review
2. justice of the peace
3. writ of mandamus
4. appointed
5. commission

a. written order giving certain powers, duties, or rights
b. court order to do a legal action
c. power of the court to decide if laws are constitutional
d. named for an office or position
e. judge who tries minor cases

QUICK QUIZ
1. Why did John Marshall rule in favor of the Bank of the United States?
2. What principle was established in the case of *Gibbons* v. *Ogden*?

THINK ABOUT IT
What is meant by judicial review? How does this doctrine add to the system of checks and balances?

36 THE MONROE DOCTRINE

During the 1800s, many Latin Americans rebelled against their Spanish colonial rulers. This 1890 painting shows the departure of one such ruler after independence was declared in his country.

"The Eagle of the United States—may she extend her wings from the Atlantic to the Pacific."

That was how people in Waterville, Maine, toasted the new nation on July 4, 1815. The toast promised great things for the United States. Only a few years earlier, large numbers of Americans had thought of their state first and their country second. Now more and more of them were thinking in national terms first.

The nation had come through the War of 1812 with some success. There was a new spirit of **nationalism** (national pride)

in the air. It could be seen most clearly in the nation's capital. Government buildings in Washington, D.C., had been burned by the British in 1814. After the war, new buildings had begun rising from the ashes of the old. The White House was being enlarged, repaired, and repainted. In September of 1817, it was ready to be occupied. A new president, James Monroe of Virginia, and his wife Elizabeth moved in.

Monroe was an old Democratic–Republican friend of Thomas Jefferson. Monroe's election in 1816 had been just another sign that the Federalist party was dying out. During Monroe's first term as president, the U.S. seemed more united than ever before. A Boston newspaper called this period an "Era of Good Feelings." The term stuck.

During these years, the spirit of nationalism grew. Some Americans took special pride in comparing their government to European ones. In Spain and France, Russia and Austria, kings and emperors still ruled. Citizens there had few rights.

The United States still had to pay attention to Europe, for the young nation was surrounded by European colonies. Britain remained in control of Canada. It also claimed to own parts of Oregon and other areas in the Northwest. Russia claimed a huge piece of land that went from Alaska to Oregon. Spain held Florida, Texas, Cuba, Mexico, and most of South America.

But Spain was growing weaker. Its huge American empire was fast falling apart. Starting in 1810, a series of revolts had broken out, from Mexico in the north to Argentina in the south. One

The son of famous parents, John Quincy Adams (1767-1848) won his own fame as President Monroe's secretary of state.

after another, new nations were becoming independent.

Unrest in Florida

Spain also had problems in Florida. The border between Georgia and Florida was an area of unrest. In 1817, the U.S. tried to drive Seminole (SEM-uh-nole) Indians from a settlement in Georgia. Seminoles in Florida became very angry at this. They staged raids over the border into Georgia. Their raids led to a wider war with the U.S.

In 1818, the U.S. sent a small army to the area. It was led by the hero of the Battle of New Orleans, General Andrew Jackson. Jackson was expected to chase Indian raiders back into Florida and punish them. But it was not clear if he should go further.

Jackson swept across the border and deep into Florida. He put two Indian chiefs to death without trial. He took two forts from the Spanish, though he had no orders to do so. Then he left the area, believing that he had conquered it.

President Monroe was shocked when he heard what Jackson had done. He did not want to go to war with Spain. He ordered Jackson to withdraw his troops from Spanish forts, but he did not tell Spain he was sorry about the **invasion**. His secretary of state persuaded him against this.

The secretary of state was John Quincy Adams, the son of Abigail and John Adams. Adams' parents had been stern patriots during the Revolution. Now he was proving to be a stern nationalist. He was furious with Jackson's military action, but approved the results. If Spain could not keep peace in Florida, Adams warned, it should turn the area over to a nation which could.

After this, Spain saw that it could not hold onto East Florida much longer. In 1819, it signed a treaty giving the area to the United States. In return, Americans gave up rights to the 5 million dollars that Spain owed them. And they gave up all claims to Texas (which the Spanish also claimed).

The treaty gave a further boost to American pride. Monroe was re-elected president by all but one electoral vote the next year. Yet his re-election did not end worries about the nations of Europe. If anything, these worries became greater in his second term.

As Spain withdrew from South America, it left behind a continent divided among weak nations. At the same time, some European nations were hungry for new colonies overseas. Was it possible that France, Russia, Prussia (today's Germany), and Austria might join forces in South America? Might they try to take hold of former Spanish colonies for themselves? There were no clear signs of this. But there were many rumors.

Threats in the Pacific

There was also a sharper threat from Russia. In 1821, Russia told other nations to keep their ships out of the North Pacific. This angered Monroe and Adams. It also angered the British. Like Russia, both the United States and Britain had claims to parts of Oregon. They were not going to let the Russians seal off the Pacific Coast.

Still, what was to prevent trouble on the high seas? And what was to prevent it in the newly independent nations to the south? British leaders thought they saw a solution. In August 1823, they suggested that the United States join them in issuing a warning. They would tell European leaders not to interfere in the Americas.

Monroe liked the idea. So did some other U.S. leaders. But John Quincy Adams had misgivings. He held high hopes of being elected president in 1824. Any pact with Britain might be unpopular with the voters. Besides, he doubted the rumors about Europe's plans for South America. And he thought it more dignified for the U.S. to make the warning by itself.

Adams was a stubborn man. He held his views even when others disagreed. Slowly he persuaded Monroe to "go-it-alone" in his warning to Europe. In the end, he won his point.

Monroe issued the warning in his regular message to Congress on December 2, 1823. In the message, Monroe made two points about Europe and the Americas. First, he said that no European nation could start a new colony anywhere in the Americas. Second, he said that the United States and Europe should stay out of each other's territory and not interfere in the other's internal affairs.

This policy became known as the **Monroe Doctrine.** The ideas it stated were not completely new ones. In 1796, George Washington had warned against permanent alliances with Europe. Now Monroe carried Washington's warning one step further. He said that all independent nations of America should stay separate from Europe.

His Doctrine was a bold one for its time. It was bolder still because it had been set forth by the United States alone. In 1823, Britain held control of shipping in the Atlantic Ocean, and only Britain could enforce the Monroe Doctrine. By "going-it-alone," the U.S. had made the separation between Europe and the Americas very evident.

The Monroe Doctrine became a key part of American foreign policy. Other presidents have followed the Doctrine which clearly states to all the world: Keep out of the Americas. Since Monroe's time, the Doctrine has provided the rationale for United States expansion and even intervention in other nations' affairs.

CHAPTER CHECK

WORD MATCH
1. Monroe Doctrine
2. nationalism
3. invasion
4. John Qunicy Adams
5. James Monroe

a. statement of government policy
b. being entered by an attacking military force
c. secretary of state under Monroe
d. pride for one's country
e. president favoring expansion and intervention policy

QUICK QUIZ
1. Name the European colonies that surrounded the United States in 1816.
2. Explain the two main points of the Monroe Doctrine.

THINK ABOUT IT
Why do you think United States citizens were interested in what happened in South America and Mexico? Do you think those are still good reasons for U.S. interest in Latin America?

A NEW NATIONALISM

History Detective

1. I am the policy President James Monroe issued to let Europe know it was no longer welcome in the Americas. What am I?

2. I am the justice who was responsible for establishing the powers the Supreme Court still relies on today. Who am I?

3. Once Daniel Boone created me, he could reach the Kentucky River and build Boonesborough. What am I?

4. When the British attacked Washington, D.C., in 1814, I was left in charge of the White House, its contents, and staff. Who am I?

5. Was there a river running to the Pacific Ocean? I led the expedition that would find out. Who am I?

Voices From the Past

Meriwether Lewis and William Clark kept a very careful journal of their trip to the West. In it, they documented, among other things, their meetings with Indian tribes. Read the entry on one such meeting from *The Journals of Lewis and Clark*, below, and answer the questions that follow.

> . . . *as I was about to leave the chief's [of the Cheyenne] lodge, he requested me to send some traders to them, that their country was full of beaver and they would then be encouraged to kill beaver, but now they had no use for them as they could get nothing for their skins and did not know well, how to catch beaver. If the [European American settlers] would come amongst them they [could teach the Indians] how to take the beaver. . . .*

1. The Indians were native to the area, and they tended to live closer to nature than the European Americans. Does it surprise you that European Americans would know how to catch beaver better than the Indians? Why or why not?

2. If they knew what you know about the European Americans' future treatment of the Indians, do you think the Cheyennes would have asked Lewis and Clark to send the European Americans to their lands? Why or why not?

Hands–On History

Writing Descriptively—In the early 1800s, most of America had yet to be explored and settled by European Americans. Imagine you were leading an expedition, like Lewis and Clark or Daniel Boone, or that you were the first European American explorer ever to reach the area you live in today. Write a journal entry describing what you would have found there.

Indians and Settlers Battle at Tippecanoe

Tippecanoe, November 7, 1811—Early this morning, Indians at Tippecanoe attacked General Harrison's forces, who were camped at the edge of the village. One hundred eighty-eight soldiers were killed. The battle raged for hours, and many Indians are also believed dead. Harrison's forces had been closing in on the territory for weeks. It is thought that the Prophet, who was in charge of the Indians in Chief Tecumseh's absence, gave the order to fight. After the battle, Harrison and his troops moved into the Indian village, found it abandoned, and set fire to it.

1.

2.

Many observers believe the confrontation at Tippecanoe was bound to happen. Tecumseh has spent the last two years uniting the Indian tribes into one confederation. He believes this is the only way to stop the European Americans from taking Indian land. "The Indians were once a happy race," said Tecumseh recently, "but are now made miserable by the [European Americans], who are never contented." Up until today's fighting, Tecumseh has been content to meet peacefully with European American leaders to discuss the problem.

At an Impasse

Throughout the conflict, General William Harrison has served as governor of the Indiana Territory. He has been under great pressure from anxious settlers to acquire the vast amounts of land under Indian control. Between 1795 and 1809, Americans took 50 million acres of Indian hunting ground. Treaties were made with Indian tribes to take more land. But once Tecumseh set up his confederacy, he refused to recognize the treaties. At last year's meeting at Vincennes, Harrison told Tecumseh that one treaty was none of his business because his tribe didn't "own" the land in the first place.

The Next Step

The American public disagrees on how to solve the problem. Settlers desire to make homes on land the Indians control. But if America uses force against the Indians, the government fears no settlers will be safe from Indian attack.

3.

You Be the Reporter

Match each question with its news item above.
1. What caption would you put with this photo?
2. How would you title this news story?
3. Finish this story with one or more suggestions for settling the conflict with the Indians.

NOTING CHANGE ON A MAP

In 1823, the Americas were in the midst of rapid change. Spain and Portugal, once powerful empires, were losing control of their former colonies. The map on the opposite page is a **geo-political** map. It shows the political boundaries of the American nations which existed in 1823. The map also shows when different Latin American countries became independent. If you were a United States diplomat at that time, you might have found useful information on the map about the new nations to the south.

Study the map's key. Then answer these questions on a separate sheet of paper.

1. Many people confuse the terms "Latin America" and "South America." Which Latin American nation on the map is actually in North America?

2. The southernmost tip of South America had not been settled by Europeans in 1823. Which two countries were closest to this area?

3. The struggle for independence was completed earlier in some areas than in others. Look at the dates near the names of Latin American countries on this map. **(a)** In what year did most of these countries become independent? **(b)** Which Latin American country shown on this map was the first colony of Europe to gain independence? Which was the last?

4. Use the map's scale to estimate the distance between countries. **(a)** In 1823, which South American country was the closest to the United States? **(b)** How far away was it?

5. Many of the new countries eventually broke up into smaller countries. **(a)** Which area on the map had broken away from Mexico by 1823? **(b)** What nations developed from this split? (Check the map on page 814.)

6. Not all of Latin America was independent by 1823. **(a)** What areas were still controlled by Spain? **(b)** What other European nations still had colonies in the Americas?

7. Modern Mexico is much smaller than it was in 1821. Use the map's scale to measure Mexico at its longest, north-south dimension on this map. What was the distance from the northwest tip of Mexico **(a)** to its southernmost point in 1823? **(b)** to the southern tip of the United Provinces of Central America?

8. Imagine you were sent as a U.S. ambassador to Brazil in 1823. You decided to travel by boat from the mouth of the Mississippi River along the Latin American coast to Brazil. Which countries and territories would you have passed along the way?

9. Because the Equator passes through it, some people believe that all of South America is hot. **(a)** How many degrees of latitude away from the Equator was the southern border of Chile in 1823? **(b)** How many degrees away was the northern border of the United States?

10. Before the 1820s, most of Latin America had been linked to the colonial empires of Europe. The Monroe Doctrine of 1823 meant, in effect, that Latin America was now linked with the United States instead. **(a)** What facts of physical geography made Latin America and the United States part of a unified "region"? **(b)** What facts of political history did these two areas share in common? **(c)** What facts of their history were different?

The Americas in 1823

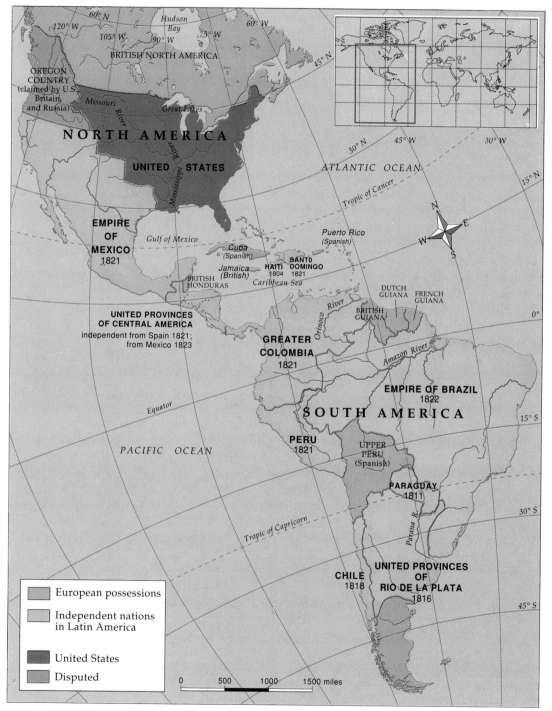

European possessions

Independent nations in Latin America

United States

Disputed

Physical Map of North America

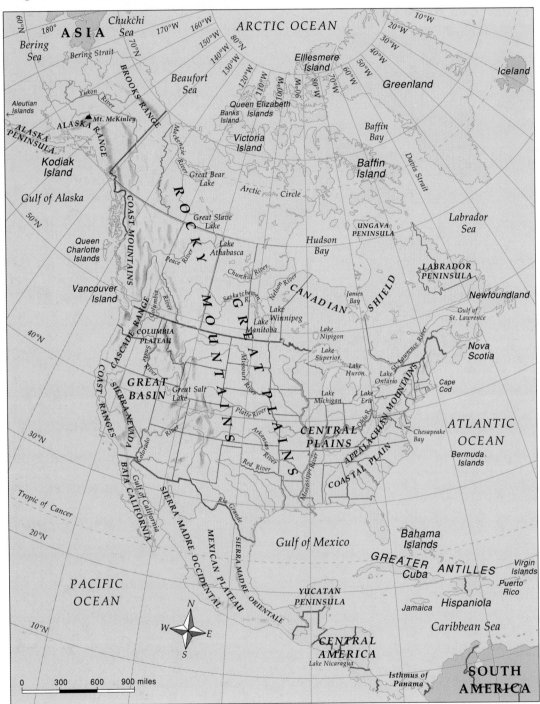

U.S. Territorial Growth Map

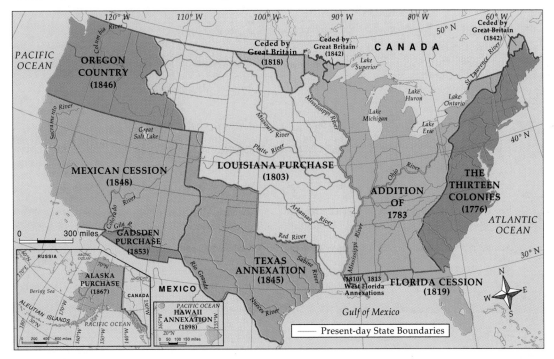

Top 10 Sources of Immigrants to the United States, 1965–1985

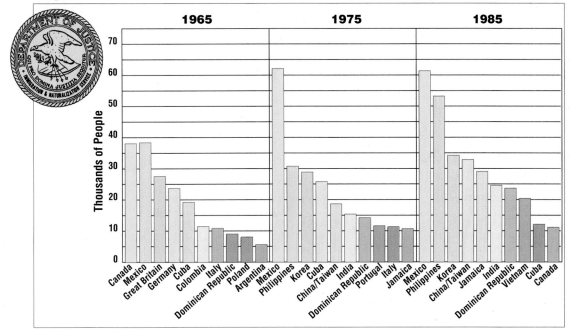

PRESIDENTIAL FACTS

President Term	Party	Vice-President	Birthplace/Born-Died	Facts
George Washington 1789–1797	None	John Adams	Westmoreland Co., Va./1732–1799	First president to appear on a U.S. postage stamp.
John Adams 1797–1801	Fed.	Thomas Jefferson	Braintree, Mass./1735–1826	Only president to be the father of another president—John Quincy Adams.
Thomas Jefferson 1801–1809	Rep.	Aaron Burr	Albemarle Co., Va./1743–1826	First president to be inaugurated in Washington, D.C.
James Madison 1809–1817	Rep.	George Clinton	Port Conway, Va./1751–1836	Was the only president to lead troops while in office—Battle of Bladensburg, Aug. 24, 1814.
James Monroe 1817–1825	Rep.	Daniel D. Tompkins	Westmoreland Co., Va./1758–1831	Was the first president to have been a senator.
John Quincy Adams 1825–1829	Rep.	John C. Calhoun	Braintree, Mass./1767–1848	Was the first and only son of a president to become president.
Andrew Jackson 1829–1837	Dem.	John C. Calhoun	Waxhaw Settlement, S.C./1767–1845	Was the only president to pay off the national debt.
Martin Van Buren 1837–1841	Dem.	Richard M. Johnson	Kinderhook, N.Y./1782–1862	Was both the eighth president and the eighth vice-president.
William Henry Harrison 1841	Whig	John Tyler	Berkeley, Va./1773–1841	Had 106 great-grandchildren, the most of any president.
John Tyler 1841–1845	Whig	——	Greenway, Va./1790–1862	Was the first president to have no vice-president during his entire term.
James K. Polk 1845–1849	Dem.	George M. Dallas	near Pineville, N.C./1795–1849	Was the first president to voluntarily retire after one term.
Zachary Taylor 1849–1850	Whig	Millard Filmore	Orange County, Va./1784–1850	Was the first president to have held no previous political office.
Millard Filmore 1850–1853	Whig	——	Locke, N.Y/1800–1874	Was the first president to have been an indentured servant.
Franklin Pierce 1853–1857	Dem.	William R. King	Hillsboro, N.H./1804–1869	Always insisted that grace be said before every meal.
James Buchanan 1857–1861	Dem.	John C. Breckinridge	near Mercersburg, Penn./1791–1868	Was the first and only president to never marry.
Abraham Lincoln 1861–1865	Rep.	Hannibal Hamlin	near Hogdenville, Ken./1809–1865	First president to be photographed at his inauguration
Andrew Johnson 1865–1869	Rep.	——	Raleigh, N.C./1808–1875	Was the only unschooled man to become president.
Ulysses S. Grant 1869–1877	Rep.	Schuyler Colfax	Point Pleasant, Ohio/1822–1885	His favorite breakfast was cucumbers soaked in vinegar.
Rutherford B. Hayes 1877–1881	Rep.	William A. Wheeler	Delaware, Ohio/1822–1893	Was the first president to visit the West Coast while in office.
James A. Garfield 1881	Rep.	Chester A. Arthur	Orange, Ohio/1831–1881	Liked to juggle Indian clubs to build his muscles.
Chester A. Arthur 1881–1885	Rep.	——	Fairfield, Vt./1830–1886	Had a French chef in the White House where dinners often lasted two to three hours.

PRESIDENTIAL FACTS

President Term	Party	Vice-President	Birthplace/Born-Died	Facts
Grover Cleveland 1885–1889	Dem.	Thomas A. Hendricks	Caldwell, N.J./1837–1908	Was the first and only president to be married in the White House.
Benjamin Harrison 1889–1893	Rep.	Levi P. Morton	North Bend, Ohio/1833–1901	In 1891, was the first president to have electricity in the White House.
Grover Cleveland 1893–1897	Dem.	Adlai E. Stevenson	Caldwell, N.J./1837–1908	First president to be elected to two non-consecutive terms.
William McKinley 1897–1901	Rep.	Garret A. Hobart Theodore Roosevelt	Niles, Ohio/1843–1901	Always wore a red carnation in his lapel for good luck.
Theodore Roosevelt 1901–1909	Rep.	Charles W. Fairbanks	New York, N.Y./1858–1919	Was the first president to win the Nobel Peace Prize.
William H. Taft 1909–1913	Rep.	James S. Sherman	Cincinnati, Ohio/1857–1930	First president to serve in the Supreme Court.
Woodrow Wilson 1913–1921	Dem.	Thomas R. Marshall	Staunton, Va./1856–1924	Was the first president to cross the Atlantic during his term in office.
Warren G. Harding 1921–1923	Rep.	Calvin Coolidge	Blooming Grove, Ohio/1865–1923	Was the first president to visit Alaska.
Calvin Coolidge 1923–1929	Rep.	Charles G. Dawes	Plymouth Notch, Vt./1872–1933	Had a reputation of never wasting a penny or a word.
Herbert C. Hoover 1929–1933	Rep.	Charles Curtis	West Branch, Iowa/1874–1964	Was the first president to visit China.
Franklin D. Roosevelt 1933–1945	Dem.	John N. Garner Henry A. Wallace Harry S. Truman	Hyde Park, N.Y/1882–1945	Was the only president to be elected to four terms.
Harry S. Truman 1945–1953	Dem.	Alben W. Barkley	Lamar, Missouri/1884–1972	Was the first president to televise a speech from the White House.
Dwight D. Eisenhower 1953–1961	Rep.	Richard M. Nixon	Denison, Texas/1890–1969	Was the first president to appear on color television.
John F. Kennedy 1961–1963	Dem.	Lyndon B. Johnson	Brookline, Mass./1917–1963	Was the first Boy Scout to become president.
Lyndon B. Johnson 1963–1969	Dem.	Hubert Humphrey	near Stonewall, Texas/1908–1973	First president to be sworn in by a woman—Sarah Hughes, a Federal District Judge.
Richard M. Nixon 1969–1974	Rep.	Spiro T. Agnew Gerald R. Ford	Yorba Linda, Calif./1913–	Was the first president to resign from office.
Gerald R. Ford 1974–1977	Rep.	Nelson Rockefeller	Omaha, Nebraska/1913–	Was the first to become president without being elected.
Jimmy Carter 1977–1981	Dem.	Walter F. Mondale	Plains, Georgia/1924–	Was the first president to be born in a hospital—the Wise Clinic in Plains, Georgia.
Ronald Reagan 1981–1989	Rep.	George Bush	Tampico, Ill./1911–	Believed in knocking on wood for good luck.
George Bush 1989–	Rep.	J. Danforth Quayle	Milton, Mass./1924–	Played first-base for his Yale University baseball team.

FACTS ABOUT THE 50 STATES

State	Admitted into the Union	Capital	Area in Square Miles	Population 1980	Population 1988	Electoral Votes
Alabama (Ala.)	1819	Montgomery	51,609	3,890,061	4,102,000	9
Alaska	1959	Juneau	586,412	400,481	524,000	3
Arizona (Ariz.)	1912	Phoenix	113,909	2,717,866	3,489,000	7
Arkansas (Ark.)	1836	Little Rock	53,104	2,285,513	2,395,000	6
California (Calif.)	1850	Sacramento	158,693	23,668,562	28,314,000	47
Colorado (Colo.)	1876	Denver	104,247	2,888,834	3,301,000	8
Connecticut (Conn.)	1788	Hartford	5009	3,107,576	3,233,000	8
Delaware (Del.)	1787	Dover	2057	595,225	660,000	3
Florida (Fla.)	1845	Tallahassee	58,560	9,739,992	12,335,000	21
Georgia (Ga.)	1788	Atlanta	58,876	5,464,265	6,342,000	12
Hawaii	1959	Honolulu	6450	965,000	1,098,000	4
Idaho (Ida.)	1890	Boise	83,557	943,935	1,003,000	4
Illinois (Ill.)	1818	Springfield	56,400	11,418,461	11,614,000	24
Indiana (Ind.)	1816	Indianapolis	36,291	5,490,179	5,556,000	2
Iowa (Ia.)	1846	Des Moines	56,290	2,913,387	2,834,000	8
Kansas (Kans.)	1861	Topeka	82,264	2,363,208	2,495,000	7
Kentucky (Ken.)	1792	Frankfort	40,395	3,661,433	3,727,000	9
Louisiana (La.)	1812	Baton Rouge	48,523	4,203,972	4,408,000	10
Maine (Me.)	1820	Augusta	33,215	1,124,660	1,205,000	4
Maryland (Md.)	1788	Annapolis	10,577	4,216,446	4,622,000	10
Massachusetts (Mass.)	1788	Boston	8257	5,737,037	5,889,000	13
Michigan (Mich.)	1837	Lansing	58,216	9,258,344	9,240,000	20
Minnesota (Minn.)	1858	St. Paul	84,068	4,077,148	4,307,000	10
Mississippi (Miss.)	1817	Jackson	47,716	2,520,638	2,620,000	7
Missouri (Mo.)	1821	Jefferson City	69,686	4,917,444	5,141,000	11
Montana (Mont.)	1889	Helena	147,138	786,690	805,000	4

FACTS ABOUT THE 50 STATES

State	Admitted into the Union	Capital	Area in Square Miles	Population 1980	Population 1988	Electoral Votes
Nebraska (Neb.)	1867	Lincoln	77,227	1,570,006	1,602,000	5
Nevada (Nev.)	1864	Carson City	110,540	799,184	1,054,000	4
New Hampshire (N.H.)	1788	Concord	9404	920,610	1,085,000	4
New Jersey (N.J.)	1787	Trenton	7836	7,364,158	7,721,000	16
New Mexico (N.Mex.)	1912	Santa Fe	121,666	1,299,968	1,507,000	5
New York (N.Y.)	1788	Albany	49,576	17,557,288	17,909,000	36
North Carolina (N.C.)	1789	Raleigh	52,58	5,874,429	6,489,000	13
North Dakota (N.Dak.)	1889	Bismarck	70,665	652,695	667,000	3
Ohio	1803	Columbus	41,222	10,797,419	10,855,000	23
Oklahoma (Okla.)	1907	Oklahoma City	69,919	3,025,266	3,242,000	8
Oregon (Ore.)	1859	Salem	96,981	2,632,663	2,767,000	7
Pennsylvania (Penn.)	1787	Harrisburg	45,333	11,866,728	12,001,000	25
Rhode Island (R.I.)	1790	Providence	1214	947,154	993,000	4
South Carolina (S.C.)	1788	Columbia	31,055	3,119,208	3,470,000	8
South Dakota (S.Dak.)	1889	Pierre	77,047	690,178	713,000	3
Tennessee (Tenn.)	1796	Nashville	42,244	4,590,750	4,895,000	11
Texas (Tex.)	1845	Austin	267,339	14,228,383	16,841,000	29
Utah (Ut.)	1896	Salt Lake City	84,916	1,461,037	1,690,000	5
Vermont (Vt.)	1791	Montpelier	9609	511,456	557,000	3
Virginia (Va.)	1788	Richmond	40,817	5,346,279	6,015,000	12
Washington (Wash.)	1889	Olympia	68,192	4,130,163	4,648,000	10
West Virginia (W.Va.)	1863	Charleston	24,181	1,949,644	1,876,000	6
Wisconsin (Wis.)	1848	Madison	56,154	4,705,335	4,855,000	11
Wyoming (Wyo.)	1890	Cheyenne	97,914	470,816	479,000	3
District of Columbia		Washington	67	637,651	617,000	3

THE DECLARATION OF INDEPENDENCE

1. This is the preamble, or introduction, to the Declaration of Independence. Thomas Jefferson was the main author of the Declaration. Jefferson and the other American colonists believed that the time had come for them to break away from England and form their own nation. In the preamble, Jefferson writes that the colonists have a duty to state the reasons for their actions. He believes the colonists must explain to the world why they are declaring their independence from Britain.

2. In this section, Jefferson describes what he believes are the basic principles of democracy. This is perhaps the most meaningful part of the document. It is certainly the most well known. Jefferson believes that all people are born equal. That means they all have the same basic rights. The most important are "life, liberty, and the pursuit of happiness." People set up governments to protect these rights. Jefferson thought that governments should get their power by agreement of the people. This is different from previous types of government which got their authority from monarchs. Jefferson argues that when a government no longer protects the basic rights of the people, the people have a right to overthrow that government and set up a new one.

3. Jefferson adds that people do not change governments for minor reasons. In fact, they often put up with many abuses rather than change to something new and untried. But when a government grows too harsh and unjust, it becomes the people's duty to overthrow that government. The colonists believe that King George III has a long history of abusing his power. That is the reason why they are establishing a new government.

4. In the long section that follows, Jefferson lists 27 injustices committed by George III. Jefferson tries to blame the king for all the actions Britain has

1 When in the Course of human events, it becomes necessary for one people to dissolve the political bands which have connected them with another, and to assume among the Powers of the earth the separate and equal station to which the Laws of Nature and of Nature's God entitle them, a decent respect to the opinions of mankind requires that they should declare the causes which impel them to the separation.

2 We hold these truths to be self-evident, that all men are created equal, that they are endowed by their Creator with certain unalienable Rights, that among these are Life, Liberty and the pursuit of Happiness. That to secure these rights, Governments are instituted among Men, deriving their just powers from the consent of the governed. That whenever any Form of Government becomes destructive of these ends, it is the Right of the People to alter or to abolish it, and to institute new Government, laying its foundation on such principles and organizing its powers in such form, as to them shall seem most likely to effect their Safety and Happiness. Prudence, indeed, will dictate that Governments long established should not be changed

3 for light and transient causes; and accordingly all experience hath shown, that mankind are more disposed to suffer, while evils are sufferable, than to right themselves by abolishing the forms to which they are accustomed. But when a long train of abuses and usurpations pursuing invariably the same Object evinces a design to reduce them under absolute Despotism, it is their right, it is their duty, to throw off such Government, and to provide new Guards for their future security. —Such has been the patient sufferance of these Colonies: and such is now the necessity which constrains them to alter their former Systems of

4 Government. The history of the present King of Great Britain is a history of repeated injuries and usurpations, all having in direct object the establishment of an absolute Tyranny over these States. To prove this, let Facts be submitted to a candid world.

5 He has refused his Assent to Laws, the most wholesome and necessary for the public good.

He has forbidden his Governors to pass Laws of immediate and pressing importance, unless suspended in their operation till his Assent should be obtained: and when so suspended, he has utterly neglected to attend to them.

He has refused to pass other Laws for the accommodation of large districts of people, unless those people would relinquish the right of Representation in the Legislature, a right inestimable to them and formidable to tyrants only.

He has called together legislative bodies at places unusual, uncomfortable, and distant from the depository of their Public Records, for the sole purpose of fatiguing them into compliance with his measures.

He has dissolved Representative Houses repeatedly, for opposing with manly firmness his invasions on the rights of the people.

He has refused for a long time, after such dissolutions, to cause others to be elected: whereby the Legislative Powers, incapable of Annihilation, have returned to the People at large for their exercise: the State remaining in the mean time exposed to all the dangers of invasion from without, and convulsions within.

He has endeavoured to prevent the population of these States: for thát purpose obstructing the Laws for Naturalization of Foreigners: refusing to pass others to encourage their migration hither, and raising the conditions of new Appropriations of Lands.

He has obstructed the Administration of Justice, by refusing his Assent to Laws for establishing Judiciary Powers.

He has made Judges dependent on his Will alone, for the tenure of their offices, and the amount and payment of their salaries.

He has erected a multitude of New Offices, and sent hither swarms of Officers to harass our People, and eat out their substance.

He has kept among us, in times of peace, Standing Armies without the Consent of our legislatures.

He has affected to render the Military independent of and superior to the Civil Power.

5 taken against its American colonies. George III is accused of deliberately trying to destroy the colonists' rights and government.

5. Jefferson begins by describing how George III has unjustly used his power. Jefferson blames the king for trying to control the colonial legislatures. George III is accused of not approving necessary laws passed by the colonists. He has dismissed assemblies that disobeyed royal governors. He has forced the colonial legislatures to meet in unusual and distant places. And he has not called for elections to replace the colonial assemblies which he has dismissed.

6 6. Here Jefferson accuses the king of prohibiting the American colonists from moving west and settling the new land. Also, George III has prevented justice from being done. He has insisted that judges serve only as long as he was pleased with them. Finally, he has annoyed the colonists by keeping British troops in America after the end of the French and Indian War. And he has sent large numbers of customs officials to harass them.

7. Jefferson then describes how the king has joined with others, meaning Parliament, to control the colonies. The colonists always argued that Parliament had no right to make laws for them because they were not represented in it. This argument was challenged by passage of the Declaratory Act in 1766. This act stated that the king and Parliament had total authority over the colonists. Still, many colonists continued to argue that Parliament had no right to tax them. Among the later actions of Parliament which angered the colonists was the Quebec Act, which kept French civil law in Quebec. Other unjust acts included the Quartering Act and the blockade of colonial ports.

7 He has combined with others to subject us to a jurisdiction foreign to our constitution, and unacknowledged by our laws: giving his Assent to their acts of pretended legislation:

For quartering large bodies of armed troops among us:

For protecting them, by mock Trial, from Punishment for any Murders which they should commit on the Inhabitants of these States:

For cutting off our Trade with all parts of the world:

For imposing taxes on us without our Consent:

For depriving us, in many cases, of the benefits of Trial by Jury:

For transporting us beyond Seas to be tried for pretended offences:

For abolishing the free System of English Laws in a neighbouring Province, establishing therein an Arbitrary government and enlarging its Boundaries so as to render it at once an example and fit instrument for introducing the same absolute rule into these Colonies:

For taking away our Charters, abolishing our most valuable Laws, and altering fundamentally the Forms of our Governments:

For suspending our own Legislatures, and declaring themselves invested with Power to legislate for us in all cases whatsoever.

8. In this section, Jefferson describes the warlike actions of the king. Instead of helping the colonists and protecting them, he has waged war on them. He has restricted their trade with other nations. He has hired foreign troops and sent them to America to fight against the colonists. He has encouraged the slaves in America to revolt against their masters. And he has persuaded Native Americans to attack settlers on the frontier.

8 He has abdicated Government here, by declaring us out of his Protection and waging War against us.

He has plundered our seas, ravaged our Coasts, burnt our towns, and destroyed the lives of our people.

He is at this time transporting large Armies of foreign Mercenaries to compleat the works of death, desolation and tyranny, already begun with circumstances of Cruelty & perfidy scarcely paralleled in the most barbarous ages, and totally unworthy the Head of a civilized nation.

He has constrained our fellow Citizens taken Captive on the high Seas to bear Arms against their Country, to become the executioners of their friends and Brethren, or to fall themselves by their Hands.

He has excited domestic insurrections amongst us, and has endeavoured to bring on the inhabitants of our

AMERICAN ADVENTURES

frontiers, the merciless Indian Savages whose known **8**
rule of warfare, is an undistinguished destruction of all
ages, sexes and conditions.

In every stage of these Oppressions We have **9**
Petitioned for Redress in the most humble terms: Our
repeated Petitions have been answered only by repeated injury. A Prince, whose character is thus marked by
every act which may define a Tyrant, is unfit to be the
ruler of a free People.

Nor have We been wanting in attentions to our
British brethren. We have warned them from time to
time of attempts by their legislature to extend an
unwarrantable jurisdiction over us. We have reminded
them of the circumstances of our emigration and settlement here. We have appealed to their native justice
and magnanimity, and we have conjured them by the
ties of our common kindred to disavow these usurpations, which would inevitably interrupt our connections
and correspondence. They too have been deaf to the
voice of justice and of consanguinity. We must, therefore, acquiesce in the necessity, which denounces our
Separation, and hold them, as we hold the rest of
mankind, Enemies in War, in Peace Friends.

We, therefore, the Representatives of the United
States of America, in General Congress, Assembled, **10**
appealing to the Supreme Judge of the world for the
rectitude of our intentions, do, in the Name, and by
Authority of the good People of these Colonies,
solemnly publish and declare, That these United
Colonies are, and of Right ought to be, Free and
Independent States; that they are Absolved from all
Allegiance to the British Crown, and that all political
connection between them and the State of Great
Britain, is and ought to be totally dissolved; and that as
Free and Independent States, they have full Power to
levy War, conclude Peace, contract Alliances, establish
Commerce, and to do all other Acts and Things which
Independent States may of right do. And for the sup-
port of this Declaration, with a firm reliance on the
Protection of Divine Providence, we mutually pledge
to each other our Lives, our Fortunes and our sacred
Honor.

9. During this time, the colonists have peacefully tried to resolve the conflict. They have repeatedly asked for relief only to receive further suffering. They even asked the British people for help, but to no avail. Therefore, the colonists now believe that they have no choice but to separate and form their own nation.

10. In this final section, the colonists formally declare their independence from Britain. The signers of this document are representatives of the people of the United States and are acting with their consent. They declare that the colonies no longer have any connection to Great Britain and are totally independent states. These states can now make war and sign treaties. And the signers promise their lives, money, and honor to defend their independence.

THE CONSTITUTION OF THE UNITED STATES OF AMERICA

1. The Preamble is the opening of the Constitution. It states the purpose of the Constitution and describes the type of government to be set up. It also explains the goals to be achieved.

2. Congress has the power to make all federal laws. It is divided into a Senate and a House of Representatives.

3. Members of the House of Representatives are elected every two years. Representatives must be at least 25 years old. They also have to live in the state which they represent.

4. The number of Representatives each state receives is based on its population. Therefore a census is taken every ten years to determine each state's population. At first, each state received a Representative for every 30,000 people. Since 1929, the total number of Representatives in the House has been fixed at 435. Each state is entitled to at least one Representative. The 16th Amendment changed the collection of direct taxes. The 3/5 reference to slaves was canceled by the 13th and 14th Amendments.

5. When a House member dies or resigns, that state's governor must call a special election to fill the vacant seat. The House has the right to elect its own officers, including a Speaker, or spokesperson. The House has the power to impeach, or formally accuse, a federal official of wrongdoing.

6. Each state shall have two Senators who serve for six-year terms. The 17th Amendment changed the way that Senators are chosen. Now they are elected by the people of the state.

7. One third of the Senate is elected every two years. The 17th Amendment changed the way vacancies are filled. Today the governor of the state may choose a replacement until an election can take place. All Senators must be at least 30 years old and residents of the states they represent.

1 **Preamble.** We, the people of the United States, in order to form a more perfect Union, establish justice, insure domestic tranquility, provide for the common defense, promote the general welfare, and secure the blessings of liberty to ourselves and our posterity, do ordain and establish this Constitution for the United States of America.

2 **Article I.** Section 1. All legislative powers herein granted shall be vested in a Congress of the United States, which shall consist of a Senate and a House of Representatives.

3 **Section 2.** The House of Representatives shall be composed of members chosen every second year by the people of the several states; and the electors in each state shall have the qualifications requisite for electors of the most numerous branch of the state legislature.

No person shall be a Representative who shall not have attained the age of twenty-five years, and been seven years a citizen of the United States, and who shall not, when elected, be an inhabitant of that state in which he shall be chosen.

4 Representatives ~~and direct taxes~~ shall be apportioned among the several states which may be included within this Union, according to their respective numbers, ~~which shall be determined by adding to the whole number of free persons, including those bound to service for a term of years, and excluding Indians not taxed, three fifths of all other persons.~~ The actual enumeration shall be made within three years after the first meeting of the Congress of the United States, and within every subsequent term of ten years, in such manner as they shall by law direct. The number of Representatives shall not exceed one for every 30,000, but each State shall have at least one Representative, ~~and until such enumeration shall be made, the State of New Hampshire shall be entitled to choose three, Massachusetts eight, Rhode Island and Providence Plantations one, Connecticut five, New York six, New Jersey four, Pennsylvania eight, Delaware one, Maryland six, Virginia ten, North Carolina five, South Carolina five, and Georgia three.~~

5 When vacancies happen in the representation from any state, the executive authority thereof shall issue writs of election to fill such vacancies.

The House of Representatives shall choose their Speaker and other officers; and shall have the sole power of impeachment.

6 **Section 3.** The Senate of the United States shall be composed of two Senators from each State, chosen ~~by the legislature thereof,~~ for six years; and each Senator shall have one vote.

7 ~~Immediately after they shall be assembled, in consequence of the first election,~~ they shall be divided as equally as may be into three classes. ~~The seats of the Senators of the first class shall be vacated at the expiration of the second year, of the second class at the expiration of the fourth year, and of the third class at the expiration of the sixth year,~~ so that one third may be chosen every second year; ~~and if vacancies happen by resignation, or otherwise, during the recess of the legislature of any State, the Executive thereof may make temporary appointments until the next meeting of the legislature, which shall then fill such vacancies.~~

No person shall be a Senator who shall not have attained the age of 30 years, and been nine years a citizen of the United States, and who shall not, when elected, be an inhabitant of that state for which he shall be chosen.

8 The Vice-President of the United States shall be President of the Senate, but shall have no vote, unless they be equally divided.

[1] Those parts of the U.S. Constitution which are no longer applicable or have been changed by ammendments are marked through.

The Senate shall choose their other officers, and also a President *Pro Tempore*, in the absence of the Vice-President, or when he shall exercise the office of President of the United States.

The Senate shall have the sole power to try all impeachments. When sitting for that purpose, they shall be on oath or affirmation. When the President of the United States is tried, the Chief Justice shall preside: and no person shall be convicted without the concurrence of two thirds of the members present.

Judgment in cases of impeachment shall not extend further than to removal from office, and disqualification to hold and enjoy any office of honor, trust, or profit, under the United States; but the party convicted shall nevertheless be liable and subject to indictment, trial, judgment, and punishment according to law.

Section 4. The times, places and manner of holding elections for Senators and Representatives, shall be prescribed in each state by the legislature thereof; but the Congress may at any time by law make or alter such regulations, except as to the places of choosing Senators.

The Congress shall assemble at least once in every year, and such meeting shall be on the first Monday in December, unless they shall by law appoint a different day.

Section 5. Each House shall be the judge of the elections, returns, and qualifications of its own members, and a majority of each shall constitute a quorum to do business; but a smaller number may adjourn from day to day, and may be authorized to compel the attendance of absent members, in such manner, and under such penalties, as each House may provide.

Each House may determine the rules of its proceedings, punish its members for disorderly behavior, and, with the concurrence of two thirds, expel a member.

Each House shall keep a journal of its proceedings, and from time to time publish the same, excepting such parts as may, in their judgment, require secrecy; and the yeas and nays of the members of either House on any question, shall, at the desire of one fifth of those present, be entered on the journal.

Neither House, during the session of Congress, shall, without the consent of the other, adjourn for more than three days, nor to any other place than that in which the two Houses shall be sitting.

Section 6. The Senators and Representatives shall receive a compensation for their services, to be ascertained by law, and paid out of the Treasury of the United States. They shall, in all cases, except treason, felony, and breach of the peace, be privileged from arrest during their attendance at the session of their respective Houses, and in going to, and returning from, the same; and for any speech or debate in either House, they shall not be questioned in any other place.

No Senator or Representative shall, during the time for which he was elected, be appointed to any civil office under the authority of the United States, which shall have been created, or the emoluments whereof shall have been increased during such time; and no person holding any office under the United States, shall be a member of either House during his continuance in office.

Section 7. All bills for raising revenue shall originate in the House of Representatives; but the Senate may propose or concur with amendments as on other bills.

Every bill which shall have passed the House of Representatives and the Senate, shall, before it becomes a law, be presented to the President of the United States; if he approves he shall sign it, but if not he shall return

8. The Vice-President of the United States serves as President, or chairperson, of the Senate. However, he or she can only vote to break a tie. The Senate chooses all its other officers.

9. The Senate has the power to try federal officials after the House has accused them. The person on trial has the same legal rights as any person on trial. Two-thirds of the Senate must find the person guilty for conviction. Punishment is limited to removal from office. But the convicted person can then be tried in a normal court of law.

10. Each state can make its own rules about elections for Congress. But Congress has the right to change these state election laws. Congress must meet at least once each year. The 20th Amendment moved the opening date of Congress to January 3.

11. Both the House of Representatives and Senate can refuse to seat members. Neither house can conduct business unless half its members are present. Each house can make rules for the conduct of its members. Each house must keep a written record of its business. Neither house can recess for more than three days without the consent of the other.

12. Each member of Congress is paid a salary by the U.S. Treasury. Members set their own pay. No member of Congress can be arrested while serving in Congress. And no member of Congress can hold another office in the U.S. government while serving in Congress.

13. All bills, or proposed laws, for raising money through taxes must be introduced in the House of Representatives. Any bill that passes both houses of Congress is sent to the President. If the President signs the bill, it becomes law. If the President does not like the bill, the President can veto, or refuse to sign, the bill. The bill is then sent back to Congress. Congress can either drop the bill or try to pass it over the President's veto. To override the President's veto, two-thirds of both houses of Congress need to approve the bill.

14. This section states the powers granted to Congress. Congress may collect taxes to pay the nation's debt and provide for the security and welfare of the country. All federal taxes must be the same throughout the nation. Congress can borrow money. It has the right to control trade, transportation, and communication between the various states and with foreign nations. Congress can decide how immigrants become citizens. It has the power to coin money and set its value, and determine how people who make fake money shall be punished. Congress may also establish post offices, patent and copyright laws, and national courts.

15. Congress can define the punishment for people who commit crimes against ships at sea. Only Congress has the right to declare war. It has the power to determine the size of the armed forces and how much money is spent on maintaining them. Congress may call up the state militias for federal service. Today the militias are called the National Guard.

13

it, with his objections, to that House in which it shall have originated, who shall enter the objections at large on their journal, and proceed to reconsider it. If after such reconsideration two thirds of that House shall agree to pass the bill, it shall be sent, together with the objections, to the other House, by which it shall likewise be reconsidered, and if approved by two thirds of that House, it shall become a law. But in all such cases the votes of both Houses shall be determined by yeas and nays, and the names of the persons voting for and against the bill shall be entered on the journal of each House respectively. If any bill shall not be returned by the President within 10 days (Sundays excepted) after it shall have been presented to him, the same shall be a law in like manner as if he had signed it, unless the Congress by their adjournment prevent its return, in which case it shall not be a law.

Every order, resolution, or vote, to which the concurrence of the Senate and House of Representatives may be necessary (except on a question of adjournment), shall be presented to the President of the United States; and before the same shall take effect, shall be approved by him, or being disapproved by him, shall be repassed by two thirds of the Senate and House of Representatives, according to the rules and limitations prescribed in the case of a bill.

Section 8. The Congress shall have power

To lay and collect taxes, duties, imposts and excises, to pay the debts, and provide for the common defense and general welfare of the United States; but all duties, imposts, and excises shall be uniform throughout the United States;

To borrow money on the credit of the United States;

To regulate commerce with foreign nations, and among the several states, and with the Indian tribes;

To establish an uniform rule of naturalization, and uniform laws on the subject of bankruptcies throughout the United States;

To coin money, regulate the value thereof, and of foreign coin, and fix the standard of weights and measures;

To provide for the punishment of counterfeiting the securities and current coin of the United States;

To establish post-offices and post-roads;

To promote the progress of science and useful arts, by securing, for limited times, to authors and inventors, the exclusive right to their respective writings and discoveries;

To constitute tribunals inferior to the Supreme Court;

To define and punish piracies and felonies committed on the high seas, and offences against the law of nations;

To declare war, grant letters of marque and reprisal, and make rules concerning captures on land and water;

To raise and support armies: but no appropriation of money to that use shall be for a longer term than two years;

To provide and maintain a navy;

To make rules for the government and regulation of the land and naval forces;

To provide for calling forth the militia to execute the laws of the Union, suppress insurrections and repel invasions;

To provide for organizing, arming, and disciplining the militia, and for governing such part of them as may be employed in the service of the United States, reserving to the states respectively, the appointment of the officers, and the authority of training the militia according to the discipline prescribed by Congress;

14

15

To exercise exclusive legislation, in all cases whatsoever, over such district (not exceeding ten miles square) as may, by cession of particular states, and the acceptance of Congress, become the seat of the government of the United States, and to exercise like authority over all places purchased by the consent of the legislature of the State in which the same shall be, for the erection of forts, magazines, arsenals, dock-yards, and other needful buildings. And,

To make all laws which shall be necessary and proper for carrying into execution the foregoing powers, and all other powers vested by this Constitution in the government of the United States, or in any department or officer thereof.

Section 9. The migration or importation of such persons as any of the States now existing shall think proper to admit, shall not be prohibited by the Congress prior to the year one thousand eight hundred and eight; but a tax or duty may be imposed on such importation, not exceeding ten dollars for each person.

The privilege of the writ of *habeas corpus* shall not be suspended, unless when in cases of rebellion or invasion the public safety may require it.

No bill of attainder or *ex post facto* law shall be passed.

No capitation, or other direct tax, shall be laid, unless in proportion to the census or enumeration herein before directed to be taken.

No tax or duty shall be laid on articles exported from any state.

No preference shall be given by any regulation of commerce or revenue to the ports of one state over those of another; nor shall vessels bound to, or from, one state be obliged to enter, clear, or pay duties in another.

No money shall be drawn from the treasury, but in consequence of appropriations made by law; and a regular statement and account of the receipts and expenditures of all public money shall be published from time to time.

No title of nobility shall be granted by the United States; and no person holding any office of profit or trust under them, shall, without the consent of the Congress, accept of any present, emolument, office, or title of any kind whatever, from any king, prince, or foreign state.

Section 10. No state shall enter into any treaty, alliance, or confederation; grant letters of marque and reprisal; coin money; emit bills of credit; make any thing but gold and silver coin a tender in payment of debts; pass any bill of attainder, *ex post facto* law, or law impairing the obligation of contracts, or grant any title of nobility.

No state shall, without the consent of the Congress, lay any imposts or duties on imports or exports, except what may be absolutely necessary for executing its inspection laws; and the net produce of all duties and imposts, laid by any state on imports or exports, shall be for the use of the treasury of the United States; and all such laws shall be subject to the revision and control of the Congress. No state shall, without the consent of Congress, lay any duty of tonnage, keep troops, or ships of war, in time of peace, enter into any agreement or compact with another state, or with a foreign power, or engage in war, unless actually invaded, or in such imminent danger as will not admit of delay.

Article II. Section 1. The executive power shall be vested in a President of the United States of America. He shall hold his office during the term of four years, and together with the Vice-President, chosen for the same term, be elected as follows:

Each state shall appoint, in such manner as the legislature thereof may direct, a number of electors equal to the whole number of Senators and

16 **16. Congress controls the District of Columbia, which includes the national capital. Congress also has the right to make all laws necessary to carry out the other powers granted to the national government by the Constitution. This clause was included to insure that Congress could adapt to the changing needs of the nation.**

17 **17. This section includes all the powers denied to Congress. This paragraph states that Congress could not outlaw the slave trade before 1808. It was abolished in that year.**

18

18. All prisoners must be told why they are being held, and no one shall be imprisoned unlawfully. No person can be punished for committing an act before that act became unlawful. The clause about direct taxes was changed by the 16th Amendment. No taxes can be placed on goods exported from any state. And no law can be passed favoring one state over another in trade. The federal government can only spend money if Congress approves it. No titles of nobility can be granted.

19 **19. This section includes all the powers denied to the states. No state can enter into a treaty with a foreign government or coin its own money. Like the federal government, no state can unlawfully imprison a person. States cannot tax imports or exports without the consent of Congress. No state can keep an army or navy without the consent of Congress or make war unless invaded.**

20 **20. The President is responsible for carrying out the laws passed by Congress. The President and Vice-President are elected every four years.**

21

21. The President and Vice-President are chosen by special electors from each state. The number of Presidential electors each state receives is equal to the number of Senators and Representatives that state has in Congress. Each state may decide how to select its electors. No federal official or member of Congress can serve as an elector. The 12th Amendment changed the way that the President and Vice-President are selected. Now each elector votes for one candidate for President and another for Vice-President. Congress has set the first Tuesday after the first Monday of November as the day each state chooses it Presidential electors.

22. The President must be a citizen of the U.S. by birth and at least 35 years old. If for some reason the Presidency becomes vacant, the Vice-President becomes President. The 25th Amendment deals with a President's inability to perform his or her duties. Presidents are paid a fixed salary for their entire term. Before taking office, the President must promise to defend the Constitution.

23. This section deals with the powers of the President. The President is the Commander in Chief of the Armed Forces. The President may order written reports from Cabinet officers and pardon persons convicted

21 Representatives to which the state may be entitled in the Congress; but no Senator or Representative, or person holding an office of trust or profit under the United States, shall be appointed an elector.

~~The electors shall meet in their respective States, and vote by ballot for two persons, of whom one at least shall not be an inhabitant of the same State with themselves. And they shall make a list of all the persons voted for, and of the number of votes for each; which list they shall sign and certify, and transmit sealed to the seat of the government of the United States, directed to the President of the Senate. The President of the Senate shall, in the presence of the Senate and House of Representatives, open all the certificates, and the votes shall then be counted. The person having the greatest number of votes shall be the President, if such number be a majority of the whole number of electors appointed; and if there be more than one who have such majority, and have an equal number of votes, then the House of Representatives shall immediately choose by ballot one of them for President; and if no person have a majority, then from the five highest on the list the said House shall in like manner choose the President. But in choosing the President, the votes shall be taken by States, the representation from each State having one vote; a quorum for this purpose shall consist of a member or members from two thirds of the States, and a majority of all the States shall be necessary to a choice. In every case, after the choice of the President, the person having the greatest number of votes of the electors shall be the Vice-President. But if there should remain two or more who have equal votes, the Senate shall choose from them by ballot the Vice-President.~~

The Congress may determine the time of choosing the electors, and the day on which they shall give their votes; which day shall be the same throughout the United States.

22 No person except a natural-born citizen, ~~or a citizen of the United States, at the time of the adoption of this Constitution,~~ shall be eligible to the office of President; neither shall any person be eligible to that office who shall not have attained the age of thirty-five years, and been fourteen years a resident within the United States.

In case of the removal of the President from office, or of his death, resignation, or inability to discharge the powers and duties of the said office, the same shall devolve on the Vice-President, and the Congress may by law provide for the case of removal, death, resignation, or inability, both of the President and Vice-President, declaring what officer shall then act as President, and such officer shall act accordingly until the disability be removed, or a President shall be elected.

The President shall, at stated times, receive for his services, a compensation, which shall neither be increased nor diminished during the period for which he shall have been elected, and he shall not receive within that period any other emolument from the United States or any of them.

Before he enter on the execution of his office, he shall take the following oath or affirmation:

"I do solemnly swear (or affirm) that I will faithfully execute the office of President of the United States, and will, to the best of my ability, preserve, protect, and defend the Constitution of the United States."

23 **Section 2.** The President shall be Commander-in-Chief of the Army and Navy of the United States, and of the militia of the several states, when called into the actual service of the United States; he may require the opinion, in writing, of the principal officer in each of the executive departments, upon any subject relating to the duties of their respective offices, and he shall have power to grant reprieves and pardons for offenses against the United States, except in cases of impeachment.

He shall have power, by and with the advice and consent of the Senate, to make treaties, provided two-thirds of the Senators present concur; and he shall nominate, and by and with the advice and consent of the Senate, shall appoint ambassadors, other public ministers and consuls, judges of the Supreme Court, and all other officers of the United States, whose appointments are not herein otherwise provided for, and which shall be established by law. But the Congress may by law vest the appointment of such inferior officers, as they think proper, in the President alone, in the courts of law, or in the heads of departments.

The President shall have power to fill up all vacancies that may happen during the recess of the Senate, by granting commissions which shall expire at the end of their next session.

Section 3. He shall, from time to time, give to the Congress information of the state of the Union, and recommend to their consideration such measures as he shall judge necessary and expedient. He may, on extraordinary occasions, convene both Houses, or either of them; and in case of disagreement between them, with respect to the time of adjournment, he may adjourn them to such time as he shall think proper. He shall receive ambassadors and other public ministers. He shall take care that the laws be faithfully executed; and shall commission all the officers of the United States.

Section 4. The President, Vice-President, and all civil officers of the United States, shall be removed from office on impeachment for, and conviction of, treason, bribery, or other high crimes and misdemeanors.

Article III. Section 1. The judicial power of the United States shall be vested in one Supreme Court, and in such inferior courts as the Congress may, from time to time, ordain and establish. The judges, both of the Supreme and inferior courts, shall hold their offices during good behavior; and shall, at stated times, receive for their services, a compensation, which shall not be diminished during their continuance in office.

Section 2. The judicial power shall extend to all cases, in law and equity, arising under this Constitution, the laws of the United States, and treaties made, or which shall be made, under their authority; to all cases affecting ambassadors, other public ministers, and consuls; to all cases of admiralty and maritime jurisdiction; to controversies to which the United States shall be a party; to controversies between two or more states, between a state and citizens of another state, between citizens of different states, between citizens of the same state claiming lands under grants of different states, and between a state, or the citizens thereof, and foreign states, citizens, or subjects.

In all cases affecting ambassadors, other public ministers and consuls, and those in which a state shall be party, the Supreme Court shall have original jurisdiction. In all the other cases before mentioned, the Supreme Court shall have appellate jurisdiction, both as to law and fact, with such exceptions, and under such regulations, as the Congress shall make.

The trial of all crimes, except in cases of impeachment, shall be by jury; and such trial shall be held in the State where the said crimes shall have been committed; but when not committed within any state, the trial shall be at such place or places as the Congress may by law have directed.

Section 3. Treason against the United States, shall consist only in levying war against them, or in adhering to their enemies, giving them aid and comfort. No person shall be convicted of treason unless on the testimony of two witnesses to the same overt act, or on confession in open court.

23 of federal crimes. The President can make treaties with foreign governments, but they must be approved by two-thirds of the Senate. The President chooses judges for the Supreme Court and other high officials. They must also be approved by the Senate. The President can make temporary appointments to federal offices when the Senate is not in session.

24 **24.** Every year, the President must give to Congress a report on the state of the nation. The President can call a special session of Congress if necessary. The President, or any other high government official, can be removed from office for any major wrongdoing.

25 **25.** The Supreme Court is the final authority in matters of law. Congress can also set up other lesser national courts. Federal judges hold their office for life unless proven guilty of any wrongdoing. Their pay cannot be lowered during their term in office.

26 **26.** The federal courts settle disputes concerning the Constitution and conflicts between the U.S. and other nations. They also settle legal questions of U.S. law and problems between citizens of various states. The 11th Amendment prohibited residents of one state from suing another state. Most of the cases appearing before the Supreme Court begin in the lower courts. All trials must be tried in the state where the crime originally occurred. The Supreme Court determines if those cases were tried correctly.

27 **27.** A person can only be convicted of treason for actions committed against the United States. A person cannot be convicted of treason for thinking treasonous thoughts.

Congress has the right to set the punishment for traitors. The family of convicted traitors cannot be punished.

27 | The Congress shall have power to declare the punishment of treason, but no attainder of treason shall work corruption of blood, or forfeiture, except during the life of the person attainted.

28. Each state must recognize the legal actions and official records of every other state. Persons who move to another state must be treated the same way as the citizens of that state. A person charged with a crime, who flees to another state, must be returned to the state where the crime was committed. The clause referring to the return of fugitive slaves was canceled by the 13th Amendment.

28 | **Article IV. Section 1.** Full faith and credit shall be given in each state to the public acts, records, and judicial proceedings of every other state. And the Congress may by general laws prescribe the manner in which such acts, records, and proceedings shall be proved, and the effect thereof.

Section 2. The citizens of each state shall be entitled to all privileges and immunities of citizens in the several states.

A person charged in any state with treason, felony, or other crime, who shall flee from justice, and be found in another state, shall, on demand of the executive authority of the state from which he fled, be delivered up to be removed to the state having jurisdiction of the crime.

~~No person held to service or labor in one state, under the laws thereof, escaping into another, shall, in consequence of any laws or regulation therein, be discharged from such service or labour, but shall be delivered up on claim of the party to whom such service or labour may be due.~~

29. Congress has the power to control all land belonging to the United States. It has the right to govern the Western territories and create new states. No new state can be made from part of an existing state without that state's consent. New states will be equal to the existing states. Every state will be guaranteed a republican form of government and protection from foreign invasion.

29 | **Section 3.** New states may be admitted by the Congress into this Union; but no new state shall be formed or erected within the jurisdiction of any other state; nor any state be formed by the junction of two or more states, or parts of states, without the consent of the legislatures of the states concerned, as well as of the Congress.

The Congress shall have power to dispose of and make all needful rules and regulations respecting the territory or other property belonging to the United States; and nothing in this Constitution shall be so construed as to prejudice any claims of the United States, or of any particular state.

Section 4. The United States shall guarantee to every state in this Union a republican form of government, and shall protect each of them against invasion; and on application of the legislature, or of the executive (when the legislature cannot be convened), against domestic violence.

30. The Constitution can be changed, if necessary, by adding amendments. Three-fourths of all the states need to approve a proposed amendment. No amendment can deprive a state of its equal representation in the Senate.

30 | **Article V.** The Congress, whenever two thirds of both Houses shall deem it necessary, shall propose amendments to this Constitution, or, on the application of the legislatures of two thirds of the several states, shall call a convention for proposing amendments, which, in either case, shall be valid to all intents and purposes, as part of this Constitution, when ratified by the legislatures of three fourths of the several states, or by conventions in three fourths thereof, as the one or the other mode of ratification may be proposed by the Congress; provided ~~that no amendment, which may be made prior to the year one thousand eight hundred and eight, shall in any manner affect the first and fourth clauses in the ninth section of the first article; and~~ that no state, without its consent, shall be deprived of its equal suffrage in the Senate.

31. The United States promises to pay all debts incurred by any previous government. The Constitution and all federal laws and treaties are the supreme law of the land. They have priority over any state laws that conflict with them. All federal and state officials must promise to support the Constitution. The Constitution became the supreme law of the land after nine of the original thirteen states approved it.

31 | **Article VI.** All debts contracted, and engagements entered into, before the adoption of this Constitution, shall be as valid against the United States, under this Constitution, as under the confederation.

This Constitution and the laws of the United States which shall be made in pursuance thereof, and all treaties made, or which shall be made, under the authority of the United States, shall be the supreme law of the land; and the judges, in every state, shall be bound thereby, any thing in the constitution or laws of any state to the contrary notwithstanding.

The Senators and Representatives before mentioned, and the members of the several state legislatures, and all executive and judicial officers, both of the United States and of the several states, shall be bound, by oath or affirmation, to support this Constitution; but no religious test shall ever be required as a qualification to any office or public trust under the United States.

~~Article VII. The ratification of the conventions of nine States, shall be sufficient for the establishment of this Constitution between the States so ratifying the same.~~

TEN ORIGINAL AMENDMENTS: **THE BILL OF RIGHTS**
(These first 10 amendments were adopted in 1791.)

Article I. Congress shall make no law respecting an establishment of religion, or prohibiting the free exercise thereof; or abridging the freedom of speech, or of the press; or the right of the people peaceably to assemble, and to petition the government for a redress of grievances.

Article II. A well regulated militia being necessary to the security of a free state, the right of the people to keep and bear arms shall not be infringed.

Article III. No soldier shall, in time of peace, be quartered in any house without the consent of the owner; nor in time of war, but in a manner to be prescribed by law.

Article IV. The right of the people to be secure in their persons, houses, papers, and effects, against unreasonable searches and seizures, shall not be violated; and no warrants shall issue, but upon probable cause, supported by oath or affirmation, and particularly describing the place to be searched, and the persons or things to be seized.

Article V. No person shall be held to answer for a capital or otherwise infamous crime, unless on a presentment or indictment of a grand jury, except in cases arising in the land or naval forces, or in the militia, when in actual service, in time of war or public danger; nor shall any person be subject for the same offenses to be twice put in jeopardy of life or limb; nor shall be compelled, in any criminal case, to be witness against himself; nor be deprived of life, liberty, or property, without due process of law; nor shall private property be taken for public use without just compensation.

Article VI. In all criminal prosecutions the accused shall enjoy the right to a speedy and public trial, by an impartial jury of the state and district wherein the crime shall have been committed, which district shall have been previously ascertained by law, and to be informed of the nature and cause of the accusation; to be confronted with the witnesses against him; to have compulsory process for obtaining witnesses in his favor; and to have the assistance of counsel for his defense.

Article VII. In suits at common law, where the value of controversy shall exceed twenty dollars, the right of trial by jury shall be preserved; and no fact tried by a jury shall be otherwise re-examined in any court of the United States than according to the rules of the common law.

Article VIII. Excessive bail shall not be required, nor excessive fines imposed, nor cruel and unusual punishments inflicted.

Article IX. The enumeration in the Constitution of certain rights, shall not be construed to deny or disparage others retained by the people.

Article X. The powers not delegated to the United States by the Constitution, nor prohibited by it to the states, are reserved to the states respectively or to the people.

AMENDMENTS SINCE THE BILL OF RIGHTS

Article XI *(1798).* The judicial power of the United States shall not be construed to extend to any suit in law or equity, commenced or prosecuted against one of the United States by citizens of any state, or by citizens or subjects of any foreign state.

Article XII *(1804).* The electors shall meet in their respective states, and

31

32 **32. The first ten amendments grant basic human freedoms. The people have the right to freedom of religion, speech, the press, assembly, and petition. The states have the right to keep armed militias for protection. No individual can be forced to keep soldiers in his or her home against his or her will. And no government official can enter a person's home without showing reasonable cause that a crime has been committed.**

33 **33. All persons accused of a crime have the right to a fair and speedy trial. The government must formally charge someone with a crime before they can be brought to trial. Individuals cannot be tried twice for the same crime, and they cannot be forced to give testimony against themselves. In lawsuits of more than twenty dollars, the people involved have the right to a trial by jury. Excessive punishments cannot be given.**

34 **34. The people have rights that are not mentioned in the Constitution. The powers not given to the federal government are reserved to the states, or to the people.**

35 **35. A citizen of one state cannot sue another state in federal court.**

36

36

36. This amendment changed the way Presidential electors vote for the President and Vice-President. Now the electors vote for only one candidate in each office. If no candidate receives a majority of electoral votes, Congress decides the election. The House of Representatives selects the President and the Senate chooses the Vice-President. The Vice-President must meet the requirements needed for the Presidency.

37

37. These three amendments abolish slavery and protect the rights of all American citizens. They were passed following the Civil War. Any person who was born in the United States or who has been a naturalized citizen is a citizen of the United States. No state can take away the rights of a United States citizen. Many Confederate leaders were prohibited from holding office, but by 1872, most were allowed to return to political life. No United States citizen can be denied the right to vote on the basis of their race or color. The 19th Amendment changed this to include women as well. The 26th Amendment modified this to include all citizens over the age of eighteen.

vote by ballot for President and Vice-President, one of whom, at least, shall not be an inhabitant of the same state with themselves; they shall name in their ballots the person voted for as President, and in distinct ballots the person voted for as Vice-President; and they shall make distinct lists of all persons voted for as President, and of all persons voted for as Vice-President, and of the number of Votes for each, which list they shall sign and certify, and transmit, sealed, to the seat of the government of the United States, directed to the President of the Senate; the President of the Senate shall, in the presence of the Senate and House of Representatives, open all the certificates, and the votes shall then be counted. The person having the greatest number of votes for President shall be the President, if such number be a majority of the whole number of electors appointed; and if no person have such majority, then from the persons having the highest numbers, not exceeding three, on the list of those voted for as President, the House of Representatives shall choose immediately, by ballot, the President. But in choosing the President, the vote shall be taken by States, the representation from each State having one vote; a quorum for this purpose shall consist of a member or members from two thirds of the States, and a majority of all the States shall be necessary to a choice. And if the House of Representatives shall not choose a President whenever the right of choice shall devolve upon them, before the fourth day of March next following, then the Vice-President shall act as President, as in the case of the death or other constitutional disability of the President.

The person having the greatest number of votes as Vice-President shall be the Vice-President, if such number be a majority of the whole number of electors appointed; and if no person have a majority, then from the two highest numbers on the list the Senate shall choose the Vice-President. A quorum for the purpose shall consist of two thirds of the whole number of Senators, and a majority of the whole number shall be necessary to a choice.

But no person constitutionally ineligible to the office of President shall be eligible to that of Vice-President of the United States.

Article XIII *(1865)*. **Section 1.** Neither slavery nor involuntary servitude, except as a punishment for crime whereof the party shall have been duly convicted, shall exist within the United States, or any place subject to their jurisdiction.

Section 2. Congress shall have power to enforce this article by appropriate legislation.

Article XIV *(1868)*. **Section 1.** All persons born or naturalized in the United States, and subject to the jurisdiction thereof, are citizens of the United States and of the state wherein they reside. No state shall make or enforce any law which shall abridge the privileges or immunities of citizens of the United States; nor shall any state deprive any person of life, liberty, or property, without due process of law, nor deny to any person within its jurisdiction the equal protection of the laws.

Section 2. Representatives shall be apportioned among the several states according to their respective numbers, counting the whole number of persons in each state, excluding Indians not taxed. But when the right to vote at any election for the choice of electors for President and Vice-President of the United States, representatives in Congress, the executive and judicial officers of a state, or the members of the legislature thereof, is denied to any of the male inhabitants of such state, being twenty-one years of age, and citizens of the United States, or in any way abridged, except for participation in rebellion or other crime, the basis of representation therein shall be reduced in the proportion which the number of such male citizens shall bear to the whole number of male citizens twenty-one years of age in such State.

Section 3. No person shall be a Senator or Representative in Congress, or elector of President and Vice-President, or hold any office, civil or military, under the United States, or under any state, who having previously taken an oath, as a member of Congress, or as an officer of the United States, or as a member of any state legislature, or as an executive or judicial officer of any state, to support the Constitution of the United States, shall have engaged in insurrection or rebellion against the same, or given aid or comfort to the enemies thereof. But Congress may, by a vote of two thirds of each house, remove such disability.

Section 4. The validity of the public debt of the United States, authorized by law, including debts incurred for payment of pensions and bounties for services in suppressing insurrection or rebellion, shall not be questioned. But neither the United States nor any state shall assume or pay any debt or obligation incurred in aid of insurrection or rebellion against the United States, or any claim for the loss or emancipation of any slave; but all such debts, obligations, and claims shall be held illegal and void.

Section 5. The Congress shall have power to enforce, by appropriate legislation, the provisions of this article.

Article XV *(1870)*. **Section 1.** The right of citizens of the United States to vote shall not be denied or abridged by the United States or by any State on account of race, color, or previous condition of servitude.

Section 2. The Congress shall have power to enforce this article by appropriate legislation.

Article XVI *(1913)*. The Congress shall have power to lay and collect taxes on incomes, from whatever source derived, without apportionment among the several states, and without regard to any census or enumeration.

38. Congress has the right to collect taxes on people's income. Congress does not have to base this tax on each state's population.

Article XVII *(1913)*. The Senate of the United States shall be composed of two Senators from each state, elected by the people thereof, for six years; and each Senator shall have one vote. The electors in each state shall have the qualifications requisite for electors of the most numerous branch of the state legislatures.

When vacancies happen in the representation of any state in the Senate, the executive authority of such state shall issue writs of election to fill such vacancies:

Provided, That the legislature of any state may empower the executive thereof to make temporary appointments until the people fill the vacancies by election as the legislature may direct.

This amendment shall not be so construed as to affect the election or term of any Senator chosen before it becomes valid as part of the Constitution.

39. This amendment changed the way Senators are elected. Before, they were chosen by the state legislatures. Now they are elected directly by the people. If a Senator cannot complete his or her term, the state's governor may appoint a temporary replacement until an election can be held.

Article XVIII *(1919)*. **Section 1.** After one year from the ratification of this article the manufacture, sale, or transportation of intoxicating liquors within, the importation thereof into, or the exportation thereof from the United States and all territory subject to the jurisdiction thereof for beverage purposes is hereby prohibited.

Section 2. The Congress and the several states shall have concurrent power to enforce this article by appropriate legislation.

Section 3. This article shall be inoperative unless it shall have been ratified as an amendment to the Constitution by the legislatures of the several states, as provided in the Constitution, within seven years from the date of the submission hereof to the states by the Congress.

40. This amendment prohibits the making, sale, and shipment of alcoholic beverages. It was later canceled by the 21st Amendment.

Article XIX *(1920)*. The right of citizens of the United States to vote shall not be denied or abridged by the United States or by any State on

41. The right to vote cannot be denied on account of a person's sex.

41 account of sex.

Congress shall have power to enforce this article by appropriate legislation.

42 **Article XX** *(1933).* **Section 1.** The terms of the President and Vice-President shall end at noon on the 20th day of January, and the terms of Senators and Representatives at noon on the 3rd day of January, of the years in which such terms would have ended if this article had not been ratified; and the terms of their successors shall then begin.

Section 2. The Congress shall assemble at least once in every year, and such meeting shall begin at noon on the 3rd day of January, unless they shall by law appoint a different day.

Section 3. If, at the time fixed for the beginning of the term of the President, the President-elect shall have died, the Vice-President-elect shall become President. If a President shall not have been chosen before the time fixed for the beginning of his term, or if the President-elect shall have failed to qualify; then the Vice-President-elect shall act as President until a President shall have qualified; and the Congress may by law provide for the case wherein neither a President-elect nor a Vice-President-elect shall have qualified, declaring who shall then act as President, or the manner in which one who is to act shall be selected, and such person shall act accordingly until a President or Vice-President shall have qualified.

Section 4. The Congress may by law provide for the case of the death of any of the persons from whom the House of Representatives may choose a President whenever the right of choice shall have devolved upon them, and for the case of the death of any of the persons from whom the Senate may choose a Vice-President whenever the right of choice shall have devolved upon them.

~~**Section 5.** Sections 1 and 2 shall take effect on the 15th day of October following the ratification of this article.~~

~~**Section 6.** This article shall be inoperative unless it shall have been ratified as an amendment to the Constitution by the legislatures of three fourths of the several States within seven years from the date of its submission.~~

43 **Article XXI** *(1933).* **Section 1.** The eighteenth article of amendment to the Constitution of the United States is hereby repealed.

Section 2. The transportation or importation into any state, territory, or possession of the United States for delivery or use therein of intoxicating liquors, in violation of the laws thereof, is hereby prohibited.

~~**Section 3.** This article shall be inoperative unless it shall have been ratified as an amendment to the Constitution by conventions in the several states, as provided in the Constitution, within seven years from the date of the submission hereof to the states by the Congress.~~

44 **Article XXII** *(1951).* **Section 1.** No person shall be elected to the office of the President more than twice, and no person who has held the office of President, or acted as President, for more than two years of a term to which some other person was elected President shall be elected to the office of the President more than once. ~~But this Article shall not apply to any person holding the office of President when this Article was proposed by the Congress, and shall not prevent any person who may be holding the office of President, or acting as President, during the term within which this Article becomes operative from holding the office of President or acting as President during the remainder of such term.~~

45 **Article XXIII** *(1961).* **Section 1.** The district constituting the seat of government of the United States shall appoint in such manner as the Congress may direct: A number of electors of President and Vice-Presi-

---

42. This amendment changes the date for the President and Vice-President beginning their terms of office. The opening date for Congress was also moved. The amendment provides for what should be done in case something happens to the President-elect before taking office.

43. This amendment canceled the 18th Amendment, and made it once again legal to make and sell alcoholic beverages.

44. No person may serve more than two terms as President.

---

dent equal to the whole number of Senators and Representatives in Congress to which the District would be entitled if it were a state, but in no event more than the least populous state; they shall be in addition to those appointed by the states, but they shall be considered, for the purposes of the election of President and Vice-President, to be electors appointed by a state; and they shall meet in the District and perform such duties as provided by the twelfth article of amendment.

Section 2. The Congress shall have power to enforce this article by appropriate legislation.

Article XXIV *(1964)*. **Section 1.** The right of citizens of the United States to vote in any primary or other election for President or Vice-President, for electors for President or Vice-President, or for Senator or Representatives in Congress, shall not be denied or abridged by the United States or any state by reason of failure to pay any poll tax or other tax.

Section 2. The Congress shall have power to enforce this article by appropriate legislation.

Article XXV *(1967)*. **Section 1.** In case of the removal of the President from office or his death or resignation, the Vice-President shall become President.

Section 2. Whenever there is a vacancy in the office of the Vice-President, the President shall nominate a Vice-President who shall take office upon confirmation by a majority vote of both houses of Congress.

Section 3. Whenever the President transmits to the President *Pro Tempore* of the Senate and the Speaker of the House of Representatives his written declaration that he is unable to discharge the powers and duties of his office, and until he transmits to them a written declaration to the contrary, such powers and duties shall be discharged by the Vice-President as Acting President.

Section 4. Whenever the Vice-President and a majority of either the principal officers of the executive departments or of such other body as Congress may by law provide, transmit to the President *Pro Tempore* of the Senate and the Speaker of the House of Representatives their written declaration that the President is unable to discharge the powers and duties of his office, the Vice-President shall immediately assume the powers and duties of the office as Acting President.

Thereafter, when the President transmits to the President *Pro Tempore* of the Senate and the Speaker of the House of Representatives his written declaration that no inability exists, he shall resume the powers and duties of his office unless the Vice-President and a majority of either the principal officers of the executive departments or of such other body as Congress may by law provide, transmit within four days to the President *Pro Tempore* of the Senate and the Speaker of the House of Representatives their written declaration that the President is unable to discharge the powers and duties of his office. Thereupon Congress shall decide the issue, assembling within 48 hours for that purpose if not in session. If the Congress, within 21 days after receipt of the latter written declaration, or, if Congress is not in session, within 21 days after Congress is required to assemble, determines by two-thirds vote of both houses that the President is unable to discharge the powers and duties of his office, the Vice-President shall continue to discharge the same as Acting President; otherwise, the President shall resume the powers and duties of his office.

Article XXVI (1971). **Section 1.** The right of citizens of the United States, who are 18 years of age or older, to vote shall not be denied or abridged by the United States or any state on account of age.

Section 2. The Congress shall have power to enforce this article by appropriate legislation.

45 45. The residents of the District of Columbia have the right to vote in Presidential elections. The District has three electoral votes.

46 46. No person can be denied the right to vote in national elections for failure to pay a tax. In 1966, the Supreme Court extended this right to include state elections as well.

47 47. This amendment determines what should be done if something happens to the President. If the President dies or cannot continue in office, the Vice-President becomes President. This person then appoints a new Vice-President who must be approved by Congress. The Vice-President may also become Acting President if the President cannot fulfill the duties of the office for a limited time.

48 48. All United States citizens over the age of eighteen have the right to vote.

GLOSSARY

A

adjourn to close a session, for a time

allies people united for a specific purpose

almanac an informational book published annually

ambushes traps

amendment change or addition to the U.S. Constitution

ammunition bullets and shells for weapons

Antifederalists people who believed in strong state government during the early history of the United States

apprentices persons learning a trade

arsenal store of arms

arson crime of purposely setting fire to property

assemblies meetings of lawmakers

B

barracks buildings soldiers live in

bayonet a long knife attached to the end of a rifle

boycotting refusing to deal with a nation, company, or organization in order to show disapproval or force a change

broadside poster featuring news

C

Cabinet officially chosen group of advisors to the president

candidate person seeking office

census an official count of people

civilization advanced stage of social development

clan group of families

colony settlement or community

column line of soldiers

command soldiers or area under an officer's authority

commission written order giving certain powers, duties, or rights

Committee of Correspondence a group of American patriots who worked to unite the colonies against Britain

communal shared ownership

compact agreement

compromise a way of satisfying both sides in a disagreement by which each side settles for less than it wants; mutual agreement

confederation a joining together in an alliance

conquistador conqueror

Constitution the document that outlines the plan of government in the United States

continent one of the main bodies of land in the world

convert to persuade people to change their beliefs

cultures the way of life of a group of people

D

Daughters of Liberty women who boycotted British products during the Revolutionary war

delegates formal representatives

democracy government of the people

deserted ran away from duty

E

economy financial affairs of a community

empire a group of cities, states, or territories under the rule of one person

Enlightenment period of political questioning in 18th century Europe

equality having the same rights, privileges, and rank

European Americans Americans of European descent

executive person who enforces the law

exile long period living away from one's own country

exports goods sent to another country

F

faction group

Federalists people who believed in strong federal government during early history of the U.S.

First Continental Congress meeting of colonial leaders held in Philadelphia in 1774

fleet ships under one command

fort permanent army post

H

Hessians German troops hired by the British during the American Revolution

homespun cloth made of yarn at home

House of Burgesses group responsible for making laws in colonial Virginia

hunter-gatherers people who move often to hunt and gather food

I

imported brought in from another country

indentured servitude an agreement to work a set number of years in exchange for passage to America

infidels non-believers of a dominant religion

J

judicial review power of the U.S. Supreme Court to decide if laws are constitutional

judiciary branch of government that makes sure laws are constitutional; system of courts of law

jury a group chosen to make a judgment

justice of the peace judge who tries minor cases

L

legislature law-making body

loyalists American colonists who remained loyal to Britain

M

Magna Carta great charter sealed by King John in 1215 that guaranteed political liberty for the people of England

merchant person who buys and sells goods

mesas flat-topped hills

militia emergency army of citizens

Minutemen farmers in colonial America who trained to fight the British

Monroe Doctrine a warning issued by President James Monroe in 1823 to keep European armies out of the Americas

Muslims people who believe in one God, whose name is Allah

N

nationalism a strong feeling of pride for one's country

Native Americans the first native peoples of North America including Eskimos and Indians

nomadic wandering from place to place

P

parliament a legislature

patriots people who are loyal and supportive of their country; 17th-century Americans loyal to the colonies

petition a written, formal statement requesting something

philosopher person who searches for wisdom and knowledge

plague a serious epidemic

plantations large farms or estates

political parties groups set up for the purpose of directing the policies of a government

preamble introduction

privateers privately owned, armed ships hired by a government

proportional representation a system in which a group (such as a state) is represented according to its population

Puritans people who wanted to change and simplify the English church during the 17th century

Q

Quakers a Christian group called the Society of Friends, they believe in simple religious services and oppose war

R

radical someone who favors extreme changes in existing laws or conditions

ratified to formally have a law approved

redcoats nickname for British soldiers during the Revolutionary war

reforms changes

refugees people who flee a country during time of conflict

repealed did away with a law

representatives people chosen to speak or act for others

republic a representative form of government; democratic nation

riots violent disturbances of the peace

S

Separatists people who wanted to separate from the Church of England in the 17th century

siege surrounding of a fort by an army trying to capture it

Sons of Liberty men who stirred up riots against the British before and during the Revolutionary war

subjects people owing allegiance to a monarchy

T

tariff a tax on goods sent from another country

treaty a formal agreement between nations

Treaty of Paris Britain's recognition of American independence in 1783

trial an examination of the facts of a case

tyrant a cruel and unjust leader

V

veterans people who served in time of war and survived

veto a refusal to approve

viceroy office similar to governor

W

Whiskey Rebellion an uprising of farmers in Pennsylvania who refused to pay new tax in the late 18th century

wilderness undeveloped land area

writ of mandamus court order to do a legal action

ILLUSTRATION CREDITS

2-3 (36). Angelo Lomeo/The Image Bank; 4. *Hunting Deer,* engraving by DeBry. Reproduced with the Authorization of the Service Hydrographique de la Marine, Paris; 5. Courtesy, The Bancroft Library, University of California, Berkeley; 7–8. Courtesy Department of Library Services, American Museum of Natural History; 9. Reproduced by courtesy of the Trustees of the British Museum; 12. Courtesy Department of Library Services, American Museum of Natural History (Photo: R. Wanamaker); 13. Courtesy of the Heard Museum, Phoenix; 16. Oronoz; 17. Michael Holford; 20 (37). *The Landing of Columbus,* c. 1837, Edward Hicks. National Gallery of Art, Washington, D.C.; Gift of Edgar William and Bernice Chrysler Garbisch; 21. *Christopher Columbus,* Sebastiano del Piombo, 1519. The Metropolitan Museum of Art, Gift of J. Pierpont Morgan, 1900; 24. John Running; 25. Oronoz; 26. Courtesy Frederic Remington Art Museum, Ogdensburg, NY; 28. Courtesy The Warner House Association, Portsmouth, NH; 29. Longyear Museum of Anthropology, Colgate University, Herbert Bigford, Sr. Collection; 30. *Codex Canadiensis,* Louis Nicholas. The Thomas Gilcrease Institute of American History and Art, Tulsa, OK; 32. *Chief of the Taensa Indians Receiving La Salle, March, 1682,* George Catlin. National Gallery of Art, Washington, D.C.; Paul Mellon Collection; 33. Primatives *Sailing by the Winnebago,* George Catlin. Courtesy of the Buffalo Bill Historical Center, Cody, Wyoming; 34. The Stokes Collection. Print Collection. Miriam and Ira D. Wallach Division of Art, Prints and Photographs, The New York Public Library, Astor Lenox and Tilden Foundations; 40-41 (62). Frank Siteman/Stock, Boston; 42 (63). Van Bergen Overmantel, 1732-33. Attributed to John Heaton. New York State Historical Association, Cooperstown; 43. From the Collections of Henry Ford Museum and Greenfield Village, Dearborn, MI; 45. *The Old Plantation,* c. 1800. Unknown artist. Abby Aldrich Rockefeller Folk Art Center, Colonial Williamsburg Foundation; 46. *James Forte at Jamestowne,* John Hull. Courtesy A.H. Robins Company, Richmond, VA. Photo, Don Eiler; 47. *Pocahontas,* after 1616, after an engraving by Simon van de Passe. National Portrait Gallery, Smithsonian Institution. Gift of Andrew W. Mellon, 1942; 48. *Village of Secoton,* John White. Reproduced Courtesy of the Trustees of the British Museum; 49. Rare Books and Manuscripts Division; The New York Public Library, Astor, Lenox and Tilden Foundations; 50. *First Thanksgiving.* Doris Lee. Courtesy John Hancock Mutual Life Insurance Company Collection, Boston, MA; 51. Courtesy of the Pilgrim Society, Plymouth, MA; 52. Worcester Art Museum, MA. Gift of Mr. and Mrs. Albert W. Rice; 54. *Penn's Treaty with the Indians,* c. 1830-1840, Edward Hicks. The Museum of Fine Arts, Houston, Bayou Bend Collection; Gift of Alice C. Simkins in memory of Alice N. Hanszen; 55. *Quaker Meeting,* c. 1800. Courtesy, Museum of Fine Arts, Boston; Bequest of Maxim Karolik; 57. *Southeast Prospect of the City of Philadelphia,* Peter Cooper. Library Company of Philadelphia; 58. The Gibbes Museum of Art/Carolina Art Association, Charleston, SC; 59. New York Public Library; 61. Collection of Butolph-Williams House (1692), a property of the Antiquarian and Landmarks Society, Hartford, CT; 66-67 (92). *Battle of Lexington,* W.B. Wollen. National Army Museum, London; 68. *A View of the Casionchigon or Great Seneca Falls, Lake Ontario, North America,* 1766, Thomas Davies. National Gallery of Canada, Ottawa; 69 (93). *The Bostonians Paying the Excise-Man,* 1774. Attributed to Philip Dawe. Chicago Historical Society; 71. *The Family of George III,* 1771, John Zoffany. The Royal Collection, St. James's Palace. Copyright reserved to Her Majesty Queen Elizabeth II; 72. *Patrick Henry Pleading the Parson's Cause,* George Cook. Virginia Historical Society, Richmond; 74. *Patrick Henry,* Artist Unknown. Shelburne Museum, Shelburne, VT; 75. Courtesy of the Essex Institute, Salem, MA; 76-77. Courtesy American Antiquarian Society, Worcester, MA. 78. Courtesy The Henry Frances duPont Winterthur Museum, Wilmington, DE; 80. *The Boston Tea Party,* A. Lassell Ripley. © The Paul Revere Life Insurance Company, Boston, MA; 82. Courtesy of The Bostonian Society/Old State House, Boston, MA; 84. *The Midnight Ride of Paul Revere,* Grant Wood, 1931. The Metropolitan Museum of Art, Arthur Hoppock Hearn Fund, 1950 © Estate of Grant Wood/VAGA 1989; 85. *Samuel Adams,* c. 1772, John Singleton Copley. Museum of Fine Arts, Boston, Deposited by the City of Boston, 1876; 87. The Connecticut Historical Society, Hartford; 88. Massachusetts Historical Society, Boston, MA; 89. Courtesy of The Bostonian Society/Old State House, Boston, MA; 90. *Battle of Bunker Hill,* Winthrop Chandler. Museum of Fine Arts, Boston; Gift of Mr. and Mrs. Gardner Richardson; 91. U.S. Department of the Interior, National Park Service, Adams National Historic Site, Quincy, MA. Photo, Jeffrey Dunn; 96-97 (130). *March to Valley Forge, Dec. 16, 1777,* William B.T. Trego, 1883. Courtesy of The Valley Forge Historical Society; 99. © National Geographic Society, Washington, D.C.; 100. *Attack against Fort Washington, 1776,* Thomas Davies. Stokes Collection. Print Collection Miriam and Ira D. Wallach Division of Art, Prints and Photographs, The New York Public Library. Astor, Lenox and Tilden Foundations; 102. *Congress Voting Independence,* Private Collection; 104. The Bettmann Archive; 105. J. Devenney/The Image Bank; 106. *George Washington,* Charles Willson Peale. The Metropolitan Museum of Art. Gift of Collis P. Huntington, 1896; 107. *Washington Crossing the Delaware,* c. 1830, Artist unknown. Philadelphia Museum of Art. The Edgar William and Bernice Chrysler Garbisch Collection; 109. *Battle of Trenton,* Richard Schlecht. © National Geographic Society, Washington, D.C.; 110. Courtesy of Continental Insurance Company, New York City; 111. Anne S. K. Brown Military Collection, Brown University Library, Providence, RI; 114. The Bettmann Archive 115. *Mrs. Richard Bache (Sarah Franklin),* John Hoppner. The Metropolitan Museum of Art. Wolfe Fund, 1901. Catharine Lorillard Wolfe Collection; 116. The Historical Society of Pennsylvania, Philadelphia; 118. *The Woolsey Family,* 1809, William Berczy. National Gallery of Canada, Ottawa. Gift of Major Edgar © Woolsey, 1952; 119. New York State Historical Society, Cooperstown; 120. Stokes Collection. Print Collection, Miriam and Ira D. Wallach Division of Art, Prints and Photographs. The New York Public Library. Astor, Lenox and Tilden Foundations; 122. U.S. Capitol Historical Society; 123. Anne S. K. Brown Military Collection, Brown University Library, Providence, RI; 125 (131). Wide World Photos; 126. The Historical Society of Pennsylvania, Philadelphia; 127. John Lewis Stage/Image Bank; 128. Detail from an announcement of the Hand-in-Hand Fire Company, c. 1753. Print Collection, Miriam and Ira D. Wallach Collection of Art, Prints and Photographs. The New York Public Library. Astor, Lenox, and Tilden Foundations; 134-135 (168). Robert Llewellyn; 136. *The Tontine Coffee House,* Francis Guy. Courtesy New-York Historical Society, New York City; 137. New York Public Library; 139 (l). Chicago Historical Society; (r) Courtesy of The Museum, U.S. Naval Academy, Annapolis, MD; 140. © Al Freni; 141. *Militia Training, 1841,* James Goodwyn Clonney. The Pennsylvania Academy of the Fine Arts. Bequest of Henry c. Casey, The Casey Collection; 144. Gilbert Stuart, c. 1870. Mead Art Museum, Amherst College, Amherst, MA. Bequest of Herbert L. Pratt; 145. Culver Pictures; 146. *House of Lords,* Thomas Rowlandson aand Augustus Charles Pugin, c. 1810. Plate 62 from *The Microcosm of London,* published by R. Ackermann, London. The Metropolitan Museum of Art. Rogers Fund, 1921; 147. *House of Commons,* Thomas Rowlandson and Augustus Charles Pugin, c. 1810. Plate 22 from *The Microcosm of London,* published by R. Ackermann, London. The Metropolitan Museum of Art. Rogers Fund, 1921; 148. Historical Society of Pennsylvania, Philadelphia; 149. *Travel by Stagecoach Near Trenton, New Jersey,* Pavel Petrovich Svinin. The Metropolitan Museum of Art, Rogers Fund, 1942; 152 (169). *Washington Addressing The Constitutional Convention,* Junius Brutus Stearns, 19th century. Virginia Museum, Richmond. Gift of Col. and Mrs. Garbisch; 155. (Detail) Maryland Historical Society, Baltimore; 157. New York Public Library; 160. Culver Pictures; 161. Museum of Art, Rhode Island School of Design, Providence. Gift of Lucy T. Aldrich; 162. Library Company of Philadelphia; 164. Courtesy Mr. and Mrs. John Harney; 165. Atwater Kent Museum, Philadelphia, PA; 166. Culver Pictures; 172-173 (202). Antoine Roux. Peabody Museum of Salem, MA. Photo, Mark Sexton; 174. Library of Congress; 175. Missouri Historical Society, St. Louis; 177. *Thomas Jefferson at Natural Bridge,* Caleb Boyle. Kirby Collecton of Historical Paintings, Lafayette College Art Gallery, Easton, PA; 178. George Caleb Bingham, 1851-52. Washington University Gallery of Art, St. Louis, MO; 179. Colonial Williamsburg Foundation, VA; 182. Charles W. Russell, 1917. Thomas Gilcrease Institute of American History and Art, Tulsa, OK; 183. Peabody Museum, Harvard University, Cambridge, MA; 186 (203). Field Museum of Natural History, Chicago; 187. McKenney and Hall. *History of the Indian Tribes,* Philadelphia, 1836. Library Company of Philadelphia; 190. Library of Congress; 191. Miniature by Aline Alaux after Gilbert Stuart. Courtesy of the New-York Historical Society, New York City; 194. Rembrandt Peale. Collection of the Supreme Court of the United States; 195. Courtesy of Penn Mutual Life Insurance Company, Philadelphia; 196. *Panoramic View of New York,* Robert Havell, c. 1840. Stokes Collection. Print Collection. Mirium and Ira D. Wallach Division of Art, Prints, and Photographs. The New York Public Library. Astor, Lenox and Tilden Foundations; 198. *Allegory for the Departure of Don Pedro II for Europe after the Declaration of the Republic,* Anonymous Artist. Courtesy Funcacao Maria Luisa e Oscar Americano, Sao Paulo, Brazil; 199. Phillip Haas, 1843. The Metropolitan Museum of Art. Gift of I. N. Phelps Stokes, Edward S. Hawes, Alice Mary Hawes, Marion Augusta Hawes, 1937.